DON'T LISTEN

TO PHIL HELLMUTH*

.and a host of other champions, TV commentators, and self-proclaimed experts

CORRECTING THE 50 WORST PIECES OF POKER ADVICE!

Dedication

For Matt Amen, who persevered with me through my early mistakes, and for all the new players starting out. May your mistakes be few and short-lived. — Dusty

For Phil Hellmuth, Chris Moneymaker, Mike Sexton, David Sklansky, and all the other authors, announcers, players and champions who've given advice ranging from excellent to awful, relevant to outdated. For our readers who have sifted through it all and not known which advice to follow. And to members of the next generation, watchful for the time when any of our advice becomes antique. — Paul

Acknowledgments

Dusty would like to thank Paul Hoppe, Nicole Schmidt, Michelle Breazeale, Lennon Schmidt, Scott Brown, Neal Rosenshine, Tracy Hopper, Sara Brown, Matt Amen, Alice Pellegrino, Hunter Bick, Korey Gillis, Phil Nagy, Jared Tendler, Rob Wise, Matt Bolt, Casey Martin, Johnny Mac, Jim Pellegrino, Brian Henninger, Justin Marchand, Steve Radulovich, Shawn Patrick Green, Ziad Kaady, Sam Montez, Clint Demaris, Allen Knecht, Scott Walker, Rickard Kling, Benjamin Wilson and Steve Day. Additionally, Paul would like to thank Mateel Hoppe, Ed Miller, Dusty Schmidt and Mary Yost.

DON'T LISTEN
TO PHIL HELLMUTH*

and a host of other champions, TV commentators, and self-proclaimed experts

CORRECTING THE 50 WORST PIECES OF POKER ADVICE!

DUSTY SCHMIDT
& PAUL CHRISTOPHER HOPPE

CARDOZA PUBLISHING

Cardoza Publishing is the foremost gaming and gambling publisher in the world with a library of more than 200 up-to-date and easy-to-read books and strategies. These authoritative works are written by the top experts in their fields and with more than 10,000,000 books in print, represent the best-selling and most popular gaming books anywhere.

Copyright © 2010, 2012 by Dusty Schmidt & Paul Christopher Hoppe

LIBRARY OF CONGRESS CONTROL NUMBER: 2012931044
ISBN 10:   1-58042-308-6
ISBN 13: 978-1-58042-308-3

ABOUT DUSTY SCHMIDT

A consummate grinder,"Dusty "Leatherass" Schmidt has played nearly 9 million hands of online poker over his six-year career. In December 2009, Schmidt released his first book, *Treat Your Poker Like A Business*, which quickly became an international sensation. Today the book has been published in eight languages. Schmidt has won almost $4 million during that period, and has never experienced a losing month. In 2007, he achieved PokerStars SuperNova Elite status in just eight months while playing high-stakes cash games exclusively. Schmidt posted the world's highest win rate in both $5/$10 NL and $10/$20 NL in both 2007 and 2008. In a four-month period between November, 2007 and February, 2008, Schmidt won in excess of $600,000 in high-stakes cash games. He is now a highly respected instructor at DragTheBar.com, and plays as high as $25/50 NL.

As a young man, Schmidt was a top-ranked golfer. He broke two of Tiger Woods' junior records and was the leading money winner on the Golden States Tour when, at age 23, he suffered a career-ending heart attack. Schmidt returned to golf in 2009, winning medalist honors in qualifying for the Oregon Amateur Championship. Later that year, Schmidt famously represented himself in federal court in his suit against the United States Golf Association, which controversially stripped him of his amateur status, in part due to his working as a poker professional.

Schmidt is co-founder of Imagine Media and the creator of 10thGreen. com, the first social network for golfers. His story has been featured in *Sports Illustrated, Card Player, Golf Magazine,* ESPN, CNN.com, wallstreetjournal.com, forbes.com, fortune.com, ESPN.com, golfdigest. com and golf.com, among others. He recently founded the House of Cards Project, a philanthropic effort to provide food and shelter to disadvantaged families. His life story will be told in the book "Raise: The Impossibly True Tale of Dusty Schmidt," to be released later. He lives in Portland, Oregon, with his wife Nicole and daughter Lennon.

ABOUT PAUL CHRISTOPHER HOPPE

Author Paul "Giantbuddha" Hoppe is a skilled martial arts practitioner, as well as an acclaimed poker player and coach. In July 2010, he released his first book, *Way of the Poker Warrior,* to critical acclaim worldwide. Hoppe is a fourth-degree black belt with Taekwon-Do International, which qualifies him as a "master." He has taught martial arts for nine years. For two years, he was the head instructor of a Dojang in Times Square.

As a poker professional, Hoppe is known for his detailed and efficient combo analysis. He played live poker professionally at games that included $20/$40 limit hold'em and seven-card stud, some Omaha 8 and stud 8, and $5/$10 no-limit hold'em. In 2006, starting with a $100 deposit bonus, he built his bankroll from that free $100 into a six-figure income, going from $.50/$1 to $10/$20, $15/$30 and $30/$60, which he plays today.

Hoppe has maintained a very solid 1.5 BB/100 win rate over 30 months. His heads-up win rate is 5 BB/100. In 2007, 2008 and 2009, he was able to double his poker income from the previous year. He is known as a versatile player, mixing limit, no-limit, Omaha, stud, and triple draw. In Spring 2010, Hoppe staged a 28-day "grind-a-thon," during which time he played poker, then recorded a Hand of the Day video and a video blog every day. He made $30,000 in profits and raised $3,000 for cancer and autism charities.

He has coached poker for more than two years, including about 50 private students, and is an instructor at DragTheBar.com, for which he has made more than 50 videos. As a writer, Hoppe has published an article on Internet poker legislation and legal issues. He authors a popular blog, Wandering Path of a Zen Madman, which he has now moved to giantbuddhapoker.com. His is a popular strategy-forum poster.

Hoppe is also a talented musician who currently plays guitar for the New York band, Villain's Lament, for which he writes music and lyrics.

T TABLE OF CONTENTS

SECTION 2: HAND ANALYSIS   181

SECTION 3: STUDY   243

GLOSSARY   265

# INTRODUCTION

What if many of the fundamental "truths" you've heard about poker turned out to be false?

Recognize any of these commonly held beliefs?

- Preflop play doesn't matter that much.
- The key to getting paid off is playing loose so no one can put you on a hand.
- Bigger 3-bets get more folds.
- Calling is weak.
- You have to bet this flop because you don't want to give up.

There is certainly an element of truth to some of these statements, but by and large they are big misconceptions. Perhaps this shouldn't bother us because, as poker pros, we profit off the mistakes of others. But when we see so many high-level players making so many fundamental mistakes in their games, and then see those moves endorsed by television announcers, it's enough to make us scream, "Stop! That's not how it's done!"

This book focuses on correcting the greatest fallacies in poker. There are an astonishing number of them, providing our common understanding of the game with an incredibly shaky foundation.

This did not come entirely as a surprise.

Like many new players, we struggled to sift through all the competing voices. One author would say this, another would say that. Hoping to give you a better leg up than we had, we systematically take on what we recognize as flawed advice. We have combed through more than four decades of conventional poker wisdom. No one is spared: world champions, on-air commentators, and other "flavors of the month." Not even Dusty is excluded from our criticism! One by one, we challenge each misconception, taking on what we believe are the top 50 ways to lose at poker. By proving these misconceptions false, you will benefit in such a way that, by implementing these newfound understandings, they can become more profitable tomorrow.

We want this book to ultimately function as a FactCheck. org or "MythBusters" for poker. We hope you'll come to look at us as watchdogs out to protect your interests by questioning the powers that be. As we did in our previous books, *Treat Your Poker Like A Business* and *Way of the Poker Warrior*, in this book we cover the game's most frequent scenarios, seeking to provide solutions to situations that arise every ten minutes rather than only once a month.

Our criteria for choosing misconceptions were simple. Are they costing you money, and can we prove it? The scenarios that vex you now once did the same to us. Unlike our previous books, this is a comprehensive manual that aims to troubleshoot the poker process from the top down, complete with hand analyses and a reader quiz at book's end.

Writing this book has led us to think about coaching. Golfers don't have ten swing coaches. Baseball players don't have ten hitting coaches. Football teams don't have ten offensive coordinators. But in poker, we tend to entertain advice from all comers, which leads to confusion and a fragmented playing style. Why do we do this?

Profit motive!

INTRODUCTION

Poker advice is one part technical or mechanical, and one part investment tip. We're all looking for that hot lead that will get us ahead of the competition. But with this wider mesh, we're letting in some voices that don't deserve to be there. In sports and money management, ascension through the coaching/advising ranks is mostly a meritocracy. The rubber inevitably meets the road. Your pedigree might have gotten you in the door, but there'll be no place to hide when they tally the wins and losses. This merit-based rise through the ranks is not yet the case in poker, where instructional straw men are still hiding in plain sight.

Several years ago, poker experienced exponential growth that was virtually unprecedented in any sport. When the World Series of Poker started in 1970, everyone started at the final table and the participants voted to determine who won. Even at its pre-2003 height, the Main Event included far fewer players than it does today. You didn't need to be the best player in the world to win. You only had to be the best player in Las Vegas. Then in 2003, ESPN made the brilliant decision to install hole-card cameras in the tables. An accountant named Chris Moneymaker won the event, and that's when things got interesting. It was great fortune meeting great opportunity— the masterstroke of letting the audience know more than the players knew, fused with an amateur with a Hollywood surname. In an instant, poker went from being ten times more boring than golf to being ten times more popular.

Within three years, the number of World Series of Poker Main Event entrants rose tenfold, from 839 in 2003 to 8,773 in 2006, with each player willing to lay down a $10,000 entry fee for the privilege. It was at this point that poker stardom took on the look of creationism rather than evolution. Television execs came looking for stars, and Phil Hellmuth, Johnny Chan, et al were the big names of the day. They managed to be standing at the right place at the right time when the guys with cameras asked, "Hey, you want to be famous?" These anointed ones made their bones at a period in poker that was much like golf was in 1910, when you could win the U.S. Open shooting twenty over par while drunk on the back nine. Even so, poker books, DVD's and announcing gigs followed for these guys, and they all proffered instruction that might not have been that good in the first place and hasn't really changed over the years.

However, they are offering commentary on a game that has moved on without them. Listening to their advice today, we feel like we're hearing Lee Iacocca profess that his 1988 K-cars remain superior to modern-day models with front-wheel drive and computer-assisted design. Germs of advice that were either misguided to begin with, or were okay in small doses but not large ones, have metastasized into bloated edicts that never deserved to be sacred in the first place. Like perfume, a little bit of this advice is fine, but too much of it is odorous.

A lot of this issue comes down to how poker is played. Once upon a time, check-raising was thought of as unethical because it was deceitful. Today, *not* check-raising is referred to as "donk" betting, as in, "You're a donkey for betting there instead of check-raising." The point is, the game evolves. Players must evolve with it or perish. We think it's time to tip these sacred cows, to set fire to these paper lions.

If you want to make seismic gains in your profitability, you need to question the fundamental things you think you know about poker. For example:

"Checking and folding the flop is weak."
Not necessarily.

"Always c-bet the same amount."
Not without considering the board texture and how your opponent will respond to different sizes.

"Save the small bets for the kiddie game."
Not even close.

"Great players never fold the best hand."
It's impossible to win without ever folding the best hand.

"Raise to find out where you stand."
A classic Hellmuthism and a total misconception.

"The key to no-limit hold'em is to put a man to a decision for all his chips."
There's a lot right about this one from Doyle Brunson, but a lot wrong as well.

"You're either a passive player or an aggressive one."
Style is no substitute for thinking. A good player makes the most profitable decision regardless of whether it's passive or aggressive.

Part of determining what's really right and wrong in the poker lexicon will start with your winnowing down the number of voices in your head and organizing the learning process. In choosing a coach, we're huge believers in following someone who is or has been a big winner in the game you're playing. Should this player be an online player or a live-game player? You can become great playing either game. We're online players and might be perceived as biased, but the fact is that we have the luxury of establishing our credentials faster. Online can put up graphs that no mathematician can argue with. We're able to play more hands in a month than a live player can play in a year; thus in 12 months of poker per year, we get in more than a decade worth of hands relative to a live-game player.

Are we saying that we know more about the game than many, if not most, of the authorities out there? Well, yes.

Fortunately we're up to the challenge of proving it, as we think we do in the pages that follow. In any case, it is our belief that we need to question the voices in our heads.

We're talking about an evolution, people!

CORRECTING THE 50 WORST PIECES OF POKER ADVICE YOU'VE EVER HEARD

MISCONCEPTION #1
AVOID TOUGH DECISIONS

Once upon a time, no-limit hold'em was a postflop game. A bunch of players would limp along, and the ones who played the best after the flop would get the money. Sometimes someone would make a little raise, there would be a few callers, and they would all see a flop.

Along came Dolly.

Doyle "Texas Dolly" Brunson started raising it up to five or ten blinds before the flop and putting pressure on everyone—pressure he knew they wouldn't stand up to. He was still playing the postflop game, but made more money than anyone else because he was juicing up the pots before he took them down.

Somewhere along the line someone saw guys like Doyle making all these aggressive preflop raises and thought to himself, "Hey, I could throw in a bunch of reraises and put the pressure back on him." At its core, this is a solid idea. When someone is making big raises with a wide range of hands before the flop, you can often steal a lot of money by **3-betting** (reraising) aggressively. Re-bullying the bully can be a profitable venture!

In today's games with 100 big-blind starting stacks, loose and aggressive **open-raising,** where players always enter the pot with a raise, is the norm. You'd be hard pressed to find an online game with a gaggle of limpers ahead of you each hand. Instead, there will typically be an open-raise and a bunch of folds. Once everyone realized that everyone else was opening with a wide range of starting hands, **3-betting light** (reraising with a less than premium hand) came into vogue. Now it's old hat. There's so much 3-betting going on that people have started to 4-bet cold with **air** (hands with no intrinsic value). There was a time when putting in the third raise meant aces or kings, so a 4-bet had a lot of credibility. Now that we all know the 4-bet can be a bluff, the next step is to shove all in against the cold 4-bets. The whole preflop street has developed into a high stakes game of chicken!

That's a lot of aggression without the cards to back it up. It was developed with the best intentions, and it can take courage to pull the trigger on these big bets without much of a hand. Instead, the motivation is often fear. What sort of fear would cause such aggression? Fear of the unknown. Fear of making embarrassing mistakes. Fear of being challenged. Players see a chance to end the hand early by getting it in with decent *equity* and jump all over it; **equity** being the amount of money in the pot multiplied by the perceived or actual chances of winning it. When you put less money into the pot than your expected long-term win, you have at minimum, *decent* equity. Players are trying to avoid tough postflop decisions with aggressive preflop action.

POKER IS A GAME OF DECISIONS

Poker is a game of decision—players who consistently make good decisions win money. Players who consistently make poor decisions lose money. When you make a good decision that your opponent would have made, you don't gain much. There's no edge there. Your edge comes from making a *better* decision than your opponent would have made.

You don't see hugely successful businesses doing the same thing everyone else is doing and following the trend. As Warren Buffet would say, "First come the innovators, then the imitators, and finally the idiots." You might not innovate something completely original, but don't be an idiot. Don't be the thousandth company trying to design a better search engine. Don't be the millionth person trying to outwit everyone before the flop. Learn the fundamentals, but once you've done that, spend the majority of your study time looking for new areas to find an advantage. Unless you find a truly innovative approach, there's little to be reaped from over-tilled land.

When everyone gets into the 3-bet, 4-bet, and 5-bet game, no-limit hold'em becomes a fairly simple one-street game. This was *not* what Doyle had in mind when he called it "The Cadillac of Poker." You need to embrace tough decisions. While everyone else is trying to get it in quick and "not that bad," you should be finding ways to see flops. Find ways to see turns. Find ways to see showdowns for the right price or to push your opponent off a hand when you have zero equity.

Don't get us wrong. There is merit to a lot of these aggressive preflop plays, and there are spots where they are clearly profitable. But many times, you have the choice of making a slightly profitable play before the flop, or giving yourself a chance to find a hugely profitable play on the turn or river. Would you rather make a little now or a lot later? Why try to get all of your value out of one street? There are three more streets after the preflop. Every time you end a hand before the flop, you deprive yourself of three opportunities to outplay someone postflop. Trying to squeeze all of your value out of preflop play is lazy and shortsighted.

THE TAKEAWAY

Don't be the guy looking for the quickest, easiest, shortest-term profit. Embrace tough decisions!

You'll get some of them wrong, but as long as you get more right than your opponents do, you'll come out on top. Have faith in your ability to outplay your opponents on the later streets. Put *them* to tough decisions after the flop. That's where the biggest edges come from. If you don't have the skills yet, keep reading—we'll show you exactly how to make these hugely profitable plays.

MISCONCEPTION #2

PREFLOP PLAY DOESN'T MATTER THAT MUCH

Some people will tell you that no-limit hold'em is a postflop game. That preflop doesn't matter. Like many misconceptions, there is an element of truth here and a blatant fallacy. The truth is that playing well preflop will not automatically make you a winning player, and making some mistakes before the flop won't prohibit you from making money. Preflop is not everything.

But these same players who claim "preflop doesn't matter" have spent dozens of hours designing their preflop 3-betting, 4-betting, and shoving games. They've sat down and calculated the equities and equations. So which is it? Is preflop barely worth a thought, or does it demand dozens of hours of study?

There is only one round of betting before the flop, while there are three streets after, so it's easy to say that postflop play is more important than preflop play. Fine. You'll spend hundreds (or even thousands) of hours working on your postflop play. But while preflop is only one of four rounds of betting, it happens to be the first one. Your preflop strategy determines what range of hands you take to the flop. It also affects the size of the pot, which hands you should commit with postflop, and how much room you have left to maneuver. Preflop sets things up for your postflop play. So yeah, it's important. It matters. The good news is that there is a lot of information out there to help you decide how to play preflop. The bad news is that some of it is of questionable value or integrity.

THE TAKEAWAY

No-limit hold'em is a dynamic game and, as such, requires a dynamic approach. As a result, a lot of advice is vague or wishy-washy. While judgment is an important component in every decision, it *is* possible to provide solid guidelines. And that's just what the next chapters will do.

STARTING HAND CHARTS ARE FOR BEGINNERS

Let's talk about the much maligned starting hand chart. Many people claim that playing from a chart will stunt your development as a poker player. This simply isn't true. Yes, learning a fixed strategy and then playing that strategy while never deviating, never reevaluating, and never looking deeper into the game would be a huge mistake. This applies to both preflop and postflop play just as much as it applies to chess, baseball, and trying to get a date. Once you've mastered one level of complexity, you should look deeper to find the next one. But you always have to start with level one.

Imagine you are playing no-limit hold'em for the very first time. When you look at your first two cards, how are you supposed to know how to play them? Or *whether* to play them for that matter? A hand chart can be a great place to start. The idea is not to learn the opening requirements, then slavishly follow them for the rest of your poker career. The idea is to create a frame of reference. The chart says: *All other things being equal, play these hands from this position.* We've included charts with the hands that Dusty defaults to in particular situations.

Chart #1 outlines the weakest hands you should play from each position when everyone has folded to you. For instance, if the chart says to raise 6-6, that means you should also raise 7-7 and better. If it says to raise A-J and K-J offsuit, you should also raise A-K, A-Q, and K-Q. If it says A-2 under the suited column, then you should raise any ace with another card of the same suit.

Do not follow this chart when a player has called or raised ahead of you. Those are different situations and each will be dealt with in its own chapter (see Misconceptions #8 and #9.) This chart is specifically for situations where no one has voluntarily put money in the pot. If the chart says you should play the hand, you should raise to about three blinds as a default, but there are situations where a different raise size would be better (see Misconception #7).

The first column in the chart indicates your position at the table, which is also the first thing you should consider when deciding whether or not to open-raise. The fewer players left to act behind you, the better chance you have of either winning immediately or having position on a player who calls you (one of the blinds). The exception here is the small blind, where you will always be out of position against the big blind when everyone else has folded (unless you're playing a one-on-one heads-up match, which is beyond the scope of this chapter).

CHART #1: OPEN RAISING			
POSITION	**PAIRS**	**OFFSUIT**	**SUITED**
Early (EP)	7-7	A-K	A-10, K-10, Q-10, J-10
Lojack (LJ)	6-6	A-J, K-J	A-10, K-10, Q-10, J-10
Hijack (HJ)	5-5	A-J, K-J	A-10, K-10, Q-10, J-10
Cutoff (CO)	2-2	A-9, K-J	A-2, K-9, Q-9, J-9, 10-9, 9-8, 8-7, 7-6
Button (BTN)	2-2	A-2, K-J, Q-10, J-9, 10-8, 9-7, 8-6, 7-5, 6-5	Any two suited cards
Small Blind (SB)	2-2	A-8, K-10, Q-10, J-10	A-2, K-9, Q-9 ,J-7, 10-8, 9-7, 8-6, 7-6
Early (EP)—4 or more seats off (in front of) the button **Lojack (LJ)**—3 seats off the button, or under the gun in a six-handed game **Hijack (HJ)**—2 seats off the button **Cutoff (CO)**—one seat to the immediate right of the button **Button (BTN)**—last to act on every round of postflop betting **Small Blind (SB)**—sandwiched between the button and the big blind			

The Big Blind (BB) is not included in the chart since you automatically win the pot when everyone folds to you. Abbreviations for all positions are listed in the chart as well. We use these abbreviations in hand examples throughout the book, so it's a good idea to learn them now.

You don't have to use this chart. If you want to, that's fine. But you can also feel free to add and subtract hands as you see fit, developing your own standards. This particular chart errs on the side of caution. It's a great fit for a novice, or an experienced player who prefers to sit at a large number of tables.

FIND WHAT WORKS FOR YOU AND DO IT ON PURPOSE

Find a style that suits your personality and deliberately build your game around it. Some players may naturally be better at playing wide ranges than others, while some may be better served by hunkering down and playing a more disciplined and conservative style. How do you find your natural style? Ask yourself if you're typically afraid of what might beat you postflop. If you err on the side of caution after the flop, it's a good idea to do the same before the flop. That way you'll have a stronger range to attack with postflop, allowing you to play aggressively despite your predilections to the contrary.

Or are you more often looking for an angle to attack? Do you like to put pressure on people and try to scare them? If you're good at finding the right spots for this, you might be able to get away with a looser style, which may be your best fit. But don't take this advice as an excuse to do whatever the hell you want. Even if you're already playing a highly dynamic game, laying out your preflop defaults can give you a better idea of what your range will typically look like when you open from a given position. This can help you **balance** (adjust) your range, determine how often to fold to 3-bets, and be more aware of your image.

THE TAKEAWAY

If you're an inexperienced player struggling with the postflop basics, try playing from the chart. This will free up mental energy to work on the other three very important streets. Playing a totally dynamic game is a waste of energy. Instead of agonizing over razor-thin preflop decisions, you could be adding more tables and making more money. You can always make your preflop game more dynamic later—but you need to start somewhere.

MISCONCEPTION #4

PICK A STYLE AND STICK WITH IT

Some players say they prefer to play loose, while others prefer to play tight. They call each other donkey-nits, clown-fish, and all manner of animal-inspired names. They may not be playing from a hand chart, but they've decided whether they prefer always to err on the side of aggression or conservatism. They pick a style and stick with it. That doesn't make much sense. Every decision you make at the poker table should be based on what you think will win the most money.

Improving at poker is just like improving in life. When you're trying to play a logic game for a living, you need to be logical in life. Is it logical to eat awful food and never exercise? No. You don't have much in life without your health. Without it, nothing else really matters. There are times when logic will shout at you to deviate from your comfortable game plan. Heed its call. Consider the following story:

One day a salesman receives a phone call.

"I need to buy a crane asap," the caller requests.

"I'm sorry, sir. We don't sell cranes," the salesman responds. "We only carry toothbrushes and dental floss." He hangs up.

"Who the hell was that?" his boss demands.

"Some guy wanted to buy a crane," the salesman laughs.

"And you hung up on him? Get back on that phone and tell that guy you're gonna get him a goddamned crane!"

"But we don't have cra—"

"What the hell does that matter? Do you know how much those things cost?" the boss asks. "If the man wants a crane, we'll sell him a crane."

The salesman calls the guy back and the boss begins furiously flipping through the yellow pages for crane dealers. He calls a few places, talks to a few guys, and thirty minutes later he's brokering a deal where the caller gets a crane, the crane company gets $600,000, and he gets a 10 percent commission. Dusty heard this story from a golfing buddy who happened to be the boss in the story. The salesman was one of his best employees, but he considered firing him for hanging up on a dude who was looking to drop over half a million on a crane.

How does this relate to poker?

Maybe you've been playing tight all day and a couple of loose players are constantly raising and cold calling each other. It's time to reraise and grab all that money that's sitting out there. Your cards don't matter! You should squeeze—put on the pressure! You already know that both players have weak and wide ranges here. The first guy will have a hard time calling your raise with a speculative hand, knowing that he'll wind up squeezed between you and the cold caller. The cold caller is even less likely to call, since he usually would have reraised himself if he had a hand worth a 3-bet.

Maybe you've been playing loose all day and a super tight and oblivious player **shoves** (goes all in) over your 3-bet. You think his range is only aces and kings. You should fold your queens. Queens are normally a powerhouse hand when you have a loosey-goosey image, but this opponent doesn't pay attention to that stuff, and he's super tight to boot. Your awesome hand has turned into muck, and that's exactly where it should end up.

It's okay to deviate from your standard play when the situation demands. In fact, that's the best way to play. Here are a few considerations that should affect your range:

(1) A big fish is at the table.

When there is a truly awful player at the table, you should do everything you can to get into pots with him. There are players who **min-raise** (raise the minimum) with any two cards preflop, then massively overbet every flop. With these ridiculous implied odds, you can play literally play any two cards against the awful player. This example is extreme, but these situations come up. Be ready when they do. Don't take it so far when the fish isn't quite so massive, but the same general concept applies. Get in there and take their money! Consider this example:

> **GAME:** $5/$10 blinds—6 players
> **STACKS:** $1,000 **effective** (size of the smallest active stack)
> **READS:** BB is a big fish
> **YOUR HAND:** You have 7♠ 6♠ in the lojack

WHAT SHOULD YOU DO?

You should raise to $30. With a very bad player in the big blind, you should play this hand that you would usually fold from such an early position. In fact, you can open-raise your regular cutoff range from any earlier position, and an even wider range from the cutoff and button.

(2) There is a raise in front of you and the bad player is in the big blind.

This is a fine spot to do some looser cold calling. You're less likely to get 3-bet (squeezed) by any good players behind you because they should prefer to just call with their playable hands in an attempt to extract more money from the fish after the flop. Since a reraise would shut the fish out of the pot, good players may even just call with aces and kings. In fact, you should consider just calling with your strong hands as well, since you're more likely to get value from the bad player in the big blind than from the solid player in front of you.

(3) The blinds are super tight.

When the blinds fold too much, you can play more marginal hands, particularly from late position. When there's free money out there, you should take it! You can open any two cards, even 7-2 offsuit, from the button if the blinds are tight enough.

(4) You are in the cutoff and the button is weak/tight.

When the button is going to fold to your raise 95 percent of the time preflop, it's almost like you get the button twice per orbit. You can open up your cutoff range considerably. If the blinds don't adjust and keep folding as much as they would against your usual cutoff range, you can almost make an argument to open the cutoff looser than you would usually open the button. You can certainly open as loose as your default button range.

(5) You have been playing unusually tight.

Sometimes you just sit around and fold almost every hand for an hour straight. If an early position player has been opening a lot of pots, you can **3-bet light** (reraise with a lesser hand that you usually raise with) and get much more credit than you usually would. This concept only applies against opponents who are paying attention. Look at this example:

GAME:	$5/$10 blinds—6 players
STACKS:	$1,000 effective
READS:	LJ is an observant player
DYNAMIC:	You've been playing crazy tight
YOUR HAND:	You have J♥ 6♥ in the hijack
PREFLOP:	LJ raises to $30

WHAT SHOULD YOU DO?

You should reraise to $90. It's generally best to save this play for times when you have a little something for back up, like suited or connected cards, or an ace or a king in your hand. When your opponents do call the 3-bet, it will often be with pocket pairs instead of the king-queen and ace-jack type hands that have you dominated. That makes you less likely to suffer from kicker problems, keeping you from losing too many big pots. An ace or a king in your hand also reduces the chances of your opponent holding a hand like aces, kings, or A-K.

(6) The player behind you is awesome.

This can be a world-class player or just someone you feel has a good edge on you. Be honest with yourself. There's no need to seek a struggle with players who are better than you. If you're willing to give position to a player of this caliber, there'd better be a big fish on your right. (Otherwise you should find a better seat.) Play pots with *that* guy. He's the one offering to pay your rent. You can't be afraid to take advantage of the bad players just because someone scary is sitting behind you—but when the bad players are out of the pot, you should be too unless you have a strong hand. As illustrated by the following example, you should often fold hands that you would play with a weaker player sitting to your left.

> **GAME:** $5/$10 blinds—5 players
> **STACKS:** $1,000 effective
> **READS:** HJ is a fish, BTN is world-class
> **YOUR HAND:** You have A♦ 9♣ in the cutoff
> **PREFLOP:** HJ folds

WHAT SHOULD YOU DO?

You should fold. In extreme cases, you should make severe alterations to your range. Most of the time, however, you shouldn't take it too far. When a moderately bad player opens in early position, you shouldn't cold call in the cutoff with

8♠ 2♠. But you can start playing suited connectors, weaker suited hands such as Q-8 and J-7, and big offsuit hands that you would fold against a more dangerous opponent. This is not an exhaustive list. You should always be thinking about other situations where deviating will be more profitable than sticking to your chart.

THE TAKEAWAY
Never be afraid to sell someone a crane!

MISCONCEPTION #5
PLAY LOOSE SO NO ONE CAN PUT YOU ON A HAND

You've probably heard people say that the key to getting paid off is playing loose so that no one can put on a hand. Some of the best players in the world play looser than the vast majority of other good players. There is often a drive to emulate them. Perhaps this stems from hero worship, or perhaps from the misconception that playing so loose is what makes these players great. But they've got it backward.

Great players often play loose *because* they're great—they're not great because they're loose. In other words, they can get away with playing many weaker hands preflop because their world-class postflop skills allow them to make up so much ground later in the hand. That's half the story.

The other half of the story is that they're frequently playing with considerably deeper stacks than the typical online game allows. If you gave these players stacks of just 100 big blinds, they would have to play much tighter simply because there is less room for postflop maneuvering. So the next time you see Tom Dwan, Phil Ivey or Patrik Antonius cold call with 5-3s, take a look at their **effective** stack sizes, the size of their stacks in relation to the blinds. Television coverage doesn't always do a great job of communicating this information, but if you pay attention you should be able to figure it out. The fact is that with 100 big-blind stacks, tight is right.

> Great players look for profitable opportunities, and they're great at finding those opportunities. That's what makes them great, and that's what lets them play so loose.

They see ways to take pots away on the flop, turn and river. They see ways to squeeze extra value out of their opponents. They find ways to get away from sick spots where a lesser player might go broke. As great players discover how big their edge is over their opponents, they often start loosening up. They do well and then keep pushing the envelope. Eventually, it just becomes their game.

Some of this crazy looseness that you see is a television illusion. How many hours do you think they play to get those five or six hands that they feature in a 42-minute episode? They don't show people folding for hours on end. It's boring. They pick the hand where the guy shoves with 10-7s, not the one where someone opens under the gun and everyone folds.

To add to this, TV time is money. Consider that a 30-second commercial slot during the Super Bowl may cost a few million dollars. Getting a hand featured on television can build up a brand and build up an image for a player. We can't know for sure why a player chooses to play a hand a certain way. It could be for deception, knowing that many people will see this hand and make broad judgments about the player's game. There's more than one player who looks like a crazy guy on TV, but who plays totally different online. Considering how much TV time is worth, it's also possible that the player wants to buy some cheap airtime for the logos he's wearing. **Taking a line** (an approach) with a little negative EV, say $1,000, can be easily outweighed by the publicity it generates. It's hard to find airtime cheaper than a grand for five minutes.

Playing loose is fun. It's great to imagine that you can find ways to outplay your opponents postflop, but imagination and reality don't always line up. Are you so much better than your opponents that you can really get away with playing inferior hands on a regular basis? If so, that's fantastic: Get in there and make some money! But there's a good chance you could make more money by reining it in a bit and adding tables. If you're that much better than your opponents, there's also a good chance that you would make more money by moving up in stakes. Adding tables or moving up might cause your win rate to shrink, but your hourly earn would increase.

Are You Playing for Money or for Fun? Decide.

To some extent, you can do both. Playing for money (if you're good at it) can be plenty fun. But you must prioritize. One or the other has to come first. Make sure that if you're playing loose, you're doing it for the right reasons. When the game conditions are right, go for it. If you're a freak who can mass multi-table and still play a larger percentage of your hands, great. If you're one of the best players in the world and you play a small number of tables at the highest stakes, even better. But that's probably not you—at least not yet. That's not most people. Most people play loose for the wrong reasons. Most people can make more money playing a bit tighter across more tables.

Say you have the option of playing either 20 percent or 30 percent of your hands at a given table. Assuming the extra 10 percent adds to your profitability, your win rate will be higher at that table if you play looser. But how much higher will it be? Those additional hands won't provide a windfall. They will be varying degrees of marginal. So you'll be playing 50 percent more hands, but you won't increase your win rate by 50 percent.

Now consider how many tables you can play if you're playing 30 percent of your hands. How many more tables could you play if you only played 20 percent of your hands? Assuming you have the proper computer set up, the answer should be at least 50 percent more. Not only are you playing fewer hands at each table, but you're specifically playing fewer marginal hands. That means you'll have fewer time-consuming decisions. More of your plays will be straightforward.

Let's say that you usually can either play loose (30 percent of your hands) and get in 400 hands per hour, or tight (20 percent of your hands) and get dealt 600 hands per hour. If playing tight will yield 10 cents per hand, maybe playing loose will yield 12 cents per hand. Would you rather make $60 per hour or $48?

THE TAKEAWAY

It's good to try different styles. Find what feels comfortable for you, but be honest with yourself. One way or another, you want to end up with the style that allows you to make the most money.

MISCONCEPTION #6

SUPERTIGHT IS BETTER THAN TIGHT

"To begin with, I recommend playing only the top ten hands and folding all others."

- Phil Hellmuth in *Play Poker Like the Pros*

The above book, written by a World Series of Poker Champion, suggests that a beginning hold'em player should play only "The Top Ten" hands before the flop. By his account, those hands would be pocket sevens and better, A-K, and A-Q. This advice would have you playing only six percent of your hands. That's absurd!

There's a lot to be said for playing tight, particularly for a beginning player. This holds true for the experienced player sitting at many tables as well. But six percent is about the range you should play in an 18-handed game. That's twice the number of players at a typical table. Paul used to play 11-handed in some New York clubs, but it's hard to find a poker table to sit more players than Jesus sat apostles. Many people will say that the preflop advice in this book errs on the tight side, but it's clearly not the tightest advice in print.

In fairness to Phil, this advice is intended for limit hold'em. In no-limit hold'em, he suggests boosting it up to fifteen hands by adding all of the pocket pairs. That's still too tight. (Ignore for a moment the fact that good limit players play approximately 50 percent looser than good no-limit players.) Aside from being ridiculously tight, this advice is a gross oversimplification of a complex game. Yes, beginners can often benefit from simplifying things. But there's a line between generalizing and overgeneralizing. And playing only the top ten hands is over that line. (A brief confession: In 2007, Paul played over 100,000 hands of small-stakes no-limit with a VPIP of 7. Voluntairly Put In Pot (VPIP) is the percentage of hands where a player puts money in the pot on purpose. Dusty had to have the "nit" beaten out of him a couple years after that.)

There is an allure to playing an extremely simple style of poker and firing up as many tables as possible. Less thinking. More rakeback and bonus money. We've included some simplified solutions for both beginners and players who want to maximize their earnings. But again, there's a line. We can't oversimplify. Hold'em is dynamic. You should have different default ranges for each position, and you should adjust those ranges for each opponent. Against a raise and a reraise, it may be correct to play only 3 percent of your hands. When it's folded to you on the button, it may be correct to play 70 percent or more. There is no one-size-fits-all hand range.

THE TAKEAWAY

Always beware of sweeping generalizations. Also be aware of where your advice comes from. Does the author have a successful track record in the games you're trying to learn? Does he have experience teaching and coaching poker? Or is he just cashing in on some television coverage by running off a quick book. Be sure the advice you adopt is backed up by logic and a track record of success.

What constitutes a track record of success? Winning a major live tournament is a big deal, and it can be great publicity. But not only is a single tournament a tiny sample size (anyone can get lucky one time—just ask Jerry Yang or Jamie Gold), it's fundamentally different from cash games. So if you're looking to improve at cash games, then you should look for someone with a track record of success over millions of hands in the same game format that you play.

And don't listen to Phil Hellmuth!

MISCONCEPTION #7

MAKE ALL YOUR PREFLOP RAISES THE SAME SIZE

A common piece of advice is to make all of your preflop raises the same size. The theory is that, by always raising the same amount, you guard against leaking information about the quality of your hand. This is a simple and safe solution to raise sizing. It has an attractive logic, and we've all played around with it. It's also really easy to do. There are players who raise to three blinds with most of their hands, but four or five blinds with only their strongest hands. This is an awful strategy and you should not seek to emulate it. These guys would do well to always raise the same amount, since their current strategy telegraphs their hand strength. But we can do better.

Many factors come into play when deciding how to size your raise:

1. Are there short stacks behind you?

Some players like to simplify the game by playing with the minimum buy in, which is as small as 20 blinds in many online games. They leverage the fact that they can shove all of their chips in against a raise and avoid playing postflop poker. If one of these players is left to act behind you, open raising to 3 or more blinds is usually a mistake. A normal to large sized raise gives them good odds to shove over your open. Instead, make your raises smaller, effectively making their stack play deeper against you. This makes their short-stacking strategy less profitable. It also costs less when you open and then fold to their reraise.

2. Are there big calling stations in the blinds?

If so, you should make your open-raises a bit larger. Calling stations will be calling with a weaker range both before and after the flop. By raising more, you bloat the pot and allow yourself to get more value on every street. They'll miss a lot of flops—everyone does—so you'll take down larger pots with your continuation bets. They'll also call too often on the turn and river those times they do flop something decent. The larger preflop pot will allow you to get more chips in with your strong hands on the turn and river. You'll have a good chance to take a calling station's stack.

3. Are there very aggressive players in the blinds?

When the blinds like to reraise a ton, min-raising can be a good option. Your opponents may call more often, but that's okay since you're getting a better price on your steal (4 to 3 instead of the usual 2 to 1). Aggressive play may also reraise a bit less frequently, since they're getting a worse price on a resteal with less money in the pot. Experience shows that many aggressive opponents will still make their "standard" sized reraise to 10 or 11 blinds. Your smaller raise size means you lose less when you fold to these raises. You also get a great price on a small 4-bet bluff when they do have a wide range. There's no need to make a large 4-bet, since they'll almost always shove or fold.

4. Do you have an edge on the blinds?

When you're on the button and the blinds play at least as well as you do, this is another good spot to min-raise. You're effectively cutting the stakes against the good players. (An ancillary benefit at small to medium stakes is paying less rake the times the blinds call and you take a flop.) With bad players in the blinds, you'll be making larger raises and playing larger pots. Just like you'd prefer to play big pots with big hands, you'd also prefer to play big pots against bad players.

5. Do the blinds call a lot preflop and fold a lot postflop?

This is a specific manner of playing poorly, and it gives you a huge incentive to make some slightly larger raises. Don't make your raises so big that the blinds start folding a bunch. You want them to call so you can pick up a more profitable spot after the flop.

6. Are there limpers ahead of you?

A common practice is to add one blind to your raise size for every limper. This is a good default, but when the limper is a big calling station, you can often extract more value after the flop by raising a bit more before the flop. Calling an extra 7 blinds may not seem much different to them than calling an extra 5 blinds, but it has a snowballing effect. Your postflop bets can be progressively larger on each street with the larger preflop raise. An extra 2 blinds now could mean an extra 4 blinds on the flop, another 8 on the turn, and a bonus of 16 blinds on the river. Those 2 blinds quickly compounded to 30 blinds. With something like a big pair or suited big cards, you should go for the bigger raise if you think the limper will call it. Let's look at two ways the same hand can play out:

GAME:	$5/$10 blinds—6 players
STACKS:	$1,000 effective
READS:	HJ is very loose, bad and stubborn
YOUR HAND:	You have **K♠ K♦** on the button
PREFLOP:	HJ calls, 1 player folds, you raise to $70, 2 players fold, HJ calls
FLOP:	**Q♠ 7♦ 2♣** ($155—2 players)
ACTION:	HJ checks, you bet $100, HJ calls
TURN:	**9♦** ($355—2 players)
ACTION:	HJ checks, you bet $240, HJ calls
RIVER:	**3♣** ($835—2 players)
ACTION:	HJ checks, you bet $590, HJ calls
SHOWDOWN:	HJ mucks **Q♣ J♣** and you win a $2,015 pot

Would you rather win a $1,415 pot or a $2,015 one?

7. Can you safely juice the pot?

When you have a small pocket pair or suited connector, it can be tempting to make a small raise after a few players limp in. This is a horrible idea in tough games, since the blinds are so likely to squeeze you out of the pot. By raising, you also reopen the action to the limpers, who can now reraise themselves. The only time you should consider using this play is when the blinds are extremely passive and you're almost certain the limpers will not reraise. These conditions usually appear only in small-stakes live games. Under these ideal circumstances it may be worth making a small raise, trying to build a big pot before the flop. This will allow you to get more chips in after the flop those times you make a monster. Be extremely careful with this play! When in doubt, either limp along or make a normal sized raise.

These are a few of the situations where you should think about varying your raise sizes. Sometimes you will have conflicting considerations, in which case you have to weigh which factor is more important. Take the following example:

> **GAME:** $5/$10 blinds—6 players
> **STACKS:** You have $1550, BB has $1320, SB has $215
> **READS:** SB is tight and aggressive, BB is very loose and bad
> **YOUR HAND:** You have **8♦ 5♦** on the button with $1,550
> **PREFLOP:** 3 players fold, you raise to $40

By raising to $40, you lose more when the short-stacked small blind shoves over your open. With a reasonably skilled big blind, you'd be better off raising to just $20. But the value of playing a bigger pot with the terrible player outweighs the risk of losing an extra $20 against the short stack. The slightly deeper stack of the bad player (132 blinds and you cover) makes the larger raise size the right play.

You will find plenty of other opportunities to vary your raise size if you look for them. It's fine to have a default open-raise size (3 blinds is good for most games). But don't get hemmed in and always raise the same amount. Overly static preflop play can lead to overly static postflop play. Before you know it, you can be auto-piloting ABC poker on all four streets. Starting your imagination and paying attention preflop is like eating a good breakfast. It gets your hand started on the right track.

THE TAKEAWAY

Don't waste chips by raising more than necessary—and don't fail to take as much off the weaker players as you can.

MISCONCEPTION #8

PUNISH THE LIMPERS!

"With this guy limping ahead of me, I can make a big raise with any two cards and the guy will fold nine times out of ten. It's even better when he doesn't fold, because he's just going to miss the flop and fold so often, I can usually take it down with a c-bet."

— Dusty Schmidt, circa 2007

Here's an outdated piece of advice you may have heard straight from Dusty. (Don't think we're above calling ourselves out!) There was a time when raising it up to 5 or 6 blinds after a guy limped in would be profitable with any two cards. Aggressive 3-betting had not yet become mainstream, and most of the limpers would fold against these big raises 9 times out of 10. On the rare occasions that they decided to take a flop, they would fold to a continuation bet 7 or 8 times out of 10. While these numbers may be a slight exaggeration, it felt like it worked every time. It went something like this:

> **GAME:** $1/$2 blinds—6 players
> **STACKS:** $1,000 effective
> **YOUR HAND:** You have 7♥ 2♦ in the cutoff
> **PREFLOP:** HJ calls with Q♣ J♠, you raise to $12, 3 players fold, HJ calls
> **FLOP:** K♠ 8♦ 4♦ ($27—2 players)
> **ACTION:** HJ checks, you bet $12, HJ folds

Eventually the limpers would get fed up with getting raised every time they limped—but would they start raising before the flop? Would they aggressively play back at you after the flop? No. They wouldn't get clever, they'd just spite-call down for their whole stack once they finally caught a piece. This meant not only would you still win all the pots where they missed, but now you could win some massive pots when you hit a little harder than they did. Consider the following hand from the next orbit:

GAME:	$1/$2 blinds—5 players
STACKS:	$1,000 effective
YOUR HAND:	You have 6♠ 3♥ in the cutoff
PREFLOP:	HJ calls with Q♦ 10♦, you raise to $12, 3 players fold, HJ calls
FLOP:	10♠ 6♦ 3♣ ($27—2 players)
ACTION:	HJ checks, you bet $22, HJ calls
TURN:	4♥ ($71—2 players)
ACTION:	HJ checks, you bet $57, HJ calls
RIVER:	A♥ ($185—2 players)
ACTION:	HJ checks, you bet all in, HJ calls
RESULT:	You win HJ's whole stack with a weak two pair

Back then no one was reraising to resteal with air. Punishing the limpers was like shooting fish in a barrel. Things change: Over the years, the game has gotten tougher. Good players constantly work on their games using books, training websites, forums, and software. It's so easy to find information about how to play better poker that even bad players have improved. The days when you could blindly raise any two cards after a limper are gone. When people limp these days, they'll actually call your raise a substantial percentage of the time. To make matters worse, the good players are aware that you'll be punishing limpers by raising a wide range. They'll call more liberally, knowing that your range is weak and that the limper will play poorly. This is a very profitable spot for the good player sitting behind you or in the blinds. It's also a decent spot for them to throw in some extra 3-bets. While the limper may be calling your raise liberally, they're still going to fold most of their range to a 3-bet. If your range is very wide here, you'll have to fold a lot as well.

Raising any two cards against a limper is out. The only time it still works is when you know that the only players left to act are tight and this particular limper will often fold to a raise. These game conditions are more likely to exist in the small stakes than either the mid-high stakes, where players are tougher, or the micro stakes, where you'll get too many calls (who's really folding for $.14?).

So what should you actually be raising after someone limps? You can still get in there with a good-sized range. With the extra money in the pot, in addition to the chance of playing a hand in position against a bad player, you should raise a wider range than if everyone had folded. Our suggestion is to loosen up your opening guidelines by one position.

GAME: $5/$10 blinds—6 players
STACKS: $1,000 effective
YOUR HAND: You have 8♣ 7♣ in the hijack
PREFLOP: LJ limps, you raise to $50

If you're following the open-raising guidelines in Chart #1, you would usually fold 8♣ 7♣ two seats off the button. Normally you would only play the hand from the cutoff, button, or small blind. But with the bad player limping ahead of you, it's worth a raise.

The exception to this guideline is when you're in the small blind. Now the limper is even more likely to call because he is in position. That means you'll be out of position and have to see more flops. In this case you should stick to your regular small blind opening range unless this particular limper folds unusually often or is inordinately terrible.

THE TAKEAWAY

Question all advice to see what brings the most profit to your game—even our advice!

MISCONCEPTION #9

PUNISH THE NITS!

When you see a player folding to a lot of reraises, it can be tempting just to hammer on him constantly. In fact, if he's folding to a ton of reraises, then reraising relentlessly is more or less the correct response. The reason it's only mostly correct instead of completely correct is that this is a fluid edge. No one wants to be exploited (no matter what misogynists, slavery apologists, or global corporations may tell you). Most players will make adjustments against you if you're too obvious about the manner in which you're exploiting them.

Some poker authorities will have you believe that folding to too many preflop reraises is a massively exploitable leak. They go so far as to suggest that you should exploit this tendency in others by 3-betting with any two cards against an opponent who folds to 3-bets more than 67 percent of the time. Here's an example to illustrate their point:

> **GAME:** $5/$10 blinds—6 players
> **STACKS:** $1,000 effective
> **READS:** LJ is tight and aggressive
> **YOUR HAND:** You have any two cards on the button
> **PREFLOP:** LJ raises to $30, 2 players fold,
> you reraise to $90

By ignoring certain considerations, the math is simple. There is $45 in the pot (LJ's $30 plus $5 and $10 blinds). By reraising to $90, you're laying the pot 2 to 1 odds. If you win uncontested 67 percent of the time or more, you'll make a small profit (.67 x $45 - .33 x $90 = $.45).

There's a handy statistic that you can put in your Heads Up Display called **Folds To 3-bet** (**FT3B**). This number reflects your opponent's behavior against all 3-bets. There's no doubt that this stat can be useful and give you a general idea of how an open-raiser will respond to getting reraised. Here's the trouble:

it doesn't tell you how the raiser responds when *you* reraise. You make adjustments against different opponents. Most of your opponents make adjustments against you. So while FT3B gives you a general idea of your opponent's tendencies, you still need to keep your eyes open and make more specific reads as you play.

There are some additional problems that you will encounter if you start 3-betting too much (even against these nits). Unless you're the big blind, there are more players left to act. They can pick up a big hand or even 4-bet bluff if they see you getting out of line too often. Further, there are three more streets to play. Let's assume that your preflop 3-bet was immediately profitable in a vacuum (i.e. your opponent will fold often enough to overcome the chances of a third player 4-betting). Theoretically, you could just give up unless you flop a monster. But once you start checking back every missed flop, your opponent will become even more likely to adjust to your aggressive 3-betting.

THE TAKEAWAY

Your alternative to giving up is to judiciously fire continuation bets, second barrel bluffs, and **thin value bets** (a bet that gets called by a better hand more than half the time). If you're a master at these things, that's great. We hope you get to that point where you know how to play J-7 or 9-5 after reraising and seeing a flop of Q-9-2. But if you're not there yet, you can get yourself in a lot of trouble by 3-betting too much. You want to set up profitable decisions that you're prepared for. So if you prepare for flopping middle pair in a reraised pot, then you can get away with a little more light 3-betting. If not, be careful with it.

Please note that we're not suggesting that you never reraise a weak hand against someone who folds a lot. The keys here are to use your judgment and not to overdo it. Small preflop edges evaporate quickly when you get burned by large postflop errors.

MISCONCEPTION #10
3-Betting A Lot Makes Me Tough

There is a machismo associated with aggressive 3-betting. The idea is to put a lot of pressure on your opponents to make yourself harder to play against. But does it really make you that tough to play against?

When someone starts 3-betting you all over the place before the flop, they're saying one of two things:

1. They can run you over preflop, or build up a big pot and exploit a larger edge postflop since there's more money out there; or

2. They *cannot* outplay you postflop, so they're willing to take a small preflop edge instead of utilizing their position in a more sophisticated fashion. In this case, they're tacitly admitting that they can't outplay you after the flop. They're trying to end the hand now by 3-betting, hoping that you fold.

Assuming that you're neither folding to 9 out of 10 reraises nor calling preflop and pitching on most flops, the edges they're trying to squeeze out of you before the flop are very small. The thing is that when they have position on you, they should usually be trying to see flops with you and create larger edges for themselves after the flop. Instead, they see a small edge now and they seize it. We call this the lazy-edge syndrome, and it results in mindlessly 3-betting hands that play better for a call. When you're in their position, you can do better.

The hands where this makes the largest difference are A-Q, K-Q, pocket twos through tens, A-J suited and the like. When you 3-bet these hands, competent opponents will usually fold the hands that you're dominating and continue only with the hands that dominate you. Furthermore, they'll often 4-bet with their biggest hands, forcing you to fold before the flop. Instead of taking a flop against a strong hand and getting a chance to stack your opponent when you flop a set, you're sticking nine blinds into the pot and folding. So before you drag the slider bar to size your 3-bet, think about what range you're likely to get called by and whether you'd prefer to play a big pot against that range, or a smaller pot against a wider range. Consider the following hand:

> **GAME:** $5/$10 blinds—5 players
> **STACKS:** $1,000 effective
> **READS:** HJ is a solid regular
> **YOUR HAND:** You have **A♦ Q♣** on the button
> **PREFLOP:** HJ raises to $30, 1 player folds, you call, 2 players fold

In the above situation, you probably have a small equity edge against your opponent's range. You can reraise, get some folds now, some more folds after the flop, and occasionally lose a huge pot against aces, kings, queens, or ace-queen. It's quite likely that this line has a small positive expected value.

Instead of reraising before the flop, however, you can call and see a flop. Now when the flop comes ace high, your opponent will likely pay you off on all three streets with hands like A-J, A-10 and maybe some weaker suited aces. When the flop comes queen high, he'll pay you off with king-queen, queen-jack, and maybe some smaller pocket pairs. Those are all hands that he would have folded to your 3-bet. You can extract more value from those dominated hands by calling than by raising. Additionally, calling preflop doesn't mean that you've given up your right to bluff at the flop. Your opponent will flop nothing more often than not. He'll usually fire out a c-bet that you can raise as a bluff, or call, planning to outplay him on the turn or river. If he checks the flop instead, you can try to take the pot away right there.

When a bad player opens ahead of you, go ahead and 3-bet a wider range. He's going to call with those dominated hands. That's half of what makes him bad. By reraising, you get to play a big pot against a bad player who will pay you off with many dominated holdings. And when he misses, he'll just fold and you'll win a nice big pot. But against a good player, you're just not going to get the response you're looking for.

Chart #2 shows a set of defaults for which hands to call and which ones to reraise when you have position against a competent opener. The first column on the left shows the open-raiser's position, which is the number one factor you should consider when deciding how to play your hand. Each hand listed in the chart is the minimum hand you should play in that situation (e.g. if you have J-J against a LJ open, you should call, whereas you should 3-bet the same hand against a CO open). If you get 4-bet, you should be happy to get the money in with the hands listed in the reraising column.

CHART #2: RERAISING AND CALLING IN POSITION					
OPPONENT'S POSITION	**RERAISE**	**CALL**			
	PAIRS	**UNPAIRED**	**PAIRS**	**SUITED**	**OFFSUIT**
EP, LJ, HJ	K-K	A-K suited	2-2	A-10, K-10, Q-10, J-10	A-Q
CO	J-J	A-K	2-2	A-10, K-10, Q-10, J-10	A-J
Note that these are defaults for stacks of 125 blinds or less. As stacks get deeper, you can generally play more hands.					

Several other factors should affect your decision as well:

1. How often does the raiser fold to 3-bets?

In the last chapter we mentioned that the mere fact that a raiser folds to 3-bets more than 67 percent does not mean you should reraise with any two cards. Still, against a player who will fold a ridiculously large portion of his range (say, 90 percent), you can use this play. This can also be an incentive to cold call more against players you'd like to see flops against.

2. How often does the raiser fold postflop?

If your opponent calls a lot of 3-bets, then folds a lot after the flop, you can profit a lot from 3-betting looser. If his strategy against your reraise is to fold his medium strength hands and 4-bet his strong ones, then you can make more from his postflop nittiness by calling with a wider range before the flop. This way you allow him to commit a few more chips after the flop before you take the pot away from him.

3. Will the cutoff play tighter preflop if you 3-bet him a lot from the button?

Whenever everyone folds to you on the button, you're in a profitable spot. If harassing the cutoff with aggressive 3-bets will make him tighten up, it's usually worth it to hammer on him until he gives up. That doesn't mean you should start reraising with any two cards. Hands like K-6 suited and 10-7 suited provide a good backup plan for the times your opponent calls your reraise and takes a flop. You can make flushes and straights, pick up profitable semibluffing opportunities, and hit your overcards to their pocket-pair-heavy calling range.

4. Do the blinds squeeze a lot?

The more often the blinds squeeze, the fewer speculative hands you should call with. Now you're better off 3-betting these borderline hands, since you're more likely to see a flop. Conversely, this is a good spot to cold call with some of your strong hands, hoping that one of the blinds will squeeze and you can make a suspicious looking 4-bet, enticing them to get it in light. Taking this to the extreme is an unbalanced strategy, but it's an effective exploitation of your opponent's aggressive tendencies.

THE TAKEAWAY

As you can see, there are many factors to consider when deciding whether to 3-bet or cold call. Only with experience and knowledge of your opponents will you learn which factors are the most important in any situation. When in doubt, start by asking yourself these three questions:

- What will happen after the flop if I call?
- What will happen after the flop if I raise?
- Which outcome would I prefer?

If you're still learning the fundamentals of the game, it's best to stick to the chart. As you develop your game, you'll learn to recognize the above conditions and take advantage.

MISCONCEPTION #11

DON'T TOUCH MY BLINDS

"Do not touch my blinds! I'm going to go all in every hand if you keep touching my *blinds."*

- Tony G

You constantly hear players, experts even, talk about defending the blinds. "Defend your blinds!" From what? The notion is that you've put a chip from your stack into the middle, and the cutoff, button, or small blind is attempting to steal it by raising before the flop. Somehow, you're supposed to fight back and not let them run over "your" blinds. This is a load of crap!

The first thing you need to do is disabuse yourself of the notion that the blinds belong to anybody. They don't. They belong to the pot. Once you put your chip in the pot, it is no longer yours. Novice players often overlook this concept when they call a flop and/or turn bet, then throw away good money chasing the bad on future streets. They see that there is a lot of "their" money in the pot, so they want it back. More accomplished players understand that this money no longer belongs to them. Its just money in the pot, the same as the money your opponent put in there.

Why should things be any different before the flop? They're not. In Texas hold'em, the player to the dealer's immediate left posts a small blind and the next player posts a big blind. Then the cards are dealt. That blind money still sits in front of the players who put it in the pot, but it's no longer their money. It's really just an ante that provides those two players a discount to play the hand. The money belongs to the pot. Everyone at the table "owns" a share of that blind money, so when the button open-raises, he's not trying to steal your blind. He's just fighting for his rightful share.

Consider the nature of theft. Think of the pot as a bag of Twinkies in a corpse's house after an apocalyptic disaster has eliminated all government. A group of survivors enters the house. Someone sees the Twinkies first, someone else is closest, and a third person might have a gun. It doesn't matter how the indestructible cream-filled pastries got there or who they belonged to, someone is going to get the Twinkies. It's usually the person in the best position, unless someone else has a gun. The money in the pot belongs to the button and cutoff just as much as it belongs to you. Where does this leave us? We're right back to square one. Our only consideration when looking down at two cards in the blinds is, "Will I make or lose money by playing this hand? Should I fight for this bag of Twinkies?"

When you're out of position, the answer is usually "only if you have a gun."

Let's focus on the hands that will make money and toss the losers. Certain hands will be playable against almost any opponent opening from any position. These include all pocket pairs, A-K, A-Q, and all suited Broadway cards. These hands will be playable almost regardless of the opener's range, since they can call strong hands and strong draws on the flop. If your opponent holds a wide range, you will have good equity. If he's opening from early position with a narrower range, your implied odds increase. You need an excellent reason to fold any of these hands before the flop for a single raise.

As the opener's range becomes wider, you can profitably play more hands. Your implied odds will be lower, but you'll have more semibluffing opportunities and have better equity against your opponent's range. Chart #3 shows good default minimums for calling and reraising from the big blind against a competent opponent opening from a particular position.

CHART #3: "DEFENDING" THE BIG BLIND					
OPPONENT POSITION	CALL	RERAISE			
	PAIRS	SUITED	OFFSUIT	PAIRS	UNPAIRED
EP/LJ/HJ	2-2	A-10, K-10, Q-10, J-10	A-Q	Q-Q	A-K
CO	2-2	A-10, K-10, Q-10, J-10, 10-9	A-10, K-J	10-10	A-Q
BTN	2-2	A-10, K-10, Q-10, J-10, 10-9	A-10, K-J, Q-J	10-10	A-J, K-Q
SB	2-2	A-2, K-2, Q-7, J-7, 10-7, 9-6, 8-5, 7-4, 6-3, 5-3, 4-3	A-8, K-9, Q-9, J-8, 10-9, 9-8, 8-7	10-10	A-Q

As with all the charts in this book, these defaults are on the tight side. In fact, if you follow these guidelines and never make any adjustments, you will be playing too tight. These are the hands you should play against another reasonably skilled player. Remember to open it up and call with more hands against weaker opponents, or when other factors play in your favor.

Also remember that these guidelines are for a typical 100-blind online game. As stacks get deeper, you can play more weak suited aces, suited connectors and gappers, offsuit connectors and Broadway hands. These cards can often be played out of position in a super deep-stacked game. Most of these hands either lose small pots or win big ones. Stack size doesn't matter much when you try to play a small pot, since you'll never be putting all the money in anyway. When you want to play a big pot, however, having more money behind will give you a chance to get more value from your monster hands and apply more pressure with your semibluffs. So, with hands that can make big draws and big hands, the deeper the better.

MISCONCEPTION #12
THE SMALL BLIND IS IMPOSSIBLE TO PLAY

Every time you take a flop from the small blind, you're out of position. This makes marginal hands difficult to play. You also don't have the luxury of closing the action like you do in the big blind. So yeah, the small blind is tough to play, but it's not impossible—not if you make it simple. Why play those marginal hands when you know you're going to be out of position? Why cold call against button opens just to watch the big blind squeeze you out of even seeing a flop?

Don't do it. Keep it simple.

When you're in the small blind against an open-raiser from any position other than the button, you should play similarly to how you would from the big blind. You may want to ditch a few of the weaker offsuit hands from your calling range, since the threat of a squeeze from the big blind makes these hands less profitable. A-10 and K-J offsuit also don't play great multiway, so that makes them even less attractive.

The spot where small-blind play differs the most from big-blind play is when you are facing a button open. In that case, you should usually reraise or fold, since the threat of getting squeezed is quite high. You should usually 3-bet all pairs, all suited Broadway hands, K-Q offsuit, and A-J offsuit and better. That's your basic value range. Against a more aggressive opponent, you can widen this value range. You can also add in some semibluffs with suited connectors, suited aces, and occasionally any two cards, depending on how the button responds to getting 3-bet.

When the button 4-bets, you should be willing to ship it in with tens and better, A-K, and A-Q. You would prefer to be the one putting the last bet in, since you can pick up some pots without even seeing a flop. This assumes that stacks are about 100 blinds deep and the button is not overly passive. With deeper stacks or a passive opponent, you should require a stronger hand to get your chips in before the flop.

THE TAKEAWAY

There are two situations where you should consider cold calling against the button:

1. You have a pocket pair or other hand with strong implied odds and the big blind is a big fish.

   Playing a pot with a big fish means big value, so you should just call and invite him to join you for a three-way party.

2. The big blind is a big squeezer.

   If you cold call with aces, kings, or other big hands and then shove over a squeeze, your line will look like total garbage. The big blind's range will be wide, but he will often call your shove light.

One hand that requires special attention is K-Q. Whether it's suited or offsuit, you should usually reraise with K-Q against a cutoff or button open. The reason for this is that A-K and A-Q will usually 4-bet preflop, allowing you to get away cheap, while K-J and Q-J will often call. This lets you take flops against the hands that you dominate while getting off the hook early against the hands that dominate you. Contrast this to playing K-Q in position, where the opener will often fold the hands you're dominating. In position, you'd rather cold call, but out of position in the small blind, a reraise is the play.

Charts #4 and #5 summarize the default minimums for calling and reraising against openers from each position.

CHART #4: CALLING FROM THE SMALL BLIND			
OPPONENT'S POSITION	PAIRS	SUITED	OFFSUIT
EP	2-2	A-10, K-10, Q-10, J-10	A-K
LJ/HJ	2-2	A-10, K-10, Q-10, J-10	A-Q
CO	2-2	A-10, K-10, Q-10, J-10	A-J

CHART #5: RERAISING FROM THE SMALL BLIND			
OPPONENT'S POSITION	PAIRS	SUITED	OFFSUIT
EP	K-K		
LJ/HJ	Q-Q	A-K	A-K
CO	Q-Q	A-J, K-Q	A-Q, K-Q
BTN	2-2	A-10, K-10, Q-10, J-10	A-J, K-Q

MISCONCEPTION #13

SUITED CONNECTORS WIN ALL THE BIG POTS IN NO- LIMIT HOLD'EM

Suited connectors such as 10-9s and 9-8s all the way down through 5-4s and 4-3s, are great hands in the right spots.

They can make straights and flushes to win big pots. They can flop strong draws, allowing you to aggressively semibluff and take down some pots without the best hand—but they are frequently overvalued. Suited connectors are great hands in the right spots. The key to playing them profitably is picking the right spots. Let's look at an example:

The cutoff open-raises and you have **8♥ 7♥** on the button. Is this a profitable opportunity to call? If there is a weak player in the blinds, yes, this is a good spot to let him in. He'll provide some nice implied odds when you hit, and play straightforwardly enough that you can win many of the pots where everyone misses. If instead, it's the cutoff who plays poorly postflop, then reraising for isolation is often better. You would rather have the weak player all to yourself.

But let's take that same **8♥ 7♥** and assume that the cutoff and blinds are all solid players. With stacks of 100 blinds, you won't have room to apply much pressure after the flop. Regardless of whether you call or reraise before the flop, it's too easy for your opponent to just go with the hand when he makes something like a pair or a draw. Consider the following example:

GAME:	$5/$10 blinds—6 players
STACKS:	$1,000 effective
READS:	CO is a solid and aggressive regular
YOUR HAND:	You have **8♥ 7♥** on the button
PREFLOP:	CO holds **K♠ Q♣,** 2 players fold, CO raises to $30, you call, 2 players fold
FLOP:	**Q♥ 9♥ 2♠** ($75—2 players)
ACTION:	CO bets $60, you raise to $180, CO raises to $970 (all in)

When your opponent shoves the flop, you're very near priced in to draw to your hand, but you'll be getting your money in with just 39 percent equity. Your opponent could just as easily have **A♥ K♥**, giving you only 19 percent equity.

With deeper stacks, your opponent would not be able to shove the flop without making a massive overbet. He'll be forced to make tougher decisions on later streets.

The flop in the example above has several different draws, which may lead the cutoff to get the money in as shown. If there were fewer draws, he might just call instead. When the board comes with an obvious draw to a straight or flush, a good hand reader will see through your semibluffs. He'll fold when the draws get there and call you down when they miss. He'll also be more willing to get it in with one pair on the flop than if the board were dry. He may even shove over your flop raise, forcing you to fold a lot of equity or commit your stack as a significant underdog.

When you're lucky enough to flop a made straight or flush, your skilled opponent will be more cautious, as the board will be scary. Your opponent is unlikely to give you his stack even with an overpair, since he'll be drawing dead against the possible nuts. Oddly enough, your best chance of getting paid is to flop a hint of a draw, call as a **float** (call with nothing), then catch runner-runner to make a straight or flush. In other words, if you really want to get paid, you need to backdoor your flush or straight. Looking back at your preflop decision, things get even worse when you throw a squeeze-happy big blind or small blind into the mix. Now you're not even going to see the flop all the time, and will be tossing away a few blinds for nothing. Without deep stacks, you won't have the implied odds or postflop maneuverability to profitably call their squeeze.

In a typical 100-big-blind game, there aren't a ton of great spots to play suited connectors. You should stick to spots where you can play multiway or against weaker players, preferably both. Once you make the stacks a little deeper, things start to look a little brighter. Now you have more room to maneuver. Your implied odds look sweeter, and your chances of moving someone off of a pair get better. No longer can your opponent shove over a flop raise for a pot-sized bet. He'll either have to make a big overbet (giving you great implied odds the times you flop a monster), or leave enough money behind for a big turn or river bet. That money will go in most of the times you improve, but not the times you miss. That extra money is like an albatross around your opponent's neck, weighing him down and letting you get away with a little more theft.

Another decent opportunity to get in there with suited connectors is when you've been playing tight and an active player opens ahead of you. You can 3-bet as a semibluff and expect to get a lot of folds. Your range should look very tight to your opponents, and even when you wind up seeing a flop, you've got a little something to fall back on.

THE TAKEAWAY

In summary, be careful with suited connectors. Pay attention and find the right spots to play them in. Look for one of the following situations:

1. **Weaker opponents**

   Bad players will provide you with both implied odds and folding equity. They miss value bets, call with hopeless hands, and telegraph their strength.

2. **Deep stacks**

   The more money there is left behind, the more there is to win with your straights, flushes, and two pair hands. There is also more postflop maneuverability, allowing you to get better odds on a draw or exert more pressure with a semibluff.

3. **Multiway pots**

   The more players in the pot, the better your immediate odds and the more likely you are to get paid off when you hit something big. Having multiple players in the pot is almost like having deeper stacks, at least in terms of how much money there is to win. You have less folding equity, but you're more likely to get paid.

Finally, remember that when you have a profitable opportunity to play a suited connector, you can often play some weaker suited hands as well. While hands like **9♣ 8♣** are more powerful than hands like **7♦ 5♦**, the difference is small enough that a single factor in your favor can suddenly make a whole group of hands profitable. You should pay at least as much attention to the current situation as you do to your actual cards.

MISCONCEPTION #14
BRING YOUR BIG GUNS TO A WAR!
"When you have a border skirmish with someone, you don't need to bring out the heavy artillery, but when a war breaks out, you'd better bring your big guns!"
- Phil Hellmuth, *Play Poker Like the Pros*

When you're sitting in the big blind and watch the button open-raise and the small blind cold call, it can be very tempting to put in a reraise. Doing this with discretion can be quite profitable. Most button raisers will have a wide range and will usually fold to a 3-bet, particularly since your pot-sized raise will be larger because of the extra money put in by the small blind. The small blind himself will rarely have a hand that is happy to see you 3-bet, since he would usually have reraised with those. Even when the small blind does decide to take a flop, you will have position on him, so it's not a poor result. It's called the squeeze play and it's very effective if used judiciously.

There was a time when you could squeeze with any two cards whenever the button opened and the small blind cold called. If you do that these days, someone will start playing back at you, or the small blind will begin cold calling with big hands trying to induce a squeeze from you. When overused, this valuable play quickly loses its effectiveness. The squeeze is a great weapon to have in your arsenal, but don't empty the clip too fast.

Just as you can squeeze against a button raise and small blind call, you can squeeze against a cutoff open and button call. Ostensibly, your opponents should give you more credit since you're 3-betting against a tighter range. Still, many opponents have wide cutoff ranges, so you may get them to fold a fairly high percentage of the time. The biggest trouble here is that the button has position on you and will be more likely to call your raise than the small blind would be. Players will also cold call on the button more often with hands like A-Q, whereas most players 3-bet those hands from the small blind. Again, squeezing in this scenario can be profitable if used judiciously. Be more cautious than you would in the first scenario.

Once we move the open-raiser up to the hijack or even further off the button, squeezing becomes a dicey proposition. Against some players, you may get an inordinate amount of respect. If the hijack is willing to fold 80 percent of his range, then go ahead and squeeze. But you still have to worry about the third player in the pot. Against an early or middle position raise, players will call with hands as strong as jacks, queens, and A-Q suited. Those hands are not folding to your squeeze. In fact, they may re-squeeze if the opener calls your reraise. When you consider everything that can go wrong, you need a special situation to make a compelling case to squeeze.

As a result of all the light 3-betting that goes on nowadays, 4-betting as a cold bluff is a viable option. This is another one of those spots where discretion is the difference between adding a valuable play to your arsenal and spewing like a madman. When you're in the big blind facing a button open and a small blind 3-bet, you have a tempting 4-bet opportunity regardless of what cards you hold. The button will usually have such a wide range that it's difficult for him to continue more than 10 percent of the time, if that often. In fact, assuming an opening range of 65 percent and a 5-bet shoving range of A-K, queens and better, he'll actually fold 96 percent of the time. Once the button folds, the small blind will be in a tough spot. His three options are to fold immediately, 5-bet all in, or call and play a large pot out of position. The last option is disgusting, so he'll almost always shove or fold. Assuming his 3-betting range in this spot is 12 percent, he's likely to fold between one-quarter and half the time.

THE SQUEEZE PLAY

> **GAME:** $5/$10 blinds—6 players
> **STACKS:** $1,000 effective
> **READS:** BTN and SB are both loose and aggressive
> **YOUR HAND:** You are in the big blind with any two cards
> **PREFLOP:** 3 players fold, BTN raises to $30,
> SB raises to $110, you raise to $240

You're spending 23 blinds to win 15 blinds, so you need both players to fold over 60 percent of the time to have a profitable bluff. If the small blind folds two-thirds of his range, then you have a slightly profitable play. So to keep this as a weapon in your arsenal, you need to keep the small blind folding closer to 75 percent than to 67 percent of the time.

THE FORMULA

To find how often a bluff needs to succeed, divide your price to bluff by the total amount of money in the pot after you raise. In this example, 23/38 = .605, or about 60 percent success is required for a profitable bluff. Both players must fold 60 percent, which is different from each player folding 60 percent. If each player folded 60 percent, then both players would fold only 36 percent of the time (.6 x .6 = .36). If the button folds 90 percent of the time, then the small blind needs to fold over 67 percent of the time (.9 x .67 = .603).

If you 4-bet too often, the button may tighten up a little on his steals and the small blind may tighten up a little on his 3-bets when you're in the blind. These are small benefits that can help you. Unfortunately, today's players are more likely to play back at you aggressively than to start folding a bunch of hands. As your success rate on the bluff goes down, the play goes from profitable to expensive.

IT'S A BALANCING ACT

Deciding how often to use this play is a balancing act. Think about the following situation: You're salivating over pocket aces in the big blind as you watch the button and small blind raise and reraise in front of you. After carefully sizing your 4-bet, you watch the button turbo-fold, then the small blind fold after pretending to deliberate. If you find that the only times you wind up getting the chips in against competent opponents is when you hold aces and they hold kings or queens, you're not bluffing enough. By bluffing a certain amount of the time, you force your opponents to either pay off your big hands, or let you run them out of some decent sized pots.

The same play can be profitable against openers from earlier positions, but it's more dangerous, particularly when the 3-bettor has position on you. It can be a useful tool to break out from time to time, particularly if you have an image on the tight side. Just keep it under control. The more you do it, the less effective it will become.

Two hands that require special consideration in these circumstances are J-J and 10-10. While you're typically far ahead of both players' ranges, the more relevant consideration is how you're doing against the hands that will get it in against you before the flop. Against most opponents, the answer is "not so hot." Their range will consist mostly of larger pairs and hands with two overcards. As a result, when you 4-bet with J-J or 10-10, your play is as much a bluff as it is a value play.

You're so unlikely to see a flop in this spot that your cards don't matter. In fact, if your opponent will never call your 4-bet and you don't plan on calling a shove, you should be more apt to bluff with any hand with an ace in it. This is because of the effect of card removal. With an ace in your hand, it is half as likely for your opponent to hold pocket aces and 25 percent less likely for your opponent to hold A-K. Those two hands make up a significant portion of most players' shoving ranges, so reducing how often your opponent can hold those hands reduces how often he'll shove. Holding a king in your hand will cause a similar effect.

Against opponents who either play very tight to your 4-bet or will 5-bet liberally as a bluff, you should go ahead and 4-bet. Against the former, you should fold to a shove; against the latter, you should be happy to call. Even if you're slightly behind when you call the 5-bet, you can make that up with the pots you'll pick up. When your opponents will 5-bet you aggressively, but not often enough that you're willing to call for your stack, just fold. Folding jacks or tens may feel weak when you're well ahead of your opponent's range, but there's just no way to play the hand profitably under those conditions. Poker is about finding profitable opportunities.

THE TAKEAWAY

It's nice to have a big gun, but sometimes a peashooter will get the job done!

MISCONCEPTION #15

MAKE BIG 3-BETS TO END THE HAND NOW

In the strictest sense, the above statement is true. If you reraise all in over the top of a 3-blind open, you're likely to get folds from everything except aces or kings and the occasional curious opponent—that is, until you start doing it all the time and your opponents take notice. So yeah, you can shove your whole stack in and get lots of folds. The problem is that it's extremely expensive. You've invested 10 times as many chips as you usually would, but is your opponent folding 10 times as often? It's not even close! Your opponent would have to be folding less than 10 percent of his range to your regular reraise for that to even be possible. (If your opponent folds 20 percent, then 10 times that is 200 percent, which is an impossibility.)

Clearly it isn't worth shoving all in as a bluff against a single raise. If you're reading this book, it's unlikely that's a mistake you're currently making, but there is a common, related mistake that many players make. When the cutoff opens to three blinds, it rarely makes sense to 3-bet to more than nine blinds from the button. The cutoff will fold a similar number of hands against a 9-blind reraise as he would against a 12-blind reraise. So why do so many players insist on making the larger 3-bet size? As discussed in Misconception #1, the motivation is often fear. They don't want to get their big hands cracked, they don't want to have their bluffs called, and they don't want to face tough decisions later in the hand. As you'll see, making the smaller raise size sets your opponent up for tough decisions.

It doesn't make sense to raise more for value, at least not with 100-blind stacks. If the cutoff calls the reraise, it will be easy to get the whole stack in after the flop with one-half to two-thirds pot-sized bets. That's part of the reason that the raise size shouldn't matter so much in terms of getting folds. The threat is the same. As shown in the example below, the 3-bettor has position and the choice to get all the chips in postflop.

> **GAME:** $5/$10 blinds—6 players
> **STACKS:** $1,000 effective
> **YOUR HAND:** You hold **K♣ K♠** on the button
> **PREFLOP:** 2 players fold, CO raises to $30,
> you raise to $90, 2 players fold, CO calls
> **FLOP:** 7♦ 6♦ 2♣ ($195—2 players)
> **ACTION:** CO checks, you bet $115, CO calls
> **TURN:** 2♠ ($425—2 players)
> **ACTION:** CO checks, you bet $240, CO calls
> **RIVER:** 4♥ ($905—2 players)
> **ACTION:** CO checks, you bet $555, CO calls
> **RESULT:** You win the $2,015 pot and CO mucks **J♥ J♦**

The larger raise size doesn't make a ton of sense as a bluff, either. Perhaps you'll shake loose a few more hands from the opener's range. Those are usually hands that have a hard time getting to showdown anyway. You actually want those hands to call before the flop so that you have an opportunity to make a more profitable bluff later in the hand, once there's more money in the pot.

In the following example, you give your opponent three chances to fold. Despite your modest preflop reraise, he's always facing the threat of committing a full 100-blind stack after the flop.

> **GAME:** $5/$10 blinds—6 players
> **STACKS:** $1,000 effective
> **YOUR HAND:** You hold **9♣ 8♣** on the button
> **PREFLOP:** 2 players fold, CO raises to $30,
> you raise to $90, 2 players fold, CO calls
> **FLOP:** 7♦ 6♦ 2♣ ($195—2 players)
> **ACTION:** CO checks, you bet $115, CO calls
> **TURN:** 2♠ ($425—2 players)
> **ACTION:** CO checks, you bet $240, CO calls
> **RIVER:** A♦ ($905—2 players)
> **ACTION:** CO checks, you bet $555, CO folds

RESULT: You win the $905 pot without a showdown as CO mucks **J♥ J♦**

There are two important exceptions to the guideline of tripling your opponent's raise size. The first is when you're up against a weak player who calls a lot preflop but gives up a lot postflop. Now you want to make a larger reraise because you think he will call with the same range he'd call against a smaller 3-bet. You want to take as many flops with this player as you can, and you want the other players behind you to fold. In this case, you should raise as much as you can without pushing the guy out of the pot. Get as many of his chips in the pot as you can before taking it away from him.

The other exception is when you're out of position to the raiser. When you 3-bet from the blinds, you should make your raise a little larger, since raising three times your opponent's raise size will now result in more calls. That wouldn't be such a problem if you had position, but as we've already discussed, you don't want to play too many big pots out of position. Good players don't often call 3-bets when they're out of position, but that changes when you give them position. By raising more, you also make the stack size shorter relative to the pot size. This usually benefits the player out of position, since there is a bit less room for postflop maneuvering. (This last effect is relatively minor here, since we're not suggesting that you reraise to something like five or six times your opponent's raise. Still, it's something you should think about when you're out of position.)

THE TAKEAWAY

While you should size your raise larger when you're out of position, don't take it too far. Add one or two blinds, making it no more than four times your opponent's raise. A reraise to 10 or 11 blinds is usually good against a 3-blind open. One mistake a lot of players make here is to reraise to 10 or 11 blinds even when the opener just makes a min-raise. Why use the same 3-bet size against just 2 blinds sitting in there? You're charging yourself too much when you're bluffing, and discouraging marginal hands from playing along with your value hands.

Don't be afraid to see some flops when you 3-bet. Whether you're in or out of position, you'll have initiative and a stronger range. Create profitable postflop opportunities, and don't spend more than you need to get the job done.

MISCONCEPTION #16
MAKE ONE DECISION AT A TIME

"I seem to look right into people's souls sometimes. I don't know what it is."

- Phil Hellmuth

"We've got to take it one day at a time" is an expression that you'll hear ad nauseam in baseball interviews, particularly when a team faces a difficult run down the stretch. While it's a terrible cliché that doesn't give a sportswriter much to work with, it's a cliché for a reason—it's the right approach. When things don't go well, you must have a short memory. Even when things do work out, you have to approach the next day with a fresh start. Yesterday's momentum is only as good as today's starting pitcher. In poker, the corollary is to approach each hand with a clear mind. Once you start grouping the results from a number of hands into a session, a rush, or even a week of play, superstition and irrationality can creep into your game.

The result of one hand should have no effect on how you play the next. The only exception is when a previous hand is likely to affect how your opponent plays another one later. Just as a pitcher must remember what a batter saw in earlier at bats, you must be aware of what your opponent has seen from you.

However, your basic approach should be to maximize your value with each hand.

This tunnel vision can be taken too far. Once you start viewing each decision in a vacuum, you're no longer just filtering out the distractions. Now you're filtering out valuable information. This information is vital to making the optimal decision on every street. Just like the pitcher and catcher need to know what happened earlier in the count to decide what to throw on 1-2, you need to know what action led up to your current decision. Furthermore, you need to project how future streets will play. A pitcher will set a batter up by throwing high and tight before dropping the hammer on the outside corner. You need to set your opponent up with your preflop and flop play before dropping the hammer on the turn and river. You need to set yourself up for profitable spots later in the hand instead of just thinking about the current street.

Long story short: Have a plan! By planning ahead, you can avoid those paralyzing big-bet scenarios. You'll be prepared for them, because you already thought about everything that could happen. You won't choke.

When live poker dominated the scene, Paul would look through his opponent's eyes and into their soul, divining their exact two cards—that was the idea anyway. Sometimes it worked better than other times. Sometimes it was the way someone smoked (or didn't smoke) a cigarette. Other times it was the way they breathed. Most of the time it was a verbal clue—more *how* they say something than *what* they say—or how they put their chips in the pot. It was possible to reduce someone's likely holdings to a much narrower range. In live poker, there is more new information on each street. Even when you're out of position, you can look for someone's physical reaction to the new board cards as they come out.

One year in Vegas during the World Series, Paul was playing a pot heads up against another competent live player.

As the board came out, both players locked eyes, waiting for the other player to react to the board first. It was funny and awkward, but also telling. That's how we play live. Since there's so much new information available from moment to moment, it's harder to make a plan and easier to handle not having one. In fact, the plan is often simply to look for some new clue on each street. A player may flop top pair with K-Q out of position and decide to check-call all three streets. But physical tells can come up that turn that call into a fold or even a raise. If you get used to waiting for new information, it's easy to develop a wait-and-see attitude. You come to overly rely on information that may or may not show up. This attitude in a live game is somewhere between "sort of bad" and "kind of okay." It's awful in an online game.

Online poker provides much less new information from street to street. All you have is bet sizing and the occasional timing tell. Online, there's no excuse for this wait-and-see attitude. What exactly are you hoping to divine over the Internet? Playing on the computer gives everyone the ultimate poker face. Don't sit around guessing. Have a plan. It can be flexible and, of course, you can take new information into account as you make future decisions.

Armed with a plan, you will be better prepared for what is to come. More than half of the "tough spots" that people post in forums could have been avoided or prepared for by having a plan. When you find yourself in a spot where you're not sure how you got there and you don't know where to go, ask yourself, "Did I have a plan?" Let's look at a possible plan for a hand, developed before the flop:

> **GAME:** $5/$10 blinds—5 players
> **STACKS:** $1,000 effective
> **YOUR HAND:** You have A♠ Q♠ in the big blind
> **PREFLOP:** HJ raises to $30, 3 players fold

What do you do? The **A♠ Q♠** is a strong starting hand, but before deciding whether to reraise or just call, you need to consider how the action will play out after the flop. You need a plan. Let's start by looking at what to do if you reraise. Some opponents will call with hands that you dominate (like A-J and K-Q) and reraise with hands that dominate you (like aces, kings, queens, and A-K). This allows you to get away from your hand cheaply when you're dominated and play with confidence when your opponent calls and you flop top pair. For example:

> **GAME:** $5/$10 blinds—5 players
> **STACKS:** $1,000 effective
> **YOUR HAND:** You have **A♠ Q♠** in the big blind
> **PREFLOP:** HJ raises to $30, 3 players fold,
> you raise to $100, HJ raises to $240, you fold

When HJ 4-bets before the flop, you should usually just fold. That result will be the exception, however. Most of the time, you'll either take it down before the flop, or your opponent will call the 3-bet. For example:

> **GAME:** $5/$10 blinds—5 players
> **STACKS:** $1,000 effective
> **YOUR HAND:** You have **A♠ Q♠** in the big blind
> **PREFLOP:** HJ raises to $30, 3 players fold,
> you raise to $100, HJ calls

On any flop where you have two overcards, top pair, or a backdoor flush draw, you should make a continuation bet of a little over half the pot. Here are a few examples:

EXAMPLE #1
> **YOUR HAND:** You have **A♠ Q♠** in the big blind
> **FLOP:** K♠ 8♣ 4♥ ($205—2 players)
> **ACTION:** You bet $120…

EXAMPLE #2
YOUR HAND: You have A♠ Q♠ in the big blind
FLOP: Q♦ 9♦ 7♥ ($205—2 players)
ACTION: You bet $120…

EXAMPLE #3
YOUR HAND: You have A♠ Q♠ in the big blind
FLOP: 7♣ 5♣ 2♥ ($205—2 players)
ACTION: You bet $120…

If you flop top pair or better and your opponent raises your flop bet, you should reraise all in unless the board is truly horrific. Here are a couple of examples:

EXAMPLE #1
YOUR HAND: You have A♠ Q♠ in the big blind
FLOP: Q♦ 9♦ 7♥ ($205—2 players)
ACTION: You bet $120, HJ raises to $360, you raise to $900 (all in)

EXAMPLE #2
YOUR HAND: You have A♠ Q♠ in the big blind
FLOP: Q♦ J♦ 8♦ ($205—2 players)
ACTION: You bet $120, HJ raises to $360, you fold

If your opponent just calls the flop on these boards, you should continue betting the turn and river for value as long as the board stays clean:

YOUR HAND: You have A♠ Q♠ in the big blind
FLOP: Q♦ 9♦ 7♥ ($205—2 players)
ACTION: You bet $120, HJ calls
TURN: 2♠ ($445—2 players)
ACTION: You bet $260, HJ calls
RIVER: 5♠ ($925—2 players)
ACTION: You bet $520 (all in)

When you flop the nut flush draw, you should also plan to go all in if your opponent raises. You will often have two overcards to go with your already strong draw, and sometimes you'll even have the best hand when your opponent has a weaker draw. There are a few exceptions to following through on the flop with a bet. The primary examples would be **monotone** (all one suit) and three-straight boards such as the following:

EXAMPLE #1
YOUR HAND: You have A♠ Q♠ in the big blind
FLOP: J♥ 4♥ 2♥ ($205—2 players)
ACTION: You check, HJ bets $120, you fold

EXAMPLE #2
YOUR HAND: You have A♠ Q♠ in the big blind
FLOP: 9♣ 8♣ 7♦ ($205—2 players)
ACTION: You check, HJ bets $120, you fold

While A♠ Q♠ suited is a strong hand, it's a good idea not to always play super straightforward. Instead of raising, calling can be an attractive option. By calling, you can capture a c-bet from the hands in your opponent's range that would have folded to a 3-bet, and still take some pots down when you whiff by check/raising almost any flop. You will have many strong semibluffing opportunities like the following two examples:

EXAMPLE #1
GAME: $5/$10 blinds, 5 players
STACKS: $1,000 effective
YOUR HAND: You have A♠ Q♠ in the big blind
ACTION: HJ raises to $30, 3 players fold, you call
FLOP: J♦ 10♥ 8♣ ($65—2 players)
ACTION: You check, HJ bets $40, you raise to $130

EXAMPLE #2

GAME: $5/$10 blinds, 5 players
STACKS: $1,000 effective
YOUR HAND: You have **A♠ Q♠** in the big blind
FLOP: 10♠ 7♠ 2♥ ($65—2 players)
ACTION: You check, HJ bets $40, you raise to $130

You can also check-raise weaker draws like overcards with backdoor flush draws on **dry** boards (boards with no apparent draws). When the turn card gives you a pair or a stronger draw, you should bet again. However, if it's a blank that is more likely to improve your opponent's hand, you should just give up:

YOUR HAND: You have **A♠ Q♠** in the big blind
FLOP: 10♠ 5♦ 2♥ ($65—2 players)
ACTION: You check, HJ bets $40, you raise to $130

You should also check-raise strong hands like top pair and better. In these cases, you should be willing to play for stacks unless your opponent calls the flop, and the turn and/or river are extremely threatening.

YOUR HAND: You have **A♠ Q♠** in the big blind
FLOP: Q♥ 8♥ 2♠ ($65—2 players)
ACTION: You check, HJ bets $40, you raise to $130

Against very nitty players who will not pay off your check-raise with worse hands, you can check and call the flop, let him keep betting his weaker hands for value, and bet the river yourself if he checks the turn. Of course, against a player who will fold so many hands to a flop check-raise, you should plan to bluff even more than you usually would.

Finally, you can lead straight out on boards like **K♦ J♥ 3♠** where you have a backdoor flush draw and a gutshot, and your opponent will fold a lot of underpairs. Some players will never raise that flop if you lead, so they may just call even with their sets, giving you a chance to spike the nuts and take their stack.

If your plan is to get all in on the flop, then check/raising and leading out are not too different.

THE TAKEAWAY

As you can see, a lot of thought goes into the preflop decision, thinking about how the hand will play out after the flop. We don't expect you to do all of this planning at the table. There are simply too many possibilities to consider. You need to work on these plans away from the table so that when the hand arises, you already have a solid sense of what you intend to do. Think of yourself as a field marshal who must pay attention to the developments in the battle around you. The planning you've put in ahead of time facilitates responding quickly to minimize losses and maximize gains. Plot your strategy so that you can deal with all the different circumstances you'll face, whether things go well or things go not so well.

MISCONCEPTION #17
MAKE 'EM DECIDE FOR ALL THEIR CHIPS

"The key to no-limit hold'em is to put a man to a decision for all his chips."

- Doyle Brunson, *Super/System*

There is still a lot right with this statement. Forcing your opponent to make a decision for all of his chips is a powerful play. What people get wrong is thinking that only an all-in bet puts them to this decision. The most critical decision you can make in no-limit hold'em is whether or not to commit all of your chips to the pot. As we've seen in the previous chapter, this is not a decision you should wait to make until you're facing an all-in river bet. It's a decision you usually should make on the flop as part of your plan for the hand.

Making your commitment decision early will keep you out of a lot of trouble and form the basis of your plan for future streets. But how exactly do you go about deciding whether to go down with your ship, or to bail early? There's no magic compass, but there are some general guidelines that can help. When you see a flop, begin by figuring out which of these three categories your hand falls into:

1. **A strong hand that you want to get all in**
   This category is made up of your strongest hands: straights, flushes, sets, and (sometimes) top two pair.

2. **A hand that you're willing to get all in**
   Exactly which hands fall into this category depends on a number of factors: your relative hand strength based on the board, your opponent's range, and how he'll behave when you put action in. This could be top pair or a big draw against super aggressive opponents, or three of a kind or better against passive players. If you flop a hand that you're not going to fold against this player, you must be willing to put in the action.

3. **A hand too weak to commit your stack**
   Aside from outright garbage, this category includes all the hands where you're doing well against your opponent's overall range, but not the range of hands he's willing to put a lot of action in with. You want to get some money in with these hands, but you don't want to get all in with them. Here are two examples of this category:

GAME: $5/$10 blinds, 5 players
STACKS: $1,000 effective
READS: BB is tight and aggressive
YOUR HAND: Q♥ J♥ in the hijack
PREFLOP: You raise to $30, 3 players fold, BB calls

> **FLOP:** J♠ 10♦ 3♣ ($65—2 players)
> **ACTION:** BB checks, you bet $40, BB raises to $120, you fold

Top pair is doing well here against your opponent's preflop range. If your opponent had called, you would be happy to make another value bet on the turn and/or the river, but when he raises, you're know you're against a much tighter range. If you only had to call this one bet, you might be getting the right price. But you can't commit to this hand because your opponent still has $850 that he can bet on the turn and river.

> **GAME:** $5/$10, 6 players
> **STACKS:** $1,000 effective
> **READS:** BB is solid and aggressive
> **YOUR HAND:** 9♦ 9♥ on the button
> **PREFLOP:** 3 players fold, you raise to $30, 1 player folds, BB calls
> **FLOP:** 10♣ 7♠ 2♦ ($65—2 players)
> **ACTION:** BB checks, you bet $40, BB raises to $120, you fold

Again, you're doing well against your opponent's preflop calling range here. But once your opponent check-raises, your hand shrinks in value. With $850 left behind, you should not commit against most opponents.

Sometimes it will be extremely obvious which category your hand falls into. When you flop the nuts, you want to get all your chips in. When you flop nothing, the only time you should ever get your whole stack in is as a bluff. Poker would be easy if every hand fell into one of those two categories—but there's a lot of middle ground where you'll have to use your judgment developed from experience. It's actually fortunate that there is so much middle ground, because that's what makes poker profitable. If these decisions were all easy, then everyone would make the right choice every time. The difficult decisions provide you an opportunity to make a better decision than your opponent would have made.

Stack size and its relation to the size of the pot is a vital consideration in deciding whether to commit to your hand. Both examples listed above had typical 100-blind stacks. If instead the stacks were 20 blinds, it would be an easy matter to commit with both hands. In general, the deeper the stacks the stronger the hand you should require to commit—you need stronger value hands and more powerful draws. With very deep stacks, the line between hands that are *willing* to get it in and hands that *want* to get it in fades away. You should usually have a hand that you're happy to commit 250 blinds to if your plan is to commit 250 blinds.

When you think you're ahead of the range that your opponent is willing to commit his chips with, you *want* to get all your chips in. Your primary task is figuring out how to get them in against as weak a range as possible. Just because you want to get your chips in doesn't mean you should always shove. Take the following example:

GAME:	$5/$10, 3 players
STACKS:	$1,000 effective
READS:	BB is bluff happy, but doesn't often fire three barrels
DYNAMIC:	You've been playing aggressively and pushing BB around
YOUR HAND:	You have 6♦ 6♣ on the button
PREFLOP:	You raise to $30, 1 player folds, BB calls
FLOP:	K♦ 6♣ 2♠ ($65—2 players)
ACTION:	BB checks, you bet $40, BB raises to $120, you raise to $280, BB raises to $970 (all in), you call
TURN:	A♦ ($2,005—2 players all in)
RIVER:	2♦ ($2,005—2 players all in)
SHOWDOWN:	BB mucks 8♣7♣ and you win $2,005 with sixes full

In this hand, your opponent is very aggressive and is likely to feel put upon by you. Calling the flop bet and raising the turn would be a reasonable option. If he held a hand like **K♠ Q♠**, you might have a chance to get this opponent's stack, but your read on him indicates that he's likely to hold a ton of bluffs in his range. You'd like to let him put as many of his chips in with as many of his bluffs as possible. With some opponents, just letting them **barrel off** (keep on raising) and then shove the river would be the best way to do this. But this guy doesn't like to fire the third barrel, so you're likely to get only one more bet from his bluffs that way.

Instead, you make a moderately sized reraise, leaving your opponent room to shove all in as a bluff. The combination of a bluff-happy opponent whom you've been pushing around and a dry board where it's hard for anyone to ever have a hand makes this an ideal situation to induce an all-in bluff. If you shoved all in yourself, your opponent would have to fold his bluffs. The only way he'll put in all his chips with those hands is if he thinks he might get you to fold.

There is no one-size-fits-all strategy for getting as many chips in as you can with your good hands. The best line to take will always depend on the board, your opponent, and the dynamic between the two of you. You have to think about your opponent's range and decide which of your possible actions will inspire him to put in the most chips with the most hands.

When your hand is too weak to commit your stack, you should often take **pot control** lines (an approach that will allow you to control the size of the pot). Sometimes you can plan to bet each street for value, but fold to a raise. This is a good line against players who will only raise you with their very strong hands, and will call down with a wide enough range to make your value bets profitable. For instance, if you raise **K♠ J♣** preflop and catch a flop of **K♦ 7♥ 2♣**, you can usually put in a value bet and fold to a raise against all but the most aggressive players. With a hand like **A♥ K♥**, you should be more willing to commit. You might not be excited to put all of the chips in, but it would be slightly profitable. This is where you need to find the line between hands you're willing to get all in with and hands you're not.

An easy rule of thumb is to be willing to commit when you're ahead of half of your opponent's value range (i.e. the strong hands that are raising because they want you to call). This isn't necessarily going to be a fist-pump get-it-in, but when there's money in the pot and you get your stack in with 50 percent equity, you're doing okay. Note that being ahead of half of your opponent's range does not equate to 50 percent equity, but it will usually be in the ballpark.

If you can't think of a single hand that your opponent could be raising for value that you can beat, you should fold. There will be occasional exceptions to this rule, but your opponent needs to have a tremendously wide bluffing range, and you need to have a solid read on how often he will barrel off with those hands. If he has a properly balanced barreling strategy, it will be very difficult for you to find a profitable way to show down your bluff catcher. (It doesn't matter how strong your hand is when you can beat no-value hands; all you have is a bluff catcher.) You should also be happy to commit your chips when you have a draw with huge equity: **K♦ Q♦** on a **J♦ 10♦ 4♠** board would be an extreme example. Your draw doesn't need to be quite so massive, but if you can get it in with very good equity, go ahead and do it.

One time when you're likely to have good equity against your opponent's all-in range is when you have an ace-high flush draw, particularly when there are straight draws on board as well. Now your opponent can call your shove or raise all in on his own with hands that you're currently ahead of. A hand like **A♦ 5♦** is doing pretty awesome on a **K♦ Q♦ 4♣** flop against hands like **J♠ 10♠** and **9♦ 8♦**. A similar situation comes up when you have the highest possible straight draw on a board with no flush draws: K-Q can get all in on a **10♦ 9♠ 5♥** board against K-J, Q-J, Q-8, J-8, J-7, 8-7, 8-6, and 7-6. It has a commanding equity edge against all of those other straight draws. Even though your draw is only to a gutshot, your equity can be good on the strength of your high-card king.

A final reason to commit all of your chips to the pot is because your opponent will fold very often. When considering whether or not to semibluff all in with a flopped draw, you should weigh the following two factors:

1. **How often will my opponent fold?**

   The more often your opponent folds, the less often you'll need to hit your draw to win. If your opponent will fold often enough, you don't even need a draw to profitably bluff all in.

2. **What will my equity be when he calls?**

   One of the best things that can happen here is for you to get it in with an ace-high draw when your opponent holds a weaker draw. Now you're not only drawing to the nuts, but you currently hold the best hand as well. If you could make accurate assessments of these factors, you would simply plug them into the following equation:

$$\text{Expected Value} = fp + (1\text{-}f)(qt\text{-}b)$$

In this equation, f = the frequency your opponent folds, expressed as a decimal; p = the current pot size; b = the money left in your stack, or the amount you must bet to be all in; q = your equity when your opponent calls, or your chances of winning the pot when all the money goes in; and t = the total pot size after your opponent calls and rake is paid.

If this equation doesn't make much sense to you right now, that's okay. During a session, it's good enough to think, "He folds a lot, therefore I can bluff. My equity will be pretty good when he calls and he'll fold sometimes, so I can bluff." Or, "He'll never fold but my equity is decent, so I'll either call or fold depending on my implied odds."

THE TAKEAWAY

The first thing you should ask every time you see a flop is whether or not you're willing to get your chips in. You should actively look to get all in with the following hands:

1. Strong hands that will be ahead of your opponent's all-in range.
2. Strong draws with excellent equity.
3. Draws that can also be the best hand right now.

You should take pot control lines with many of your marginal hands, and you should bluff when the folding equity is there.

MISCONCEPTION #18
CALLING IS WEAK

"Amateurs would be better off removing the call button from their computer."

- Chris Moneymaker, 2003 WSOP Champion

"Be Aggressive!" you constantly hear poker authors and coaches shout. "When you bet, you have two ways to win." This is true: You can show down the best hand or everyone else can fold. Either way, you win the pot. But poker is not about winning pots. "The secret to successful poker is being aggressive!" Once poker commentators began spouting this off on ESPN, it became much less of a secret. Still, there was a lot of truth to this statement. The quickest way to make a typical recreational player stop losing is to say, "Bet when you have it. Fold when you don't." Easy game, no? Well, no. The secret here is knowing what exactly "it" is.

Properly applying aggression is integral to playing winning poker. When it comes to value betting, it's critical to know whether you're ahead of your opponent's calling range. This requires judgment and experience. When it comes to bluffing, you need to correctly assess how often your opponent will fold and compare that to the odds you're getting on a bet. So yes, be aggressive when it's your most profitable option. But knowing that betting is profitable doesn't mean that it's more profitable than checking. Knowing that raising is profitable doesn't mean it's more profitable than calling.

Good players call a lot.

Calling can be very powerful, especially when you have position. Compared to raising, calling often gets you to the river with an opportunity to outmaneuver your opponent. Let's say you're on the button and cold call a cutoff open. Your opponent bets five blinds on the flop and you raise to 17 blinds. With 100-blind stacks, you've essentially put your opponent to a decision for all his chips, which is supposed to be a very powerful play. He has to decide right there whether or not to commit his stack. If he calls your raise, he has to know that there's a good chance you'll put the rest of the stack in on the turn and river. If his hand is good enough to call, he'll often prefer to just get the money in on the flop. Making a small raise to 40 blinds would mean investing almost half of his stack, committing him to the hand. (Reraising to 40 blinds and then folding to a shove would be a terrible play with almost any hand.)

In this situation, many players are either going to shove or fold. Here's the problem: good players are going to play very well in this spot. They'll get it in good against your range and get away from their troublesome hands with ease. They won't be making huge mistakes. As a result, you've created a huge pot where you're not going to have a huge edge. It's fine to take a small edge now, but not if you can find a bigger one later in the hand.

A good way to create bigger edges for yourself on later streets is to call. Now, if you're calling a lot, you're going to let cards peel off all the time. You need a plan for different ways the board can develop. Yes, there will be some volatility. Sometimes an opponent who would have folded the flop will outdraw you. Sometimes the board will get gross and you'll wind up folding. That's okay. There's a lot of volatility in playing large pots on the flop as well. Sometimes you'll hate the way the board comes out and wish you still had the option of folding.

One spot where it's a good idea to call instead of raise is when you flop a strong hand, but there's no great way to put in action and expect to get paid. If your opponent is betting the turn with more hands than he would call your flop raise, you get more value by calling both streets than by raising the flop. Here's an example:

GAME:	$5/$10 blinds—6 players
STACKS:	$1,000 effective
READS:	CO is a decent player
YOUR HAND:	You have A♠ 10♠ on the button
PREFLOP:	2 players fold, CO raises to $30, you call, 2 players fold
FLOP:	10♦ 5♥ 2♣ ($65—2 players)
ACTION:	CO bets $50, you call
TURN:	7♠ ($165—2 players)
ACTION:	CO bets $120, you call
RIVER:	2♠ ($405—2 players)
ACTION:	CO checks, you bet $350, CO calls
SHOWDOWN:	CO mucks Q♣ 10♣ and you win the pot

Top-pair/top-kicker is a strong hand on that dry flop. It loses only to overpairs and sets, which is a total of 28 combinations of hands. There are some decent second-best hands that the cutoff can hold as well—K-10, Q-10, J-10, and 10-9—but none of those decent hands will feel very good when they get raised on this flop. They may call the raise and fold the turn, but a lot of times they'll just fold the flop outright. If there were a flush draw possible or a straight draw you could hold, the cutoff might talk himself into committing with a weaker hand. But when you raise this flop, you're either bluffing or you have him crushed.

By calling the flop and again calling on the turn, you let him stay in the pot with those hands. He won't have a lot of outs. When he finally gets to the river with a decent hand, he can't help checking and calling, since he feels so close to the showdown. By playing passively, you've gotten three streets of value from your hand—but those were aggressive calls. You were extracting the maximum from your opponent by exploiting his tendencies and using his own aggression against him. Always ask yourself what you're trying to accomplish with a given play before you make it. Most of the times that you raise, you should either be bluffing or going for value. Occasionally you will be raising for information, but even then, there's a value component to the play.

A word of caution: This chapter is not about taking a generally passive approach to the game. Do not start calling all the time because it's always better than raising. It's not. It depends on the situation. There are many situations where calling will allow you to get more value out of both your bluffs and strong hands. There are other situations where betting and raising will do the same. The "secret" to successful poker is learning to tell the difference.

Don't call without a plan. Don't call because you don't know what else to do. Make sure you have a solid reason for calling and a plan for the rest of the hand. Here are a few reasons to consider calling:

7 REASONS TO CONSIDER CALLING

1. You're out of position with a hand that is too strong to fold, but not strong enough to raise.

   For example, you have a value hand that's doing well against the range of hands your opponent's betting, but poorly against the range of hands he would call a raise with).

2. You're out of position with a draw that's strong enough to call, but you don't expect your opponent to fold if you raise.

3. You're in position with either of the two types of hands above.

4. You're in position and think you can represent a hand on later streets.

   This works well on draw heavy boards where your opponent is making a mistake to bet into you, since he's not going to be able to barrel off.

5. Your opponent is straightforward.

   He will bet the flop a lot, but only continue on the turn when he has a strong hand. You can float almost any flop, since he'll check/fold so many turns.

6. The flop is unlikely to have hit your opponent.

   For example, on a 9♣ 5♦ 2♠ flop against a hijack opener, all his overcards have likely whiffed, so only his pocket pairs are any good here.

7. You have a weak draw with strong implied odds.

Look at this example:

GAME: $5/$10 blinds, 6 players
STACKS: $1,000 effective
YOUR HAND: You have 5♠ 4♠ on the button
PREFLOP ACTION: 2 players fold, CO raises to $30, you call, 2 players fold
FLOP: J♠ 6♦ 2♣ ($65—2 players)
ACTION: CO bets $40, you call

THE TAKEAWAY

If the cutoff holds a strong hand like an overpair or a set, you can often win a whole stack when you spike a 3 on the turn. When your opponent has a weak hand and you both miss the turn, he will often check, allowing you to take the pot away with a bet. This lets you take it down with much less risk than a flop raise and ensures that you'll always see the turn. In other words, your opponent won't have a chance to blow you off your draw with a flop reraise.

MISCONCEPTION #19

YOU CAN'T MAKE THAT PLAY UNLESS YOU BALANCE IT

Not so long ago, balance and game theory became the coolest things for a poker player to talk about, and for good reason. They're powerful concepts and tools that will prevent you from getting exploited by a skilled opponent when you use them properly. Game theory is a branch of mathematics used to study behavior in games of strategy, including chess, checkers, and poker—plus war, economics, and dating. Unsurprisingly, proper application of game theory can be a powerful tool for a hold'em player, though it's far from necessary to have a thorough understanding of the subject. In fact, a number of wildly successful poker players seem to have little understanding of what game theory actually is.

The ultimate goal of applying game theory to poker is to find an equilibrium strategy, where even if you told your opponents your entire strategy, there is no counterstrategy they can employ to defeat you. Theoretically, by playing a "game theory optimal" (GTO) strategy, you can prevent your opponents from having any opportunity to outplay you. Against truly world-class opposition, that's just about the best you can do. In theory, it's a perfect defense.

Playing a perfect GTO strategy sounds like a nice plan, doesn't it? The problem is that no-limit hold'em is a complex game, complex enough that computers have yet to derive a complete GTO solution to the game. Even when they can, and someday that time will come, there are so many branches of the game tree that it will probably be impossible for a human to memorize the complete solution. While a global solution is out of our reach, it is possible to solve more local problems. For instance, it is possible to find an unexploitable balance of bluffs and value bets on the river. Often the best we can do is to find some way to play that approaches this solution. That's what we call "balancing your range."

Balancing your range is less extreme than creating a perfect GTO strategy. The idea is that, by having a balance of strong hands and bluffs in your range, you will become more difficult to read. Since your opponents cannot simply narrow your range down to either bluffs or value bets, they will face difficult decisions that require accurate judgment. This concept of balance is vital in many situations. If every time you cold call from the button, you raise your draws on the flop but slowplay your monsters, observant opponents will start to notice. You'll be playing so predictably that your bluffs won't work and your strong hands won't get paid off. In this case, you will pay the price for being unbalanced. Here's an example:

GAME: $5/$10 blinds—4 players
STACKS: $1,000 effective
READS: CO is an observant regular
YOUR HAND: You have 10♠ 10♣ on the button
PREFLOP: CO raises to $30, you call, 2 players fold
FLOP: J♥ 10♥ 3♦ ($75—2 players)
ACTION: CO bets $50, you balance your range

This is a spot where you absolutely need to balance your range. If you want to raise flush draws and straight draws on this flop, you have to be raising strong hands like your sets. If you prefer to just call with your draws and raise the turn, then you need to play your sets like that some of the time as well. You don't always have to play all of your hands the same way. But your opponent needs to know that it's possible for you to hold a set when you actually have a draw, and that it's possible for you to hold a draw when you actually have a set. There are two keys to this situation:

1. **Your opponent is observant.**

   The balanced approach is great for playing against good, perceptive players. However, when you're playing against poor, oblivious opponents, you should play exploitatively. Take advantage of their weaknesses for as long as they'll let you get away with it.

2. **The situation is common.**

   An observant opponent can only take advantage of your unbalanced play when there is information for him to observe. You will play a fair number of pots from the button against a cutoff open-raise and you'll be facing a continuation bet the majority of those times. As a result, your opponent will quickly get a decent sample of hands in which to observe your behavior in that spot. If the spot came up less frequently, you would have less need for balance.

Before deciding how to play your hand, ask yourself, "Do I need to balance this?" The answer depends on how exploitable you become by not balancing, and how likely your opponent is to exploit you. Will your opponents see the hole in your defense, and if so, will they be able to take advantage? If you have to ask, most of the time the answer will be "no." Don't balance plays that don't require it. Take a look at this example:

GAME:	$5/$10 blinds—6 players
STACKS:	$1,000 effective
READS:	BTN is a decent regular
YOUR HAND:	You have 2♦ 2♥ in the big blind
PREFLOP:	4 players fold, BTN raises to $30, 1 player folds, you call
FLOP:	K♥ 7♠ 2♣ ($65—2 players)
ACTION:	You check, BTN bets $40, you call
TURN:	5♠ ($145—2 players)
ACTION:	You bet $100

Flopping bottom set usually gives you a great feeling, but flopping bottom set on a dry board when you're out of position comes with a catch: How do you get value for your hand? Against aggressive players who love to barrel off, you can check-call the first two streets and either **donk** (bet into your opponent out of position) or check-raise the river. With the right dynamic, you can check-raise some opponents, hoping they'll reraise the flop as a bluff, but these are exceptions. For example, against a lot of opponents, check-calling the flop and donking the turn can be the best way to get value from marginal hands such as K-J. Your opponent will want to play a small pot, but you want to get three streets of value. If you check-call the flop and check the turn, there's a good chance that your opponent will check it back, trying to get to showdown while keeping the pot the right size. By checking the flop, you collect a c-bet from your opponent's entire range. (This is a prime flop to c-bet.) By donking the turn, you make sure to get value from hands that would have checked back.

But how will you balance this play?

Who cares? Just because you can't balance a play doesn't mean that you can't make it. Is there more value in playing this hand in an optimal fashion, or is there more value in playing your entire range in a particular way? This is an infrequent situation with a hand that will infrequently go to showdown. That means it will take a long time for your opponent to know that you're not balanced. Remember this: Your opponent will never know that you can never do something. Just because they see you take this line twice with a set doesn't mean they know you can never have air here.

THE TAKEAWAY

In these types of spots that come up infrequently, look for ways to capture immediate value. If it's there, grab it. If it's not, then worry about balance.

MISCONCEPTION #20

I HAVE TO BET THIS FLOP BECAUSE I DON'T WANT TO GIVE UP

You only get dealt two cards for yourself in Texas hold'em. Combined with the three cards on the flop, you're supposed to make some sort of a hand, hopefully a pair or better. It turns out that it's pretty hard to make a pair. In fact, only one-third of the time will you flop a pair with two unmatched hole cards. Given that it's so hard to make a hand, the player who bets first often wins the pot. Armed with this knowledge, players will usually fire out a continuation bet when they are the preflop raiser. Most of the time, this is exactly what you should do— but before we look at all the good reasons and situations to c-bet, let's look at some of the reasons not to c-bet.

Stabbing at the pot when you've raised before the flop is a natural thing; it's almost an emotional thing for many players. "Good players try to pick up pots that no one wants," they think. "That pot is mine. I'm going to take what's mine, and put pressure on my opponent." The only time they want to check back is for pot control when they have a marginal hand. If you bet $40 when there's $60 in the pot, you only need your opponent to fold 40 percent of the time to show a profit. Most players will fold the flop between 40 percent and 50 percent (a typical regular may fold 60 percent or more), so c-betting is often profitable. But that doesn't mean it's the best play.

At the heart of this matter is a false dichotomy: You can either c-bet the flop with your air, or give up. That's the mindset of many otherwise good players, but it's dead wrong. Just because you check the flop doesn't mean that you've given up your right to attack the pot. When you c-bet the flop, you'll wind up giving up on a lot of turns that don't help you. Maybe you'll fire a scare card like an ace or a king, or you'll try to move someone off of a marginal calling hand, but in general, your turn edge will be thin.

Instead of c-betting, you can wait for an opportunity to do something more profitable later. Here's an example: Let's say you have 7♠ 4♠ on a board of A♥ Q♦ 8♣. There's nothing exciting that can happen on the turn. Not only are there no cards to give you a strong hand or a strong draw, there aren't even any good bluffing cards. When you bet, your hand looks like top pair or better, a straight draw, or total air. If you check back, your hand looks more like a marginal hand (e.g. K-Q that wants to control the pot size). If your opponent bets the turn, he usually has something. After all, you've implied that you have a marginal hand that wants to go to showdown, and he bet anyway.

When he checks, though, you've gained valuable information. Your delayed c-bet will still shake loose the same range that your flop c-bet would have. The difference is that this same range of hands now makes up a larger portion of your opponent's range because his good hands, the ones that would bet the turn, can be removed. Despite having nearly zero equity when called, it is possible that a flop bet may have been profitable—but a turn bet was more profitable, thus a better play.

There's another way to use this delayed c-bet. Let's look at an example to see how:

GAME:	$5/$10 blinds—6 players
READS:	BB is competent
STACKS:	$1,000 effective
YOUR HAND:	You have 8♥ 7♥ on the button
PREFLOP:	3 players fold, you raise to $30, 1 player folds, BB calls
FLOP:	A♥ Q♠ 6♣ ($65—2 players)
ACTION:	BB checks, you check

When you check back here, there are a number of things that can happen:

1. **Turn: 2♣** ($65—2 players) **Action:** BB bets $40, you fold.

   When your opponent bets the turn and you don't improve, you just give up. You've probably saved yourself $40.

2. **Turn: 2♣** ($65—2 players) **Action:** BB checks, you bet $40, BB folds.

   When your opponent checks the turn, he's usually folding. Your turn bet is more profitable than a flop bet would have been, since you have better information.

3. **Turn: 4♥** ($65—2 players) **Action:** BB bets $40, you raise to $120.

There are about 15 cards you could play the same way, anything that gives you a straight or flush draw. If your opponent calls, you should typically bluff the river when you miss and value bet when you improve. Your opponent will almost never reraise, but even if he makes it $360, you still have enough money behind to call. You're only risking $240 to potentially win up to $1,155. Assuming that you raised with eight or nine outs, you'll improve between 17 and 19 percent of the time, which makes it a borderline call.

There may be other ways to win the pot on the river. For example:

> **TURN:** 4♥ ($65—2 players)
> **ACTION:** BB bets $40, you raise to $120,
> BB raises to $360
> **RIVER:** 3♦ ($785—2 players)
> **ACTION:** BB checks, you bet $610 (all in), BB folds

Your turn call of the reraise represents so much strength, that it sets you up to take the pot when your opponent gives up on the river. When he checks, he's waiving the white flag. The only reason to bet all in instead of making a smaller bluff is to prevent him from taking another shot at the pot.

A similar scenario could have played out if you bet the flop and bet the turn, but turn barrels are easier for your opponents to deal with than turn raises. Most opponents will have statistics to rely on to judge your propensity to barrel off. They're used to dealing with this situation. When you check back the flop and raise the turn, you take your opponent out of his comfort zone. Even if he has some stats on the situation, they will be less reliable since the situation arises less frequently. Your opponent will have to actually *think!* Many moderately successful players are surprisingly bad at this. The use of a **HUD**—short for Heads Up Display, a tool that online players use to analyze their opponents' play—has become so prevalent that any time you can make a play that your opponent's HUD won't help them understand, there's value in it. By rendering their tools useless, you can set your opponents up to make bad decisions.

THE TAKEAWAY

The moral of the story is not that you should avoid c-betting. You should c-bet a lot. But pause to think about why you're firing off that c-bet on this exact hand against this exact opponent. C-betting should not be a reflex—it should be a decision. It is often a profitable option, but instead of asking yourself if it's a profitable option, ask if it's your *most* profitable option.

MISCONCEPTION #21

CHECKING AND FOLDING THE FLOP IS WEAK

When deciding whether or not a continuation bet with a hopeless hand will be profitable, the first consideration is how hard the board hits your opponent's range. A board such as J♥ 9♥ 2♠ hits smack in the middle of a big blind's preflop calling range. Another example of a board where little to no good can come of betting is A♠ Q♠ 8♠. You won't get a lot of folds from most opponents.

If your opponent is extremely straightforward, you can probably get away with c-betting almost every flop. Even the most threatening boards will only give your opponent a pair or better about half the time, and a straightforward player won't bluff enough to keep you from taking a profitable stab at the pot. However, if your opponent is intelligent, aggressive or tricky, your c-bets will show considerably less profit. And on boards like J♥ 9♥ 2♠ and A♠ Q♠ 8♠, c-betting becomes a losing play. Your more sophisticated opposition will be stubborn with their made hands, semibluff with their draws, and do everything in their power to force *you* to have a hand, since they know you'll rarely flop a strong one.

Giving up is fine when there's nothing to look forward to. Checking back isn't necessarily giving up anyway. When there are no good cards to fire a second barrel on the turn, you may as well wait for more information before firing your c-bet (i.e. wait for the turn). With a hand like 7♦ 4♦ on a Q♠ 8♣ 2♥, you want to throw in a bet, since the board won't hit a big blind caller's range as hard. If you check back on a board like this, though, you won't get 7♠ 7♣ to fold on a 3♣ turn. So, this is a spot where betting the flop is superior to waiting for the turn.

It's not just about how often your opponent flops a pair or better. Hands that want to get to showdown are an obvious impediment to stealing the pot on the flop, but draws sometimes present an even larger problem. For instance, a weak pair may call a flop bet and fold to a turn bet. A slightly stronger pair may call the flop and turn, but fold to a river bet. Very passive opponents will often play their draws this way, but aggressive players will usually raise the flop. This means that you don't even get to see the turn when they hold a draw. They won't give you a second chance to get them off of their hand. They won't wait to miss their draw, then let you take the pot away from them. They'll use their draw as a way to subsidize their own attack on the pot. Again, this is not to say that you should rarely c-bet. On the contrary, you should c-bet more often than not. We don't want you to play weak and passive poker. But like everything else, you should use discretion. Consider ranges and how they hit the board.

THE TAKEAWAY

Don't throw money at a pot that your opponent is unlikely to give up on.

C-betting too often may seem like a small error. Taken on its own, a bad c-bet won't cost that much; the pot is small and so is your bet. But whether or not to c-bet is a decision you'll have to make so often that those small mistakes will add up quickly. It's not just the size of a mistake that matters, it's also the frequency. To measure a leak in your game, you have to multiply the magnitude by the frequency. If you make a c-bet error that costs you one blind every 40 hands, it costs you 2.5 blinds per 100 hands. That's half of a good player's win rate!

As we saw in the last chapter, checking back does not always mean giving up. When you have position on your opponent, you can often check back the flop and play the turn with better information. You don't have this option when you're out of position. For that reason, if you think a c-bet will be profitable, you should go ahead and fire one out. Checking the flop usually does mean giving up when you're out of position—so if there's value now, take it!

MISCONCEPTION #22
NEVER LEAVE YOUR CHILDREN OUT THERE

If c-betting properly in a once-raised pot is important, then perhaps it stands to reason that c-betting in a 3-bet pot is three times as important. Whether or not that fuzzy math holds up in court, it is true that you should usually continue to attack the pot once you've 3-bet before the flop. The pot is substantial and you've shown substantial strength, so you should bet liberally. In the old poker lingo, you should never leave your children out there.

You still want to consider the texture of the board, and how it relates to both your and your opponent's range. On boards that you're *supposed* to hit, like **A♥ K♠ 4♣**, you should always bet. You should usually bet the turn as well, even with complete air like **6♦ 5♦**. It's very easy for your opponent to give you credit for a hand, since so much of your range hits this board. With **A♠ K♠** on a **J♠ 5♣ 2♦** board, you've flopped nothing, but there are a number of excellent turn cards that could help you. You should bet. When your opponent just calls and you turn an ace or a king, you're in very good shape. With a queen on the turn, you may be able to get him to fold small pairs. A spade will give you the nut flush draw, and even a 3, 4, or 10 will give you a gutshot.

The only time you should not c-bet is when the board smashes your opponent's range and nothing good can happen on the turn. Take that **A♠ K♠** again but make the flop **10♥ 9♥ 8♥**. Say your opponent opened on the button and you reraised from the small blind. Not only does this board hit your opponent's range in the face, there is not a single good turn card. Even when you hit an ace or a king (and hopefully not a heart), are you really all that happy? Now you've got top pair/top kicker in a bloated pot, but it's not a strong hand on this highly coordinated board. What are you going to do with that? Put yourself in your opponent's shoes. Why would he fold the board when you bet the flop? He knows your range is vulnerable on this coordinated board and that there are a million and one bad turn cards (okay, so there are about 21, but you get the point) and few good ones. Many players will never fold this board against a c-bet, regardless of what they hold. They'll call the flop in position, looking for opportunities to take the pot away on later streets.

Players who c-bet these boards out of position are always looking for something they can beat. Yeah, there will be some air in your opponent's range, and when you check you're going to let him take the pot away from you. But don't worry about getting outplayed: This is just a flop where your opponent's range is stronger than yours, and you have to respect that. There isn't enough air in his range for you to bet.

THE TAKEAWAY

Don't make loose calls and hopeless bets to avoid giving up on the pot. It's okay to leave your kids out there sometimes. Maybe they have soccer practice today. The only legitimate reason to c-bet is because it's profitable. When it's not, don't do it.

MISCONCEPTION #23
ALWAYS C-BET THE SAME AMOUNT

Many players are under the impression that their flop c-bets should always be the same size. There is a certain logic to this. It's easy to have a standard sized bet, something like two-thirds the pot. Just like using a fixed preflop raise size, this simplifies a very common decision and prevents giving out too much information. If you bet the same amount every time, your opponents won't be able to learn anything about your hand from the size of your bet.

Sometimes you should vary your c-bet size based on the board texture, but there's a more important reason to deviate from your regular bet size—you want to make more money with a big hand. Let's say you have A♠ K♠ on A♣ 5♥ 5♦ against a single big blind caller. Your hand is almost always ahead, and your opponent can never have very many outs. You want to extract as much money from your opponent as possible. When you're up against an observant opponent or a very tight one, you may want to make a standard sized bet. This will avoid giving information to the observant player and avoid pushing the **nit** (very tight player) out of the pot. However, when you're playing against a mediocre to bad player, you should build the pot up early.

In a $5/$10 game, the pot will likely be about $60 on the flop. If you bet $40, then the pot will be $140 on the turn. If you bet two-thirds the pot again, that's about $100. Now you're at $340 on the river, so you fire out $290, close to a pot-sized bet, which may throw up some flags after your smaller flop and turn bets. You've put $430 into the pot after the flop, or a little less than half a 100 blind stack. If you instead bet $50 on the flop, the pot will be $160 on the turn. If you bet a little larger there, say $140, the pot will be $440 on the river. Now you can bet $390 instead of $290. If all three bets get called, you've managed to get $580 in the pot. That's $150 more than if you'd bet just $10 less on the flop. Even if you're playing $.50/$1 instead of $5/$10, that's still $15. This situation comes up a few times a day. Over the course of a month you could have close to $1,500 extra spending money. In a year you might be able to buy yourself a new car. If you're playing $5/$10, call it a new house. That's a big reward for tossing in one extra blind on the flop!

There are also situations where you should bet less than you usually would. Sometimes a "standard" sized c-bet is going to be very marginal against a particular opponent. Against the right player, a good compromise can be to bet less. Particularly against straightforward opponents, instead of giving up, it's okay to bet half the pot instead of a regular two-thirds pot bet. Here's an example:

> **GAME:** $5/$10—6 players
> **STACKS:** $1,000 effective
> **READS:** BTN is tight, aggressive and fairly straightforward
> **YOUR HAND:** You have A♦ 9♦ in the cutoff
> **PREFLOP:** 2 players fold, you raise to $30, BTN calls, 2 players fold
> **FLOP:** Q♥ 8♥ 2♠ ($75—2 players)
> **ACTION:** You bet $40

Your smaller bet size won't make a significant difference in which hands your opponent folds, but it gives you a better price on your bluff. If you c-bet two-thirds pot, you need your opponent to fold 40 percent of the time ($50 / ($50 + $75) = .4, or 40 percent). If you c-bet half the pot, you only need them to fold 33 percent of the time. ($40 / ($40 + $75) = .35, or 35 percent. Note that $40 is slightly larger than half the pot here, and a half the pot bet of $37.50 would only need to work 33 percent of the time.) So if you expect your opponent to fold somewhere between 35 percent and 40 percent of his range, your bet size can make the difference between slightly profitable and slightly unprofitable.

The question arises as to whether we're balancing this play. We're probably not. But we're only using it to exploit bad players, so we really don't need to balance it.

Let's go back to the **A♠ K♠** on the **10♥ 9♥ 8♥** flop from the previous chapter. You might feel pretty weak giving up in this $230 pot with a pretty hand like A-K suited. You have to realize that you're in a terrible situation against a tough player and should cut your losses. However, against a weaker player, there may be a way to salvage the situation. Against someone who plays a fit or fold style, you can make very small c-bets on bad boards like these. Something like $75 into $230 only needs to succeed 25 percent of the time. A tough player won't fold anywhere near that often, but a fit or fold player might. Making a small bet like this can be an alternative to "leaving your kids out there." It's basically a compromise between giving up and making a normal c-bet.

THE TAKEAWAY

In deciding how to size your c-bet, you should always consider the board texture and how your opponent will respond to different bet sizes. Be careful to balance your plays against tough opponents, but against less observant ones, you can squeeze out some extra value using outside-the-box thinking.

MISCONCEPTION #24

SAVE THE SMALL BETS FOR THE KIDDIE GAME

Most people over invest in 3-bet pots. We looked at proper 3-bet sizing earlier, so let's assume that the open-raise was 3 blinds and your 3-bet was 3 times that, to 9 blinds. Assuming the blinds fold and the cutoff calls, the pot will be 19.5 blinds. Almost regardless of the flop texture, there's no need to bet much more than half the pot. You'll get about as many folds when you bet 11 blinds as when you bet 16 or 17 blinds, and betting 11 blinds is much cheaper. Let's look at an example:

> **GAME:** $5/$10 blinds—6 players
> **STACKS:** $1,000 effective
> **READS:** BTN and SB are both solid players
> **HANDS:** BTN has K♠ Q♠ and SB has K♥ J♥
> **PREFLOP:** 3 players fold, BTN raises to $30, SB raises to $100, 1 player folds BTN calls
> **FLOP:** 10♥ 7♣ 4♦ ($210—2 players)
> **ACTION:** SB bets $110, BTN folds

Sitting in the button's position, have you ever once thought to yourself, "Man, I'm glad this guy didn't bet $170? That would have changed everything." No, you haven't. That's because betting $170 would change almost nothing. It would risk more chips to cause the same effect. There's a simple reason that the smaller bet size will work just as well as the larger one: The threat is the same. If your opponent calls 11 blinds on the flop, the pot will be about 43 blinds on the turn. You can bet 25 blinds on the turn, putting the pot at 93 blinds after a call. With 54 blinds left in your stack, it's easy to get the rest of the money in, so the hammer is there regardless of how you size your flop bet. Your opponent knows that you can force him to commit all of his chips if he wants to see a showdown.

In fact, with the smaller bet sizes, you give your opponent more chances to fold. If you had bet 16 on the flop and 35 on the turn, then you'd be left with only 40 blinds to bet into a 120 blind pot on the river. That third barrel is only one-third the pot. (In some situations this is a good thing, and against certain players you would be milking them for more by building a larger pot and then taking it away, but it should not be your default approach.)

By making the larger bet on the flop, you're effectively reducing your skill advantage on future streets. The larger raise makes the stacks smaller relative to the size of the pot, which reduces maneuverability. It is this maneuverability that gives you a chance to outplay your opponent. If you happen to be playing against Phil Ivey, maybe it's a good idea to make bigger bets and cut down on his room to maneuver, but most of the time you'll want that room to play for yourself. Consider the following hand, played two different ways:

HAND #1A

GAME:	$5/$10 blinds—6 players
STACKS:	$1,000 effective
YOUR HAND:	You have A♣ K♣ in the small blind
BTN'S HAND:	BTN has K♦ J♦
PREFLOP:	3 players fold, BTN raises to $30, you raise to $100, 1 player folds, BTN calls
FLOP:	Q♦ J♣ 8♣ ($210—2 players)
ACTION:	You bet $170, BTN calls
TURN:	5♦ ($550—2 players)
ACTION:	You bet $480, BTN makes a decision for all his chips

By betting so much on the flop, you force yourself to commit on the turn. This forces the button to make a decision to play for all of his chips. You'd be better off giving yourself a chance to have a profitable draw, and also the chance to make a significant river bluff. By making such large flop and turn bets, you lose the chance to get him off of his mediocre hands with a river bluff.

HAND #1B

GAME:	$5/$10 blinds—6 players
STACKS:	$1,000 effective
YOUR HAND:	You have **A♣ K♣** in the small blind
BTN'S HAND:	BTN has **K♦ J♦**
PREFLOP:	3 players fold, BTN raises to $30, you raise to $100, 1 player folds, BTN calls
FLOP:	**Q♦ J♣ 8♣** ($210—2 players)
ACTION:	You bet $110, BTN calls
TURN:	**5♦** ($430—2 players)
ACTION:	You bet $250, BTN calls
RIVER:	**2♠** ($930—2 players)
ACTION:	You bet $540, BTN has a tough decision

By betting less on each street, you've left enough money behind to make a credible river bluff. The button's range maxes out at K-Q. With anything stronger you would expect him to raise the flop or turn. Your $540 bet is enough to push him off of almost his entire range. Even if you get called on this river, those are chips you would have lost anyway when your opponent jammed the turn. But you've spent them intelligently in this hand, instead of carelessly like you did in the last hand. You've given your opponent three chances to fold, and you've put him to three tough decisions.

An understandable concern is that by betting less, you might encourage your opponent to take more shots at you. Maybe you want to c-bet larger to "define the hand" and make your decision clear if you get check-raised. First of all, it's okay if your opponents play back at you to some degree. They can't do that without spilling off some chips to your good hands in the process. You also have the option of playing back at them when they get out of line. Unless they're check/raising all in, you get the final word on the flop. Second, a larger c-bet does not always make your decision clear. Good opponents who observe that you frequently make large c-bets and then fold to further action will start playing back at you anyway. They'll define the hand the way *they* want, telling you what you expect to hear (but not the truth). Now you've only succeeded in building a bigger pot for them to steal.

One flop that deserves special attention is the dry, ace-high board. On these hit-or-miss flops, you can bet as little as one-third of the pot, since your opponent will either have a made hand or absolutely nothing. You want to size all of your c-bets well, but in 3-bet pots the importance is magnified. The pot is larger so mistakes are larger.

THE TAKEAWAY

Spend what you need to get the job done. No more, no less!

MISCONCEPTION #25

CALL NOW—REEVALUATE THE TURN

Posting hands on poker forums is a great way to improve your game. Hearing how your fellow players would handle a tough spot and what they think about your play can be helpful. Just look out for advice like the following: "Call the flop. Reevaluate on the turn." This is a common, well-intentioned suggestion, but it's also bad advice.

Let's say you open-raise A♦ J♦ from the hijack and one player calls behind you. Both blinds fold, and you see a flop of A♠ 9♣ 2♥. You **bet for value**; that is, you bet to build the pot with either the best hand or close to it, not to get your opponent to fold. Your opponent raises.

Now what do you do?

Against an insanely aggressive player, it's easy enough to call the flop and allow him to blow off the rest of his stack on the turn and river. Against an extremely conservative player, it's easy enough to fold since you would be lucky to have three outs against any of the hands in his range. Against anyone in between these two extremes, this is a difficult spot. Many players will suggest that you should call the flop and decide what to do next after the turn card falls. Six percent of the time a jack will hit the board and your hand will improve from weak to marginal: You pull ahead of A-K, A-Q, and flopped two pair, but still lose to sets. The other 94 percent of the time you will check, your opponent will usually bet, and you'll be playing the same guessing game you played on the flop, but for higher stakes. If you call again, you'll face a similarly larger decision on the river.

There's an easy way to avoid this game of shells for growing stakes: Make your decision on the flop. Instead of calling and hoping that your opponent will give up, make a plan now. Your plan should not rely on something unlikely occurring. You wouldn't jump out of an airplane at 32,000 feet without a parachute just because one guy did it and walked away unscathed. Plan for the rule, not the exception.

In this particular example, you're either way ahead or way behind. When you have the best hand, your opponent will have at most five outs (e.g. **10♥ 9♥**). More often he'll have three, two, or zero outs. When you don't have the best hand, you have six outs against A-2, three outs against A-9, A-Q, or A-K, and zero outs against 9-9 and 2-2. There will be a few backdoor outs here and there, but that doesn't change the overall situation. This hand is not about improving, it's about whether or not you have the best hand right now.

Few players will have more bluffs in their range than value hands. Since you beat no legitimate value hands, you should fold against all but the most aggressive players. This may sound like weak and exploitable advice. Worrying about being weak and exploitable will only get you so far. It's more productive to think about being profitable. When you find yourself in a difficult situation like this one, ask yourself, "Is this a profitable situation? Why is it profitable? How can I make money from my hand?" If you can't come up with a coherent answer to these questions, then you're better off bailing out now.

Poker is about finding opportunities to make money. You *find* these opportunities, you don't *create* them.

There are spots where an expert player will find value (either by bluffing, betting for value, or finding a cheap way to showdown) that seems to be created out of thin air. But they're not actually creating these opportunities. These opportunities are there for everyone. The expert player is just better at recognizing them and taking advantage. What they're not doing is forcing the action.

THE TAKEAWAY

There are a few opponents who will raise the flop with a wide range and then shut down on the turn. It's okay to call the flop against these players with the intention of folding to a turn bet. That's different from re-evaluating on the turn. It's making a plan for the turn based on your opponent's playing style. Most players, however, will not shut down on the turn. Most players will keep betting their strong hands for value. Most players will either decide on the flop, "This guy's rarely going to have better than one pair, so I'm going to **bomb** (bet big) all three streets and get him to fold," or they'll fold their air right away.

So you have to make a decision right away: Is this hand worth a lot of chips?

MISCONCEPTION #26

GREAT PLAYERS NEVER FOLD THE BEST HAND

Folding the best hand in a large pot is one of the most expensive mistakes you can make. When your opponent makes a pot-sized bet on the river, folding a hand that beats more than one-third of your opponent's range is an error. Just how big an error it is depends on the size of the pot, and how much of your opponent's range you beat.

It's easy to take the above advice and apply it to the wrong situations. Let's say you have **A♣ 10♦** in the small blind. Everyone folds to you and you raise to three blinds. The big blind reraises to nine blinds. Against an aggressive player, you figure to have the best hand more often than not. You're ahead of your opponent's range, but what are you going to do about it? An A-10 offsuit plays poorly heads up and out of position, particularly without the initiative and against a reasonably strong range. If you just call, you're in for some nasty reverse implied odds. Unless your opponent is terrible and/or transparent (i.e. you have an iron-clad read), you won't be able to get to showdown profitably. You'll either end up folding a lot of your equity, or you'll pay too steep a price to call down.

You can consider 4-betting, but you're only going to fold out the hands that you're already ahead of, and face a shove from the hands that have you crushed. There may be some 5-bet shove bluffs in there as well, since you've given your opponent the right of last bet. You've invested lots of money on little information. Against the right opponent, your 4-bet may be profitable. Realize that you're not raising because you're ahead of your opponent's range, but because you think he'll fold a lot. You've turned your hand into a bluff. That's fine against some players, but a lot of the time you'll just be burning money.

Against most good opponents, you should just fold right now. This scenario is very different from calling a river bet in a big pot. In that case, you knew exactly how much it costs to see the showdown. In this case, you have no idea. It may cost your whole stack, it may be free. Your opponent has the luxury of barreling as he sees fit, giving up when you're planning to call down, and charging you the maximum when he has you dominated. There are many situations in no-limit hold'em where you have the best hand more often than not, but there's no way to monetize it. Sometimes you'll be sitting there and have to fold three or four decent hands in a row against the same opponent. You're thinking, "I'm just going to catch a piece of something and go with it."

We've all been there.

THE TAKEAWAY

Everyone faces those spots where they have a strong hand, but due to the structure of the game, they can't cash in. The difference between you and them will be that you recognize those spots where you can't make money off the best hand, and you'll cut your losses. You're only going to lose three blinds. Your opponents will lose a lot more!

MISCONCEPTION #27
IF YOU HAVE THE BEST HAND, RAISE!

It's always tempting to raise when you think you have the best hand—but it's not always the best play. This is a mistake that even some high profile players make.

Take this example from *High Stakes Poker*: Playing eight-handed with blinds of $500/$1,000 and antes of $300, Daniel Negraneau posts a straddle of $2,000. Eli Elezra picks up two black queens under the gun and raises to $7,200. Four players call behind him, including Tom "Durrr" Dwan. The flop comes out **3♠ 7♥ 9♣**. Elezra bets $23,300 into a $38,900 pot. Next to act, Dwan raises to $71,000. Everyone folds back around to Eli, including Phil Galfond, who flopped top pair. Elezra is in one of the least comfortable spots in no-limit hold'em. He holds an overpair, which was strong enough to lead into a field of five, but now he's facing a raise from a very strong player who has position on him. If there were no more betting to be done, this would be an easy call. Pocket queens figure to be good often enough to justify calling down for another $47,700. The trouble is that there is another round of betting and over $350,000 left behind.

Dwan's range is probably something like top two pair, a set, and straight draws. Elezra will have the best hand against that range about 60 percent of the time, but he'll only have 40 percent equity since Dwan's draws all have 8 outs. Furthermore, those straight draws should probably be discounted since Dwan may choose to just call with them, knowing that Eli is stubborn and may be unlikely to fold a hand like an overpair; and knowing that the flop raiser, Durrr, is one of the biggest action players in poker. Considering his reverse implied odds—it will cost a third of a million dollars to call down—Elezra could just fold right away. Some players will tell you that this is too weak and will allow your opponents to run you over. The truth is that in a five-way pot against the range in question, folding is the best option.

The only other reasonable option would be to call the flop raise, and let Dwan continue to bluff when he holds a draw. If the draws come in, Elezra can fold. He may have a hard time knowing what to do when an ace or a king comes off. These should be bricks, but only a strong hand reader will recognize this. Taking this line would only be correct if bluffs and draws were a large part of Durrr's range. Given that Eli is out of position against a world-class player, folding is still the better option.

Instead of calling or folding, Eli raises to $173,300! The only rational reason to do this would be to get all in against a weaker range—but not only is Elezra behind Dwan's range, he proceeds to fold after Durrr shoves all in!

Presumably he's reraising in an attempt to "define the hand" or something. What he's really doing is turning his pocket queens into a total bluff. His cards have become totally irrelevant. If his plan is to raise and fold to a shove, then he will never see the turn as Durrr will never call the flop reraise; he's either folding or shoving. If Elezra never sees the turn, his hand has no value and is a complete bluff.

THE TAKEAWAY

You should usually only raise the flop against a good player when you're either bluffing or willing to get all of your chips in. If you're thinking of raising for information, you have to consider the value of that information (i.e. how actionable and reliable is the intelligence?) and how much it will cost to obtain it. When you crunch the numbers, you'll find that it's rarely worth the price.

MISCONCEPTION #28

RAISE TO FIND OUT WHERE YOU STAND

"You've got to raise to find out where you stand."

- Phil Hellmuth

One of the most common phrases you'll hear in a poker room is, "Don't let 'em draw out on you. You've gotta raise to protect your hand." This notion of protecting your hand came primarily from limit poker, where the price of a bet is small compared to the cost of losing a pot. "Protecting your hand" has become passé in limit hold'em. In no-limit hold'em, it's downright silly.

Here's an example taken from a $.50/$1 table. Everyone folds to the small blind, who open-raises to $3; the big blind reraises to $10. The small blind calls with his pocket fours, and the flop comes out **8♠ 5♥ 2♥**. The small blind checks, the big blind bets $13, and the small blind raises to $37. When asked why he raised, the small blind replied, "I want to protect my hand and find out where I'm at." We'll leave the grammar alone, as this is a perfectly legitimate construction in Standard Poker English, just like "two pair." The trouble is that it's an awful play.

Before tossing a third of your stack into the middle, take a moment to consider the value of the information you're obtaining. When your opponent folds, you find out that you had the best hand. Was it worth it? When your opponent reraises, you find out that you didn't have the best hand— unless you did. Just because your opponent reraises the flop doesn't always mean that he has you beat. Many opponents can shove over your raise with semibluffs like 7-6 and heart draws, or even just two overcards like A-K. Check-raising the flop and getting reraised doesn't tell you "where you're at." You're asking a question with your raise, sure, but don't expect an honest answer. This is poker, not go fish.

Calling a shove here would be as bad as the check-raise, but it would at least make that first play make sense. The only legitimate reason to check-raise here would be if your opponent is so aggressive that you can actually put all of your money in on the flop and still be ahead of your opponent's range. Just like in the previous chapter, being ahead of your opponent's betting range is not the same as being ahead of his shoving range.

So what's the correct play on this flop? Well, calling is okay if you know one of the following pieces of information:

1. **Your opponent is extremely passive and straightforward and will never bet the turn unless you're drawing almost dead.**

   In this case, you could call the flop bet and get to the showdown for no additional charge when you hold the best hand. When he bets the turn, you can fold with a clear conscience. While your opponent will still draw out on you about a quarter of the time, you'll never end up folding the best hand against this passive player.

2. **Your opponent is insanely aggressive and will barrel all three streets blindly.**

   Against a player with a huge number of bluffs in his range, you can call down the whole way, allowing him to bluff off his stack.

Unfortunately, most opponents fall somewhere in the middle, and you'll wind up folding too much equity or paying too much to get to showdown. It's not that the cost is too high in absolute dollars. The problem is that you won't be getting the right price. If there is $20 in the middle before the flop with $90 left to bet after the flop, you'll have to win 45 percent of showdowns to justify calling all the way down (90 / (20 + 90 + 90) = .45, or 45 percent). If your opponent bluffs and barrels with discretion, that's not going to happen. Your other alternative is to call the flop and fold the turn or river, but the showdown value of your hand isn't worth anything if you don't get to showdown. You've got a rock/hard place situation on your hands.

So what's the answer?

Fold! In fact, you should fold to the preflop reraise against most opponents. You'll miss the flop 7.5 out of 8.5 times, and usually just check-fold. You're just not getting the right odds to play this hand out of position against most players. Against a very strong range, you can call the 3-bet hoping to spike a set. Against a player who will fold a huge portion of his range to a 4-bet, you can consider playing back. But against most players, just avoid the situation entirely.

THE TAKEAWAY

Good players often fold the best hand. It costs less than trying to "find out where you're at!"

<hr>

MISCONCEPTION #29

LEAD OUT TO FIND OUT WHERE YOU STAND

Two of the most difficult challenges in no-limit hold'em are learning to play marginal hands for a profit and handling being out of position. In fact, being out of position is what makes many hands marginal in the first place. We'll start with a basic scenario:

> **GAME:** $5/$10—6 players
>
> **STACKS:** $1,000 effective
>
> **READS:** BTN is a solid regular
>
> **DYNAMIC:** Neither you nor BTN have been getting out of line against each other
>
> **YOUR HAND:** You have 10♠ 10♣ in the big blind
>
> **PREFLOP:** 3 players fold, BTN raises to $30, 1 player folds, you call
>
> **FLOP:** 9♦ 4♥ 2♥ ($65—2 players)

You ponder the possibilities in this frustratingly tricky spot. You have a strong hand relative to your opponent's range, but you're not doing so hot anymore if you play your hand fast and all the chips go in. You can't start thinking of folding hands this strong, but how do you make money off it? How do you go about reducing your positional disadvantage? Unfortunately, there's no simple answer. That's why you should play tight out of position, though no amount of tight will eliminate situations like these completely.

Back to your pocket tens. There are downsides to every option. Checking and calling allows bad cards to come off the deck, giving your opponent a chance to outdraw you or move you off the best hand when the board gets ugly. Checking and raising almost turns your hand into a bluff, where better hands will call or reraise and worse hands will fold. Folding forfeits all of your equity and lets your opponent run wild over you. What about leading out into the preflop raiser, making a so-called "donk" bet? This may sound reasonable enough. After all, you've heard it on television a hundred times from World Poker Tour announcer Mike Sexton and others.

But the strategy is unsound.

Start with the etymology of the donk bet. Donk is short for donkey, a not so affectionate term for a bad player. Since donking is something that donkeys do, it stands to reason that you shouldn't do it. While there are exceptions to this rule, it's not a bad place to start. The intentions behind this flop donk are benign. Your hand is pretty strong, and checking feels like it misses value. Perhaps you can reduce your positional disadvantage by seizing the betting lead. Perhaps you can collect value from all of your opponent's weaker hands, preventing him from checking back for pot control.

There's one problem with this line—it doesn't work!

Maybe it's okay against weak players who will call down out of curiosity and only raise when you're crushed. But good players will generally exploit the dickens out of you. First of all, you won't pick up c-bets from the weak hands in your opponents' range. They'll either fold their air immediately, or play back at you on the flop or turn with it. The only reason to donk with a hand like this against a good player is to incite action from him, hoping to get it in against a wider range than you would with a check-raise.

Donking and folding is not a good option, since you're essentially telling your opponent that you have a marginal hand. You can try to balance this by also donking sets, but there are two problems with that. You might lose value with your strongest hands, and you don't flop that many of them.

So if donking is out, what are you left with? Against a hyper-aggressive opponent, you can check-raise, hoping to get played back at by either top pair, a flush draw, or total air. That's the exception, though. When facing a player of no more than average aggression, you're left checking and calling the flop. You can usually check-call the turn again, unless it's a complete disaster. When your opponent barrels the river, though, you should usually fold. Yeah, they *can* be bluffing, but they're not betting worse hands for value, and they're not bluffing often enough to justify a calldown unless they offer you fantastic pot odds.

Just because you've played the flop passively doesn't mean you have to stay in the back seat for the turn and river. Let's look at another example:

> **GAME:** $5/$10 blinds—6 players
> **STACKS:** $1,000 effective
> **READS:** BTN is a solid regular
> **YOUR HAND:** You have **8♥ 8♦** in the big blind
> **PREFLOP:** 3 players fold, BTN raises to $30,
> 1 player folds, you call
> **FLOP:** **10♦ 5♣ 2♠** ($65—2 players)
> **ACTION:** You check, BTN bets $40, you call
> **TURN:** **A♥** ($145—2 players)
> **ACTION:** You check, BTN bets $90, you raise to $250

After calling the flop in the hopes of a cheap showdown, you watch one of the ugliest possible turn cards slide off the deck. The A♥ hits your opponent's range hard, so you could make a strong argument for check/folding here. In fact, that's what you'd normally do. So why did you decide to check-raise your marginal hand on the turn, after explicitly being told not to do that on the flop? The answer is that your opponent knows that this turn card will look scary to you, so he'll bet it approximately 100 percent of the time with 100 percent of his range. That means two things:

1. You can put your opponent on a very precise range; and
2. Despite having a large number of top pair combinations, your opponent's overall range is quite vulnerable.

Put yourself in your opponent's shoes for a moment. He's bet the flop and gotten called. Now he bets the turn and gets check-raised. Unless he holds a set, he can only beat a bluff. He has no draws to call or re-bluff with. You could be bluffing, but does he think you're doing that often enough to justify calling the turn raise and likely river shove? Unlikely. There are no semibluffs in your range. You would have to be turning a made hand into a bluff or floating out of position. Few players do either with any level of frequency. It's true that you're representing a narrow range, since you basically have to have slowplayed a set or hold A-10. That's a drawback to this play, but if he thinks there are no bluffs in your range, then he has to give you credit for that narrow range.

Putting your own shoes back on, this awful turn card actually looks like a pretty good place to bluff now. Even if your opponent always calls with top pair or better, he'll still be folding two-thirds of his range. And there's a good chance that he'll bail with his weak aces, knowing that he can only beat a made hand that was turned into a bluff. Your check-raise risks $250 to win $235, so it needs to succeed just over half the time.

Unless your opponent suspects that you're getting out of line, you're likely to win the pot immediately over two-thirds of the time. The play is clearly and immediately profitable. Even if your opponent calls, you have a 4 percent chance of spiking an 8, giving you a good chance to win your opponent's stack. That's not a major factor, but it does provide a small discount on the bluff.

"But hold on!" you might say. "Assuming that the button is open-raising the 55 percent range recommended in this book, then betting the flop and turn with 100 percent of that range, don't pocket eights have 51 percent equity on the turn? What about check-calling?"

That's a reasonable question, and we're glad you asked. If there were no more money left to bet on the river, check-calling this turn would be a profitable play. Getting 2.6 to 1, you only need 28 percent equity to justify a call—but there is one more street to play. Your opponent can draw out on you and value bet the river. He can give up with his bluffs. Check-calling the turn can be profitable, but check-calling the river can be a costly mistake that cancels out the profitability of the turn call. In other words, you suffer from reverse implied odds here.

"But what about calling the turn and folding the river?" you press. Well, now your opponent can bluff the river and get you to fold the best hand. As we've seen in earlier examples, it doesn't matter how much showdown value you have if you can't get to showdown. The trouble here is that you don't know which approach your opponent will take. If you have a strong read on a particular player, then you can try to play the leveling game. But you're playing with imperfect information on the river. On the turn, you should have a very clear vision of your opponent's range. This almost perfect information gives you the opportunity to grab some value now. You should seize it. Note that if your opponent does call your turn check-raise here, you should usually give up on the river.

THE TAKEAWAY

You won't always have such a clear idea of your opponent's range, so then how do you reduce your positional disadvantage? There's not a lot that you can do. Your best course of action is to try to get to showdown for a reasonable price, and keep your eyes peeled to take an occasional shot at an off-balance foe.

MISCONCEPTION #30

DON'T DONK

Some successful players suggest that you should never, ever lead out with a bet when you just called the street before. The notion is that your opponent has the initiative after betting or raising on the previous street, and you should let him keep the initiative. If you want to get more money in the pot, you should check, let him bet, and then raise. Never lead out into a player who has initiative. Never donk.

In the last chapter, we saw that there are spots where leading out is a bad option. It would be easy enough to generalize and say that it's always a bad option. But it's not—sometimes it's your best option. Poker is all about playing against ranges and knowing how your opponents will respond to your actions. In the flop scenario we looked at, your opponent was not going to respond to your flop donk the way you wanted him to. That's not always going to be the case. Sometimes a donk will accomplish what you want it to.

A common situation occurs when your hand improves on the turn. You've called with **A♦ J♦** in the big blind against a hijack raise. You check-call a flop of **A♠ 8♣ 2♦**. The turn is the **J♠**. You should donk. Just lead right out into the preflop raiser/flop bettor. The idea of checking to the raiser or the player who bet the previous street comes from the fact that you don't flop a lot of monster hands. More often than not, checking is the correct play. You usually want to keep the pot small or plan to give up. Your opponent's range is wide, and if you hold a marginal hand you want to keep it that way. You want to encourage bluffs.

When you turn top two pair on a dry ace-high board, these concerns do not apply. You have a strong hand that wants to get money in the pot, so there's no need to keep the pot small. If your opponent happens to have a set, you're going to go broke no matter how you play the hand. There are only eight combinations of sets and nothing else beats you, so don't worry about the few times you get busted. There are three combos each of 8-8 and 2-2, and only one each of A-A and J-J, as the ace and jack in your hand significantly reduce your opponent's chances of holding trips. Taking a line that results in a fold would be awful. There are too many weaker hands that you can extract value from. The only reason to check would be if your opponent's betting range is wider than his calling range. That's unlikely. Unless he's very aggressive, your opponent is unlikely to bet the turn with garbage on this board, as your flop call indicates a desire to show down. You have a better chance of getting money in the pot by putting it in there yourself.

You may be tempted to check-raise, perhaps thinking that's the best way to get value from hands like A-8 and A-2. Along with A-K and A-Q, these are the primary hands you're looking to get value from. If you check-raise, your opponent is likely to fold these hands since your hand looks very distinctly like A-J or J-J. There's nothing he beats that you could be raising for value, and your play would be a very unusual bluff. By donking, you'll collect turn and river bets from all of your opponent's strong hands, and sometimes get all the money in against his weaker two-pair hands.

The scenario is even more pronounced when you improve on the river. Let's begin with an example:

GAME: $5/$10 blinds—6 players
STACKS: $1,000 effective
READS: BTN is passive
YOUR HAND: You have **Q♥ J♥**
PREFLOP: 3 players fold, BTN raises to $30,
1 player folds, you call
FLOP: 10♥ 5♥ 2♦ ($65—2 players)
ACTION: You check, BTN bets $40, you call
TURN: K♣ ($145—2 players)
ACTION: You check, BTN bets $110, you call
RIVER: 3♥ ($365—2 players)
ACTION: You bet $350

You call the flop, planning to fold the turn unless you make a flush, top pair, or pick up a gutshot to go with your draw. Against an aggressive player, you would raise the flop as a semibluff, but it's better to let this player check the turn and save your bluff for the river. If the passive button bets a blank turn, you should fold. His range will be very strong, you will need to make a flush to win the pot, and even your implied odds will not justify a call.

The **K♣** on the turn gives you a straight draw to go with your flush draw, so now you have an easy call. When the **3♥** shows up on the river, you lead straight out, even though your opponent bet the turn. As a passive player, he's likely to be scared of the flush and check back. You're also unlikely to induce bluffs by checking, since his turn bet almost always represents a strong hand.

By donking, you also get to set the bet size. Even if a bet goes in just as often when you check as when you bet (it won't), there is more value in making a well-sized bet yourself, since your opponent is unlikely to make a big bet on the scare card. Not only will he be afraid of *you* having a flush, he may also realize that you will be concerned that *he* has the flush. He will still be afraid of the flush when you donk, but passive players like to call. His range will contain mostly sets and two pair, none of which will fold to your pot-sized bet. When you complete your hand against a passive player, make sure the money goes in and he calls as much as he's willing to pay.

Lest you think that you should only donk when you improve (a hideously unbalanced strategy), here's an example of how you can balance the play:

GAME: $5/$10 blinds—6 players
STACKS: $1,000 effective
READS: BTN is solid regular
YOUR HAND: You have A♠ J♣ in the big blind
PREFLOP: 3 players fold, BTN raises to $30,
1 player folds, you call
FLOP: K♥ 10♥ 8♦ ($65—2 players)
ACTION: BTN bets $40, you call

As in the previous hands, you check-call the flop with the intention of donking if you hit your gutshot, but your plan is also to donk when a heart comes off. This gives you seven or eight fake outs here and balances the times you would lead out after actually making the flush.

THE TAKEAWAY

Whether you're looking for value or an opportunity to bluff, you should often lead right out on the cards that will discourage your opponent from betting. The philosophy of "check to the raiser" mostly stems from the expectation that the previous aggressor will continue betting. But when the board comes out in a way that will slow the aggressor down, checking becomes a terrible way to get money in the pot.

MISCONCEPTION #31

ALWAYS PLAY YOUR DRAWS AGGRESSIVELY

When you flop a strong draw, it's often a good idea to play it aggressively. This gives you two ways to win: You can make your hand and win a showdown, or your opponent can fold, ceding you the pot automatically. Deciding whether or not to semibluff involves a number of factors. How strong is your draw? Are you willing to commit your stack? How often will your opponent fold to aggression? What are your implied odds when you get there? Will raising the flop or turn set you up for a profitable bluff later in the hand? The answers to these questions will frequently instruct you to play your draw aggressively. Right now, though, we're going to take a look at a particular situation where they do not.

Let's get back to the **Q♥ J♥** example in the previous chapter, where you called in the big blind and took a heads-up flop of **10♥ 5♥ 2♦**. You may have wondered why you would check-call that board instead of semibluff. Against aggressive opponents, you should usually check-raise with a flush draw and two overcards. That's a big draw. You have a chance to get it in pretty good on the flop, and your opponent's range will have tons of air that will fold outright. But the example in question was against a passive player. A passive player will only bet the turn when he has a hand, and will give up with all of his air. In other words, he'll tell you on the turn whether your flop semibluff would have worked—but only if you're patient enough to listen.

You may be able to put in a profitable raise on the flop with this hand. You probably can, but instead you could wait until the river to bluff and find yourself in an even more profitable situation. Why waste your bullets early when you can wait and let your opponent tell you now whether or not you'll hit your target?

Semibluffing is very often going to be correct, but don't do it out of reflex. Take the time to consider your opponent, his range, and how he'll respond with different parts of that range on the flop, turn, and river. You'll need to rely on judgment and experience to find the best way to play each draw, but here are some guidelines that may help:

1. **How strong is your draw?**

    If your draw is so strong that you want to get all in, then playing it aggressively makes a lot of sense. With a very strong draw, you can have the best hand so often that you're actually getting your chips in for value. For example, **A♠ Q♠** on a **J♠ 10♦ 6♠** board is a monster draw that has great equity against anything other than a set. You'll even win one time in three against the nuts. Ace-high flush draws are often good candidates for semibluffing since you can win with ace-high when your opponent gets it in with a lower draw.

2. **Are you willing to commit your stack?**

    In general, you should be more willing to semibluff if you're willing to get all your chips in the middle. The converse is that you don't want to put in a semibluff and get moved off of your equity when your opponent plays back at you. That doesn't mean you should never raise with **5♣ 4♣** on a board of **J♣ 6♦ 2♦**, but getting reraised off your 4-outer is a risk you should consider.

3. **How often will your opponent fold to aggression?**

    The more often your opponent folds, the weaker the draw you need to have a profitable semibluff. Put another way: As your folding equity increases, you don't need as much showdown equity. The more often your opponent calls down, the less frequently you should be bluffing, but the more often you should be jamming with your super-strong draws for value.

4. **What are your implied odds when you get there?**
When you have a chance to win a huge pot, you shouldn't risk that without a compelling reason. Sometimes it pays to let your opponents stay in the pot so they can pay you when you make your draw. Other times you'll do better to build up a big pot early so that you can win more when you get there. Knowing the difference takes experience, plus being aware of the current situation and your opponent's tendencies.

5. **Will raising the flop or turn set you up for a profitable bluff later in the hand?**
A lot of players will call a flop bet or raise, thinking you can have a draw, but they're unwilling to put in a big turn bet. If you raise **Q♥ J♥** on a **9♥ 7♥ 2♦** flop, you don't need your opponent to fold the flop to make your raise profitable. If you're likely to earn folds with turn and river bets, that's even better. This way your opponent has contributed more money to a pot that you're likely to win.

6. **Will just calling the flop set you up for a more profitable turn or river play?**
If your opponent will frequently give up on the turn, you may have a more profitable bluff on the turn or river than you would have on the flop.

THE TAKEAWAY

Many times you'll have one factor telling you to do one thing and another factor telling you to do something else. The key is determining which factor is more important in any given hand.

MISCONCEPTION #32
DON'T GET BLOWN OFF YOUR HAND

You raise before the flop and only the big blind calls. You flop nothing and he checks. You fire out a continuation bet. He calls. The turn is no help; you still have nothing. Your opponent checks again. "Should I bet again?" you ask. "Will he fold ace high?" you wonder. "What if I get check-raised?" you worry. "I don't want to get blown off my equity," you might consider. "I think I'll just check it back," you decide.

There was a time when a turn bet usually meant a strong hand. Most players were afraid to fire out a big bet when they held nothing. Those same players were also afraid to make thin value bets or continue semibluffing their draws, worried that they'd get check-raised off their hand. Those would be legitimate concerns if guys were check-raising turns left and right—but they weren't then and they're still not now.

Don't fear the turn check-raise. That's our advice to you. Could this be a misconception of the future? Certainly. Game conditions change and maybe players will start taking check-call, check-raise lines more often, but we doubt it. The following hand example illustrates one reason why:

> **GAME:** $5/$10 blinds—6 players
> **STACKS:** $1,000 effective
> **YOUR HAND:** You hold **K♥ J♥** in the cutoff
> **PREFLOP:** 2 players fold, you raise to $30, 2 players fold, BB calls
> **FLOP:** **10♥ 7♥ 2♦** ($65—2 players)
> **ACTION:** BB checks, you bet $40, BB calls
> **TURN:** **8♣** ($145—2 players)
> **ACTION:** BB checks, you bet $100, BB raises to $300

Think about the situation for a moment. Some players will check back this turn, fearing they'll get pushed off their big draw by a turn raise. If the big blind were to check-raise all in, then yes, folding would be the correct play. But that would be a massive overbet, shoving $930 into a $245 pot. Most of the time, the big blind will make a more reasonable raise. Against a reasonable raise like $300, the cutoff is getting better than 2.7 to 1 odds with a flush draw, a gutshot, and two overcards. While the overcards are rarely good and the immediate odds are not good enough to justify a call, there will be $630 left behind on the river. That helps the cutoff for three reasons:

1. If the big blind has a big hand, the extra money left behind gives the cutoff good implied odds for completing his draw.
2. If the cutoff thinks the big blind is weak or bluffing, he has room to make a big semibluff shove.
3. If the cutoff calls the turn and the big blind checks the river, the cutoff may have a profitable bluffing opportunity.

While this is a specific situation, the math will always work out the same with 100-blind stacks. Sometimes the bet sizes will be a little larger or a little smaller, but the out-of-position player will always have to worry about the extra money left behind. And the player in position will always have an advantage deciding whether that money goes in.

So like we said, don't fear the turn check-raise. It doesn't happen that often, and all is not lost when it does. But that doesn't mean you should bet the turn every single time. If you're the sort of player who's afraid of betting the turn, if you're asking yourself right now, "Well, when *should* I fire the second barrel?" here's our advice: Look for reasons to bet the turn. Find any excuse you can. Here are a few good ones:

4 REASONS TO BET THE TURN

1. Your hand is strong.

This one's simple. When your hand is doing well against your opponent's range, it's usually a good idea to keep value betting. It's important to consider what range of hands your opponent will call you with and whether he'll bluff the river if you check. A good rule of thumb is that if you think you can bet the turn and river for value, then you should not check the turn hoping to induce a river bluff. Getting those two value bets in is more valuable than collecting some small bluffs. For example:

GAME:	$5/$10 blinds—6 players
STACKS:	$1,000 effective
READS:	BB is a decent regular
YOUR HAND:	You have A♣ J♠ in the cutoff
PREFLOP:	2 players fold, you raise to $30, 2 players fold, BB calls
FLOP:	J♦ 2♣ 2♠ ($65—2 players)
ACTION:	BB checks, you bet $40, BB calls
TURN:	6♥ ($145—2 players)
ACTION:	BB checks, you bet $110

2. The turn should be scary to your opponent.

If you bet, your opponent is likely to fold now. This comes up when you c-bet the flop and your opponent calls with what you suspect is a marginal made hand. If the turn is an ace, you can credibly represent one, while your opponent is unlikely to have one. If the turn completes one or more draws, that's another time you can expect your opponent to fold often, particularly if he'd usually have semibluffed draws of his own on the flop.

3. Your opponent is likely to fold to a river bet if you bet the turn.

Sometimes you should make a turn bet that has immediate negative expectation. That's because it sets up a bluffing opportunity on the river that's so profitable it makes up for any money you might lose on the turn. Let's look at an example:

GAME:	$5/$10 blinds—6 players
STACKS:	$1,000 effective
YOUR HAND:	You have K♦ 6♦ on button
PREFLOP:	3 players fold, you raise to $30, 1 player folds, BB calls
FLOP:	9♦ 5♣ 2♥ ($65—2 players)
ACTION:	BB checks, you bet $40, BB calls
TURN:	Q♠ ($145—2 players)
ACTION:	BB checks, you bet $100

The big blind here is very unlikely to have a hand that wants to check-call three streets. Yes, there are a few sets in his range. But there are many more hands like pocket threes through eights, weak nines, and ace-five in his range that will fold immediately. There are also hands that may call the turn but fold the river, like A-9 and pocket jacks or tens. When you see your opponent check-call this flop, ask yourself how often you would want to call the turn and the river in his spot. The answer should be, "Not very often."

(4) You've picked up a draw.

Straight and flush draws certainly qualify, but so do hands like bottom pair. Having a strong draw can give you good enough equity to bet and call a raise. Even having just a sliver of equity will subsidize your turn bets, making a borderline barrel into a clearly profitable opportunity. Take the following example:

GAME: $5/$10 blinds—5 players
STACKS: $1,000 effective
YOUR HAND: You have **A♣ 2♣** on the button
PREFLOP: 2 players fold, you raise to $30,
1 player folds, BB calls
FLOP: **K♦ 8♣ 4♠** ($65—2 players)
ACTION: BB checks, you bet $40, BB calls
TURN: **2♥** ($145—2 players)
ACTION: BB checks, you bet $100

Turning bottom pair gives you some showdown value, but it's not the sort of hand where you want to check back the turn hoping to induce a river bluff. Your opponent will usually have better than a pair of twos after calling this flop, and will have a good chance of improving even if he doesn't have you beaten yet. By betting this turn, you can take down the pot immediately; you can get called and bluff successfully on the river; or you can improve to the best hand and win a big pot. A lot of people claim that second barreling can be easily taught and learned. It can't. It takes experience. We can give you some guidelines here, but it's up to you to determine which guidelines apply and when. You need to think and practice.

Another area where experience and skill can provide an advantage is playing the river. By knowing when to fire the third barrel, when to put in a third value bet, and when to give up can justify some turn bets that might otherwise be unwise. Knowing how to properly size your river bets adds to this edge. There are a lot of spots where you will have a close decision between either betting or checking the turn. Having confidence in your ability to play the river can provide the swing vote. The **9♦ 5♣ 2♥** flop example from earlier in this section demonstrates a hand where betting the turn may or may not be profitable, but by knowing when to fire the third barrel (in that example, almost always) you can put together an extremely profitable line.

Let's assume now that you've gotten to the point where you're confident in your river play. You know how to get your value and you know how to steal pots away with a final stab. You should no longer be looking for reasons to bet the turn. Now you should be looking for reasons *not* to. Betting should be your default. That means that once you become a solid, well-rounded player, you should always bet the turn unless you have a compelling reason to check.

Here are some circumstances that should make you think twice about firing off an aggressive turn bet:

4 REASONS TO THINK TWICE BEFORE AGGRESSIVELY BETTING THE TURN

1. Your opponent is very good.

Against highly skilled opposition, you can't get away with representing narrow ranges. If your line can only represent a big hand or a bluff, excellent players won't believe you. They'll call you down and force you to have the unlikely big hand.

2. Your opponent is very bad.

The biggest mistake that very bad players make is calling down too often. That's what makes them very bad. Don't justify their mistake by having too many bluffs in your range. Exploit their mistake instead. Value bet more aggressively against these players, and bluff much less often.

3. The turn card does not affect your opponent's ability to call down.

This one is a bit tricky. It depends on your opponent's flop calling range, your perceived range, and the texture of the board. When a blank comes off, it's less likely to affect your opponent's ability to call down than when a scare card comes off.

4. Your opponent doesn't expect you to bluff.

If the combination of board texture and recent history suggests to your observant opponent that you would be unlikely to bluff, this is actually a good spot to bluff. Take the following example:

GAME:	$5/$10—6 players
STACKS:	$1,000 effective
READS:	SB is observant and likes to play the leveling game
DYNAMIC:	You have recently been caught triple barreling by SB
YOUR HAND:	You have **K♦ J♦** in the cutoff
PREFLOP:	2 players fold, you raise to $30, 1 player folds, SB calls, 1 player folds
FLOP:	**10♦ 7♣ 2♥** ($70—2 players)
ACTION:	SB checks, you bet $50, SB calls
TURN:	**4♠** ($170—2 players)
ACTION:	SB checks, you bet $130, SB checks
RIVER:	**4♥** ($430—2 players)
ACTION:	SB checks, you bet $365, SB levels himself

The small blind may think that you should be unlikely to bluff now. The river has not improved your range and there isn't much you can threaten to hold. You've been caught bluffing recently. Given his line, he knows that you know that he has showdown value—but you're betting anyway, so you can't be bluffing, right? The question becomes whether he knows that you know that he knows this.

"What?"

Yeah, it gets confusing. The trick is to stay one step ahead of your opponent and use what he thinks he knows about you against him.

In general, the lower the highest card on the flop the more likely you'll be able to represent a strong hand on the turn. Let's look at the difference between two flops: **9♦ 5♣ 2♥** and **K♦ 5♣ 2♥**. The only difference between the second and the first is the **K♦** instead of the **9♦**. Let's say that your opponent calls your bet on each flop with top pair and a **J♠** kicker. On the first board, there are 16 overcards that can fall on the turn. Ignoring your two cards, that will happen 34 percent of the time. With the **K♦** on board instead, there are only four overcards that can hit. There's only an 8.5 percent chance of an ace hitting. So it's less likely for a card to come off and scare your opponent.

But that's not all. On the first board, your turn bet can represent at least 42 combinations that beat your opponent: A-9 and five different overpairs, not to mention sets. On the second board, there are only pocket aces, A-K, K-Q, and sets, just 29 combos. The actual turn card will affect these numbers, but you get the point. Top pair on a 9-high flop is weaker than it is on a king-high flop. It's fairly intuitive, but it's still important. You should be more likely to fire second and third barrels when your opponent's hand is weak and vulnerable. You're more likely to earn a fold.

If you're reading through this discussion of aggressive turn betting and still thinking that you'd rather not risk a lot of money trying it out yourself, we have two suggestions for you. The first is to drop down in stakes and muck around. You can drop down one limit or ten, whatever makes you comfortable. Most players don't barrel the turn often enough, so why not just try it out, taking into consideration the factors we've listed in this chapter. If you don't want to play at a lower limit, or if there is no lower limit available, then try our second suggestion. When you're unsure of whether or not you've found a good spot to bluff, make a note. Write down the board texture and the action up to that point. The next time this situation arises and you have a strong hand, make a value bet. Keep track of how often you get paid off. If you find that you're not getting paid as often as you'd like, then you've found a good spot to bluff. If you're getting paid nine times out of ten (unlikely), then it's probably a good spot to give up on your bluffs.

The last method can be applied to any bluffing situation, not just the turn.

THE TAKEAWAY

If you have a flop line, a special turn play, or a river scenario where you're contemplating bluffing, try that line out with your value hands. Take notes. Find out whether you get paid or get folds. That will inform your decisions. Notes don't always have to be about a specific player. Don't be afraid to take broader notes about the game conditions you typically face. Once you have these notes, take action! Whether it's on the turn or any other street, be proactive.

MISCONCEPTION #33
NEVER BET THE MINIMUM

You're on the button and call a cutoff open with **K♦ Q♣**. The flop comes **J♦ 6♣ 2♥** and you call a bet. Folding the flop is an option, but you decide that even if you don't improve, you can outplay this opponent on the turn. When the **8♠** falls on the turn and your opponent checks, you have a number of options:

1. **You can check back and take a free shot at hitting one of your overcards.**
    The downside here is that you let your opponent see the river for free while giving him a chance to take back control of the hand.

2. **You can make a reasonable sized bet, which would be the standard play after the flop float.**
    There's a good chance you'll shake loose ace high hands from your opponent's range, and possibly set up a profitable river barrel against small pairs.

3. **The third option is one that few players give much thought to. Bet one chip!**
    A few good things can happen when you bet the minimum. First of all, you're likely to confuse the hell out of your opponent. He'll probably call, since

you're offering such fantastic pot odds, but check-fold the river if you make a pot-sized bet. You can also get a call, then catch top pair on the river and squeeze out a value bet on the end.

4. **Finally, sometimes your opponent will check-raise you, thinking that your tiny bet looks like weakness.**

Since you already know that his range is so weak, you can actually come back over the top and jam the money in. Now it looks as though you made your one-chip bet to merely bait your opponent, and that you've sprung a trap on him. This is not a play that you should use all the time. It's like a fake punt. It's almost always going to work, as long as you use it sparingly. The element of surprise and confusion is what lends it its effectiveness. If you use it too often, you can get exploited; but using it every so often will keep your opponents on their toes and make them uncomfortable. And you may even get some hands to fold that wouldn't have folded to a more traditional line.

The real lesson here is not just that you can sometimes confuse your opponents with weird bet sizes. The lesson is that you should never fail to consider all of your options. Be creative. Assess all your options objectively. Most of the time, the best play will be the obvious one, but sometimes you'll find a gem that a more close-minded player would have overlooked.

Let's take a look at an effective use of the **min-bet** (the minimum bet allowable) in a televised high stakes cash game in which Dusty participated. With deep stacks and blinds of $25/$50, Jennifer Tilly opens to $150 in early position. Holding 10-8, David "Viffer" Peat makes a small reraise to $300 and Luke Schwartz cold calls in the small blind. Tilly calls the reraise. The flop comes out 9-8-6. Schwartz decides to lead out for $750 with 7-7 in the pocket. Tilly folds and Peat calls. The turn is an ace, so the board now reads 9-8-6-A. Schwartz checks in a questionable play that makes his marginal hand transparent. Viffer could check back with his own marginal hand here, but he instead bets the minimum $50 into a pot of $2,450.

If he didn't want to check, why didn't he make a regular sized bet? Well, a large bet would build a big pot with a marginal hand. He'd lose more against a hand like A-7, and win nothing from hands that he beats.

So why not check back? While checking back wouldn't necessarily be a bad play, it would give Schwartz the opportunity to bluff the river. While tossing $50 into the pot doesn't technically prevent Schwartz from bluffing the river, it does tie him up psychologically. It's hard to know what a min-bet means since it occurs so infrequently. If everyone did it all the time, maybe people would respond to it properly and essentially ignore the fact that the player bet at all. But the fact is that min-bets are uncommon (and frequently frowned upon), so few players are prepared to handle them effectively.

This play comes down to defining a range. By checking back, Viffer would essentially be saying that he holds a marginal hand at best. By making the min-bet, he introduces some element of doubt into the equation. It forces Schwartz to think, "What the hell is this guy doing this with?"

It also forces Schwartz to expose the fact that he holds a marginal hand at best. While the turn check has already declared this as fact, the min-bet is like saying, "Oh yeah? You have nothing? You don't want to make a big bet? Yeah, I didn't think so." In a way, it's almost like a taunt. So by taunting Schwartz in this way, Viffer essentially locks him up on the river. The bet shuts down any marginal value bets that Luke may otherwise consider making on the river.

Let's look at one more example of the min-bet at its finest, from a hand that Dusty played:

GAME:	$5/$10 blinds—6 players
STACKS:	$1,000 effective
DUSTY'S HAND:	Dusty has **K♠ J♠** in the big blind
PREFLOP:	3 players fold, BTN raises to $30, 1 player folds, Dusty calls
FLOP:	**Q♦ J♦ 6♥** ($65—2 players)
ACTION:	Dusty bets $40, BTN calls
TURN:	**2♠** ($145—2 players)
ACTION:	Dusty bets $110, BTN calls
RIVER:	**2♣** ($365—2 players)
ACTION:	Dusty bets $10

After donking his marginal hand on the flop and following up with a turn bet, Dusty makes the tiny min-bet on the river. Why? Marginal to moderately strong made hands and passively played draws should make up almost the entirety of the button's range. If Dusty checks, everything that beats K-J will likely bet, and so will some missed draws. Perhaps check-calling would be profitable here. But what happens when Dusty bets the minimum? Strong hands like pocket aces, pocket kings, and **A♦ 2♦** will raise to approximately what they would have bet had Dusty checked. No change there. Missed draws will probably do the same. They were waiting to bluff and this tiny bet won't discourage them from doing so. Against a strong hand or a draw, the min-bet is a wash with a check. But what about the rest of the button's range? When the button holds a marginal hand like A-J, Q-10, or K-Q, he would usually bet when checked to, but against a tiny bet, he's much more likely to just call. So, making the min-bet allows Dusty to save a bunch of chips against these hands.

These are just a few of the situations where betting the minimum can be superior to making a more conventionally

sized bet. There are probably some other spots that we haven't even thought of yet where you can do the same.

THE TAKEAWAY

As with other trick plays, overuse can erode effectiveness, but adding this play to your arsenal can give you more tools than your more close-minded opponents possess.

MISCONCEPTION #34
REAL MEN MAKE REAL RAISES

While a number of women have had tremendous success in poker, some people are still under the impression that poker is somehow a man's game. This attitude is reflected in many areas of their strategy, including bet sizing. It often becomes as ridiculous as driving a Hummer in the city. Seriously, who needs to drive to the movies in a truck that was designed to have anti-tank missiles mounted on it? Traffic can be rough, but come on! This point is best illustrated with an example:

GAME: $5/$10 blind—2 players
STACKS: $1,000 effective
READS: CO is aggressive
YOUR HAND: You have 9♥ 8♥ on the button
PREFLOP: 2 players fold, CO raises to $30, you call, 2 players fold
FLOP: K♠ 7♥ 2♦ ($75—2 players)
ACTION: CO bets $50, you call
TURN: 4♣ ($175—2 players)
ACTION: CO bets $120, you raise to $280

You call preflop and float the flop specifically because you know this player will fire the second barrel here most of the time. On this dry board, he won't have a hand very often at all. The turn is a good card to apply the pressure, since it's so unlikely to have improved your opponent's hand. The fact that it's a total brick also means that your opponent cannot put you on a draw that's semibluff raising the turn, and he can't hold a draw himself to launch a semibluff reraise of his own.

Many players are inclined to make a big raise to $420 and blow him out of the pot. That's just silly. What does $420 accomplish that $280 would not? Put yourself in the cutoff's shoes. Have you ever once bet $120 on the turn, gotten raised to $280, and thought to yourself, "Thank god he didn't bet $420! That would have changed everything." Maybe if you had a draw. But there are no draws on this board. It's much more likely that the cutoff is thinking, "What the hell do I do with my K-J now?" The only hand that the cutoff can hold that cares whether you raise to $280 instead of $420 is a set—and those hands will be disappointed that you didn't raise more.

Playing your opponent off of his hand is not a macho thing, it's a math problem. How much must you invest to get him to fold how often, and will it be profitable? Raising to $420 may be profitable. (The larger raise size risks $420 to win $295, so it has to work 59 percent of the time: 420 / (295 + 420), or roughly .59.) In fact, if your flop float was a good idea, it probably is profitable, but it's still a mistake if raising to $280 would be more profitable. Raising to $280 risks less to win the same amount, so it only has to work 49 percent of the time: 280 / (295 + 280), or roughly .49. The goal is not just to find a profitable option—it is to find the *most* profitable option, and raising to $420 is not it.

The only conditions where the larger raise size would make sense are:

1. A lot more hands will fold to the bigger raise; and
2. Your opponent will often call the raise but fold to a river shove.

On this board, the first condition is almost certainly not met. This is the sort of board where your opponent either has a hand he's willing to go with, or he has air. He'll fold his air and go with his strong hands. Furthermore, you still have the threat of a river shove when you raise to $280, so he should be committing his stack to the hand if he decides not to fold. The second condition is false for the same reason. Any halfway intelligent opponent will know that he can't call only the turn and hope you give up on the river. (If you believe your opponent would often call the turn and fold the river, then you should constantly raise the turn and bet the river against him. This is a big leak in your opponent's game and you should exploit it.)

THE TAKEAWAY

Don't spend more than you have to. Making big plays is not some test of testosterone, it's a logical decision. Use logic to determine your bet size. Don't drive a Hummer to the movies.

MISCONCEPTION #35

YOU NEED A MONSTER TO GET INVOLVED AGAINST A BET & A RAISE

When a straightforward player bets the flop and a tight player raises, you're usually looking at two pretty good hands. If you're looking at a spot where ranges are tight to begin with, you may need a hand very close to the nuts to justify getting involved in the pot. That's good poker. When two people like their hands very much, you're not going to win the pot without the goods.

The mistake here would be to assume that whenever someone bets and someone else raises, they both hold strong hands. But like every decision in poker, you have to start by considering ranges. If both players are conservative, it's usually safe to assume they both have strong hands. But not all players are conservative. When bad passive players lead out into the preflop raiser, they frequently have nothing. It's hard to say why they do it, but bad players have a tendency to make the most irrational plays. That's part of what makes them bad players (and so fun to play with).

Let's look at a hand from a $2/$4 game: You open-raise to $12 from the cutoff with **Q♠ J♠**. A terrible player cold calls in the small blind, and the super-aggressive big blind comes along as well. The flop comes out **10♠ 8♣ 2♦**. The terrible player leads out for $22 into a $36 pot, and the hyper-aggressive player in the big blind raises to $73. With just queen high, this may look like an easy fold, which would keep you out of trouble—but is there a better option?

Calling doesn't appear to be a very good option. It's hard to say what the big blind will think you have if you just call, but being aggressive, he's likely to jam the turn or at least make a bet large enough to commit himself if he has a sliver of equity. So calling is out. But what about raising? We've already established that the small blind will rarely have a strong hand here. The big blind knows this, so he can be raising with a lot of nonsense as well. Despite the fact that their ranges look weak to you, an all-in shove will look strong to them. You should take the pot down immediately 8 times out of 10, which is more than the 75 percent necessary to make the bluff profitable even if you were drawing dead every time your opponent called.

In this scenario, however, you have two overcards, a gutshot, and a backdoor flush draw. That's good for 17 percent equity against a set, and 41 percent against a hand like top pair/top kicker. That equity provides a substantial discount on your bluff. In the actual hand, the big blind wound up calling with **J♦ 9♦**, the turn and river came **4♥** and **K♣**, and the player with **Q♥ J♥** (you, in our example) took it down with queen high. Sometimes there are even more ways to win than you initially estimate!

This play requires a disclaimer. If you're playing the micro-stakes or you're at a table with several fish (including the flop raiser), this play is much more dangerous. Use discretion when trying to pull off these big moves. In games at the "professional" level online ($.50/$1 and higher), most games have only one bad player at the table. A dynamic develops where the five skilled players are fighting tooth and nail for the fish's money. Here's a hand played by Dusty that illustrates this dynamic:

> **GAME:** $3/$6 blinds, $1.20 ante—5 players
> **STACKS:** Dusty has $1437, SB has $568, BB has $1509
> **READS:** SB is loose and bad, BB is solid and aggressive
> **DUSTY'S HAND:** Dusty has A♣ 8♦ on the button
> **PREFLOP:** 2 players fold, Dusty raises to $12, SB calls, BB calls
> **FLOP:** K♥ K♣ 5♠ ($42—3 players)
> **ACTION:** SB bets $18, BB raises to $68, Dusty calls, SB folds
> **TURN:** J♥ ($194—2 players)
> **ACTION:** BB checks, Dusty bets $145, BB folds

The keys to this hand are the small blind's donking range and the big blind's perception of that range. As observant and experienced players, Dusty and the big blind both realize that the small blind is donking this flop primarily with garbage. Sure, he might hold a pocket pair or a 5, but it's rare that he'll lead out with trip kings or a full house. It's hard to make those hands, so the fact that he'll usually check with them makes it very unlikely that he has a strong hand.

Armed with the read that the small blind's range is weak, the big blind's logical play is to raise, trying to take down a medium-sized pot. If Dusty were cruising on autopilot, this would work. Without holding a strong hand, few players will get involved in a multiway pot facing a flop raise. But just as surely as he knows the small blind's range is weak, Dusty knows that the big blind's range is also weak. After all, why would he raise the flop with a strong hand? The big blind is a strong player and raising the flop with a big hand would be a bad play. What could possibly pay him off?

Knowing that both of his opponents have weak ranges, Dusty chooses the play that should scare his opponents the most. He calls. Using the same logic we just applied to the big blind's play, why would Dusty reraise with a strong hand? He can't get paid unless he has something like K-5 against pocket fives. It makes more sense for him to play it slow and allow his opponents to bluff back at him. When the small blind folds the flop and the big blind checks the turn, Dusty bets and wins the pot.

THE TAKEAWAY

Accurately recognizing situations for what they are can make a big difference to your bottom line.

MISCONCEPTION #36

DON'T BLUFF IN MULTIWAY POTS

In the majority of cases where you flop nothing in a multiway pot, you should simply give up. Check and fold. The major exception to this is when your opponents can rarely have a good hand. Take this example:

> **GAME:** $5/$10—6 players
> **STACKS:** $1,000 effective
> **READS:** HJ is a straightforward regular, BTN and BB are both weak and passive
> **YOUR HAND:** You have 8♦ 7♦ in the cutoff
> **PREFLOP:** 1 player folds, HJ raises to $30, you call, BTN calls, 1 player folds, BB calls
> **FLOP:** A♥ J♥ 2♣ ($120—4 players)
> **ACTION:** BB checks, HJ checks, you check, BTN checks
> **TURN:** 6♣ ($120—4 players)
> **ACTION:** BB checks, HJ bets $80, you ponder

When the hijack bets this turn after checking the flop, you may be thinking to yourself, "So he didn't like his hand on the flop but now he does? I don't trust him, but since I only have 8-high, what can I do?"

You can raise!

Think about the hijack's range. The only hand that can be excited to get raised here is pocket sixes. Every other strong hand would have bet the flop. Besides sixes, the hijack will have A-10 or K-J that didn't want to play a big pot, a turned flush draw, or total air. There's only a very small part of that range that can withstand pressure. If you raise to $240, you'll probably win outright 8 times out of 10.

> **TURN:** 6♣ ($120—4 players)
> **ACTION:** BB checks, HJ bets $80, you raise to $240,
> BTN folds, BB folds, HJ calls
> **RIVER:** 4♣ ($600—2 players)
> **ACTION:** HJ checks, you check

If the hijack calls your turn raise, you should check back when a club comes on the river. While you could make an argument for betting no matter what comes—your hand will look like a flush or a turned monster—your opponent's range is too heavily weighted toward flushes on this river. You should only continue bluffing here if you think your opponent would always bet into you on the river if he made a flush. If that's the case, then you can remove flushes from his range and make a profitable bluff.

On any non-club river card, you should continue your bluff. For example:

> **RIVER:** 2♠ ($600—2 players)
> **ACTION:** HJ checks, you bet $350

Your opponent's range should be made up of busted club draws and a few stubborn pairs. But you still have only 8-high, so you need to bet to win. While a flop bet into a large field often indicates strength, a turn bet after a flop check doesn't mean nearly as much. Keep your eyes open for turn bets from players who can rarely hold a strong hand. If you use this play judiciously, you'll find some free money to add to your coffers.

THE TAKEAWAY

There's a more general lesson to be learned here as well. While this exact scenario will come up infrequently, you should always keep your eyes open for situations where your opponent can never hold a strong hand. Those are excellent times to take the pot away with aggressive turn plays, following up with conviction on the river.

MISCONCEPTION #37

YOUR BLUFF SHOULD TELL A STORY

This is very good advice when you're playing against observant opponents who have some good hands in their range. If you play your hand in a way that you would never play a strong hand, good opponents will often look you up whenever they hold anything at all. Your line needs to represent something in order to maintain credibility. To induce a fold, you need your opponents to think about all the good hands you could have. When your opponent has nothing to call with, however, it doesn't matter what you represent. There are times when both players know that the other player is full of it. The one who puts in the last bet wins these confrontations.

Here's an example from a hand that Dusty played: Dusty opens to $20 with **A♥ 10♥** from the button and gets called by a psychotically aggressive small blind. The flop comes **K♥ 7♣ 2♦**. Dusty bets $30 into $60. The small blind raises to $90 and the big blind folds. The small blind can almost never have a good hand here. He 3-bets all pocket pairs before the flop, as well as A-K, K-Q, and K-J, so he can never hold a set or a strong top pair. Maybe he has K-7 suited some of the time, but that's just two combinations. The plan is to let this guy bluff off as many chips as possible without allowing him to get the last word in. If Dusty raised to $270, the small blind might just reraise all in. When Dusty reraises, the small blind will very accurately observe that Dusty is unlikely to play a strong hand this way. (With something like a set, calling in position is better, allowing the small blind to barrel off).

Instead of making the larger raise, Dusty makes it only $170. With $330 in the pot and $1190 left behind, an all-in move from the small blind would be excessive. If he decides to 4-bet, he's more likely to raise to about $400. This would give Dusty a chance to come back over the top and get the last word in. Surprisingly, the small blind just calls the flop and checks the **9♠** turn. It appears that he's trying to find a way to get the last word in himself; his plan is probably to check-raise the turn. Dusty thwarts his plan by checking back. The river is the **9♦** and the small blind bets $370. Dusty now shoves all in and the maniac folds. The very next day, an almost identical situation occurred against the same player. Dusty took the same flop line with a set of sevens, bet the turn, and the guy check-raised all in with air.

THE TAKEAWAY

The moral to this story is that your bluff doesn't need to tell one, unless your opponent has something to call you with. If he doesn't, then bombs away! Just make sure you get the last word.

MISCONCEPTION #38

SELL YOUR HAND

Before finding the world of online poker, Dusty worked for his parents' company that distributed non-food items to grocery stores. The inventory included toothbrushes, pots and pans, toys, balloons and other everyday items. While the retail business was not as fun or lucrative as poker, it had a lot to teach about pricing. Have you ever been in a store, seen something priced $19.99, and wondered, "What idiot thinks this is cheaper than $20 in any significant way?" Well, there's a reason they price things at $19.99. They do it because it works!

"But it doesn't work on me!" you may say. Fair enough. It doesn't have to. If an item were knocked down from $2 to $1.99, it would only have to make a difference to 1 percent of the population to make more money. This tiny markdown causes a psychological effect. There's a reason iTunes sells songs for $.99. "C'mon mom, it's not even a buck!" The amazing thing is that marking an item down from $1.99 to $1.89 or even $1.79 has less of an effect than the one-penny difference between $2 and $1.99. That's what we call an inflection point.

Getting back to the retail business, after doing some market research at the grocery stores Dusty was responsible for, he took all the items marked $1.79 and $1.89 and bumped them up to $1.99. There was no change in the quantity of items sold, but the profit margin expanded. He took items marked $2.29 and bumped them to $2.49. Items that were $2.79 went up to $2.99. Much to Dusty's delight, the quantity of items sold remained virtually unchanged, while sales and profits soared. What he avoided was bumping prices above inflection points.

Assuming that most of you don't run a grocery store distributorship, how does this relate to you? You should treat your poker like a retail store. We'll go with an example. You have **K♣ Q♥** and open-raise the button. Only the big blind calls. The flop comes **K♠ 7♥ 2♦**. You bet and get called. The turn is another deuce, the **2♣**, you bet again, and again you get called. The river is the **5♠**. The pot is about $350. How much should you bet?

You figure your opponent's range to be K-J, K-10, and pocket eights through tens. You decide that he'll almost always fold his underpairs to a bet, but he'll almost always call with top pair. You should ask yourself, "What number will present a barrier for this guy. At what price will he no longer buy what I'm selling?" With the pot at $350, $300 may look too much like a pot-sized bet. He'll think your range is too **polarized** (concentrated on bluff hands or value hands) to contain the weaker kings he was hoping to beat. Don't break that barrier. You can start with a number like $220 (about two-thirds pot) that you're pretty sure he'll call. But don't stop there. Why bet $220 if he's just as likely to call $240 or $260? Drag the bar to the right until you find the biggest number you can that won't break the retail barrier. Don't stop at $260 if he's just as likely to call $290.

THE TAKEAWAY

When people talk about selling their hand, they're usually referring to betting small to induce a call. But don't bet small just because your opponent may be more likely to call. Take the time to think it through as you size your bets.

Sell your hand, but make them pay!

MISCONCEPTION #39

BET BIG WITH YOUR BIG HANDS

In no-limit hold'em, there are a number of situations where you will find yourself on the river with a huge hand, but your opponent will almost never have a strong hand. This usually happens when more than one draw gets there at the same time. If your opponent will call with the same range against a large bet as he will against a small bet, you should go ahead and make the larger bet. Your expectation will be higher. Sometimes you can go so far as to make a fishy looking overbet, hoping to arouse suspicion. Unfortunately, these tactics won't work that often against most opponents.

What you're left with is the task of selling your hand. Here's an example: You call in the cutoff with **Q♥ J♥** against a hijack opener. Stacks are 200 blinds deep. The flop comes out **10♥ 8♣ 3♥**, and the plan is to raise. When the preflop raiser makes a full pot-sized bet, however, it's time to change plans. This guy's range is now too strong to push him off of many hands. It looks like he's happy to play a big pot.

The turn is the **2♠**, so no help there. Again, the opponent fires off a pot-sized bet. With a flush draw, gutshot, two overcards, and position, you call again. Given the deep stacks, implied odds should be strong, particularly if the straight comes in. The river is the **A♥** and the aggressor checks. Unless he's getting tricky with the nut flush, this must look like the worst card in the world to him: Flushes got there and A-10 just pulled ahead of his overpairs. Firing off a large bet in this situation is a large mistake. The hijack will almost never have a strong hand. He's not happy about the river card. When he looks at that river card and a large bet, he's going to flip his cards in the muck without thinking twice.

This is a time to sell your hand. We know that you want to win a big pot when you make a big hand. We do too! But your opponent is clearly unhappy with his hand now, and won't let you win a big pot. There is a chance that he'll call a smaller bet, though. Bet half the pot, or even a little less. Against some sophisticated opponents, it's not worth trying to sell your hand. But this is a situation where many players simply can't resist calling down. They want to fold, but they think about how strong their hand was on the turn, look at the attractive pot odds you're offering them, and click the call button. That could be 20 or more blinds in your pocket every time this situation occurs.

Don't make small bets to sell your hand to players who are willing to call more, but you can't always blow weak hands out of the pot either, especially not when your opponent can't be strong.

THE TAKEAWAY

Recognize when your opponent hates the river card—and make him an offer he can't refuse!

MISCONCEPTION #40

GREAT PLAYERS ALWAYS MAKE THIN VALUE BETS

Many players have the notion that at high stakes poker, you need to make super thin value bets. As with most misconceptions, there's both truth and fallacy here. The truth is that when your opponents become stubborn and willing to call you down light to keep you from running them over, opportunities arise to value bet three streets with some surprisingly marginal hands. Your opponent may expect your range to be heavily polarized, so he'll call down with all of his bluff catchers. By betting some of your weaker hands for value, you depolarize your range and make some extra money.

This situation is nothing special, it's simply good poker. You put your opponent on a range. You think about how he'll play that range. You choose the most profitable option: one, two, three. Easy game. The only thing that changes is your opponent's range and how he plays it. Your thought process should always be the same.

There will be other spots in high-stakes games where your opponent's range is very strong and thus not a good time for thin value bets. Take this example: Dusty has **K♠ K♣** in a full ring game and cold calls a tight, early position raiser, hoping to get squeezed behind. No one obliges, but the big blind calls.

The three-way flop comes **K♦ A♠ 4♣.** It is an excellent flop for Dusty, and the tight opener makes a three-quarters pot c-bet. Dusty calls and the big blind folds. The turn is the **A♣** and the raiser fires out another three-quarters pot bet. Dusty calls. The river is the **Q♥** and the raiser checks. Dusty checks.

It may seem insane to check kings-full on the river. After all, there are only nine combinations of likely hands that can beat it—A-A, A-K, and A-Q—but what on earth can call a value bet? An A-J? This tight player might not even raise with A-J under the gun, except possibly suited. That's only two to eight combinations that would be calling just hoping to chop. While the better hands can be discounted after the river check, it's not unreasonable for the preflop raiser to go for a check-raise with them. In fact, he turned up an A-K in this hand, the stone cold nuts.

While kings-full may be a surprising river check back, there are spots that are more difficult to deal with than that one. The most confusing situation is the one where you figure to have the best hand almost all the time, but there is nothing in your opponent's range that can pay you off. You don't want to check behind because your range will become overly polarized, making it easy for your opponents to call down against your bluffs. But you don't want to value bet way too liberally either. Sometimes you'll get raised and either fold the best hand or end up paying off an unlikely monster.

The good news is that by the time you get to the river, you've accumulated a lot of information. You can use all of this information to decide whether to bet and how much. Consider the following factors:

1. **The strength of your hand.**
   This is pretty straightforward. If you hold the nuts, you'll obviously want to value bet. As your hand becomes weaker, there will be fewer and fewer

hands that you beat. You can only make money from hands that you beat.

2. **The strength of your opponent's range.**

   As your opponent's range becomes stronger, the relative strength of your hand will decrease (unless you hold the nuts).

3. **The strength of your perceived range.**

   The weaker your opponent thinks your range is, the lighter he will call you down; therefore, the thinner you can value bet.

4. **The table play dynamics.**

   If you've been betting and raising a lot, your opponent is likely to perceive your range as wider, which usually means you can value bet more aggressively. If you've been caught bluffing recently, there's a good chance your opponent will call you down lighter. This is where the leveling game comes into play.

To learn to squeeze that extra value out of the right hands, you need to develop strong reads. Pay attention to everything your opponents do. Watch how often they fold and what hands they call you down with. Ranges are usually pretty wide on the flop. As more action goes in, they get tighter. Ranges contract as the pot expands. By the river, you're often looking at some well refined ranges. Just remember, in order for you to have a profitable value bet, it's not good enough to be ahead of your opponent's range. You have to be ahead of the range of hands that will actually call your bet.

THE TAKEAWAY

Keep your finger to the pulse of your opponent if you want to keep your foot on his throat.

MISCONCEPTION #41

CALL IF YOU CAN BEAT ANYTHING AT ALL

Given how many people do this, you'd think every poker coach is telling players to find a hand they can beat and call down—but you won't hear coaches saying to do that. Nevertheless, many players go to great lengths to justify a calldown.

First of all, you should never try to put someone on a specific hand. You can only do that if you're using a marked deck. Since you can't actually see their cards, you should instead put them on a range. Ask yourself what hands this player could play this way, and how likely he is to have done so. Look at his range objectively. You can always find a hand or two that you can beat. Assuming that your opponent is betting and you do not hold the nuts, you'll also come up with some hands that beat you.

You have to compare the likelihood of the hands that beat you to the likelihood of the hands that don't. Take the following example: You raise with A-K and your very aggressive opponent calls. For the past several hands, this guy has been betting and raising and you've been folding hand after hand. You're a bit frustrated and feel like you're getting run over. The flop comes **K♥ J♥ 3♣**. You're already plotting your revenge! You bet and your opponent calls. The turn is the **7♦** and the action is the same as the flop. You hate the river card: It's the **Q♥.** You check. You're frustrated that you were all set up to get back at this guy who seems to have your number, but the truth is you're doing awful against his range now. When your opponent bets here, you have no business calling. What do you beat? You could have been losing already, and now you lose to K-Q, Q-J, A-10, 10-9, and heart flushes.

People don't want to fold in this spot because they're afraid to get run over. Maybe occasionally your opponent will be turning J-10 into a bluff or value betting K-10, but that will be way too small a portion of their range for you to call down. If you look at their range objectively, you will fold, knowing that the odds are too short and their range is too strong. Here's another example:

> **GAME:** $5/$10 blinds—4 players
> **STACKS:** $1,320 effective
> **READS:** CO is loose, aggressive and sane
> **DYNAMIC:** CO has been hammering on you
> **YOUR HAND:** You have A♠ Q♠ in the big blind
> **PREFLOP:** CO raises to $30, 2 players fold, you reraise to $100, he calls
> **FLOP:** Q♦ 10♦ 5♣ ($205—2 players)
> **ACTION:** You bet $140, CO calls
> **TURN:** 4♣ ($485—2 players)
> **ACTION:** You bet $300, CO calls
> **RIVER:** A♦ ($1,085—2 players)
> **ACTION:** You check, CO bets $780 (all in)

We all find ourselves in spots like this one on the river. You just made top two pair and it feels like there should be some way to get value. But when you pause to think about your opponent's range, what can he possibly call you with? Sure he could have A♣ 10♣ and make a crying call. That's exactly one hand, and he'll probably fold it to a river bet. He's not doing very well against your river betting range.

So what about checking and calling? Now it's possible to come up with a few more hands that you beat. He could try value betting that A♣ 10♣. He could also have called two streets with J-9, missed his straight draw, and then decided to bluff the river. After calling the turn, though, he usually has a flush draw to go with his straight draw—J♦ 9♦ or J♣ 9♣— and one of those just made a flush. He could be betting A♣ Q♣, allowing you to chop, but he usually 4-bets that preflop. Ace-king is out since he 4-bets that before the flop. There are also **K♣ 10♣, Q♣ 10♣, K♣ Q♣, Q♣ J♣, 10♣ 9♣,** and **10♣ 8♣**. All of these hands have at least one pair to go with a flush draw on the turn, so it's reasonable that he'd get to the river with them—but it is unlikely that he'll turn them into a bluff.

Even if you assume that he can turn third pair into a bluff, there are only six combos of hands that you beat on the river. Getting 2.4 to 1 pot odds on the river, you need the cutoff to have fewer than 15 possible combos that beat you, and K-J is 16 combos right off the bat. Throw in the flushes your opponent just made and you're up to at least 20 combos. That's a clear fold.

"But can't I discount K-J and diamond draws because my opponent will semibluff with them? Doesn't that mean I can call?" you may ask. The answer is "yes and no," in that order. You should certainly discount the combos that could have semibluffed the flop or turn; that's everything that beats you. But you should also discount the combos that you're ahead of. In fact, you should discount the hands that you beat even more than the ones that you don't, because most of them require your opponent to turn a made hand into a bluff. That's a less common play than taking a passive line in position with a draw. So no, you should not call.

THE TAKEAWAY

Making top two pair on the river may seem like a weird time to check and fold. Granted, that won't be your usual line. But when you think about your opponent's range in this exact situation, putting money in the pot reveals itself to be a mistake. Also remember that by checking with the intention of folding, you're not automatically giving up the pot. Your opponent can check back with his one-pair hands and his weaker two-pair hands; you'll still win the pot on those occasions. You just won't win the pot when you're beat, but at least it won't cost you any money.

MISCONCEPTION #42
WHEN A LINE MAKES NO SENSE, CALL DOWN

There are times when you get raised on the river and ask yourself, "What the hell could this guy possibly have? His line makes no sense." When a tough player, an erratic player, or an aggressive player makes a raise in a spot where there are very few legitimate hands that he could hold, you should usually call down with your bluff catchers. If it's hard for them to have a strong hand, they don't need to bluff that often for you to have a profitable calldown. Take the following example: You raise with pocket aces from the hijack. You get called by the big blind. The flop comes out K♠ 7♦ 4♦. He checks and calls your bet. The turn is the 4♣ and another check-call from the big blind. The river is the 2♠. You bet, expecting that you always have the best hand, and that your opponent will pay you off with a king. Instead, he check-raises all in.

What could he possibly have? Why would he slowplay a set here? How could he have a 4? Why would he call the flop and turn with pocket twos? It's so unlikely for your opponent to have anything worth check-raising all in for value. Slowplaying flopped sets or turned trips makes no sense, especially with all the draws on board. Pocket twos would usually fold before the river, and even if they didn't, that's only three combinations.

Against a player with any level of trickiness, you should call down. But what about when you're up against a typical rake-back pro? You know, the sort of player who's grinding 16 to 24 tables all day long, playing a rote strategy and piling up the VPPs on PokerStars. As unlikely as it is for him to hold a strong hand, it's even less likely for him to hold a bluff. That move isn't in his playbook. It doesn't matter how unlikely it is for your opponent to have you beaten if he's simply not capable of bluffing like this.

Against a tight, straightforward player, you're just giving money away by calling that river. If you do call, you're always going to look at the nuts. Why pay for the privilege? You already know what he has. Don't put 100 percent of your money in the pot with 0 percent equity. It's as bad as folding the nuts against a shove.

THE TAKEAWAY

The most useful note you can have on a player is that he's capable of doing something that you wouldn't expect from him. Anyone can make a move on the flop. For some players, this will just be a c-bet. Others can raise with air. The population of players who can raise the turn with air is thinner still. And the population of players who can run a complex multi-street float and shove-the-river bluff? Well, it's as thin as the Rocky Mountain air. Ever seen someone hit a baseball in Colorado?

MISCONCEPTION #43
DON'T CALL WITHOUT A HAND

As you move up in limits, you may begin to face opponents who seem to bet and raise at every opportunity. The pressure can be hard to deal with. When you start raising them back as a bluff, they just shove over the top of you, forcing you to be the one holding a real hand. So what do you do in these spots? How can you win a pot when you can't make a strong hand and your opponent never shows any weakness? Well, it turns out that betting at every turn *is* a weakness, and there's a very simple way to exploit it.

Most of the time that you bluff, you're going to be betting or raising. That's usually the only way to get someone to fold.

While eventually you have to put a bet in to elicit a fold, there's nothing to say that you have to do it on the flop. When your opponent c-bets the flop but frequently gives up on the turn, it's a good time to float. You call the flop with the plan of betting the turn when your opponent checks. The idea is to get the same folds you would get with a flop raise, but to wait until you have more information. This play generally works best in position.

If your opponent frequently fires a second barrel on the turn (but checks marginal made hands), you may be set up for a profitable bluff-raise on the turn. This has the advantage of getting more money in the pot than a flop bluff-raise would. A more effective option can be to float a second time. Just call the turn. When they check the river, their range is extremely weak. Against this range, you have the opportunity to make the ultimate bluff. We mentioned earlier that few players will call both the flop and turn with absolutely nothing and then shove all in on the river. That's reasonable enough. It's a lot of money to invest on nothing but a prayer that your opponent will check and fold after putting in two barrels himself.

Here's the thing: No one does it, so no one expects it—so expect it to work! Affectionately known as the Mississippi Bluff, perhaps originating from the riverboat roots of poker, this is the ultimate "my balls are bigger than yours" play.

One situation where it can be effective is against very aggressive players who 3-bet a lot, bet lots of flops, barrel lots of turns, but won't bomb off a whole stack on the river. (If a player has a tendency to shove all in as a bluff, the play obviously won't work.) You want them to bet as much as possible while still leaving room for you to make a threatening river shove.

You can set this play up with a min-raise, keeping the pot on the smaller side. If your opponent reraises to eight blinds, the pot will be about 16 blinds going to the flop. A bet and call of 10 blinds on the flop puts the pot at 36 blinds. If each player puts another 22 blinds in on the turn, the pot is now 70 blinds. When your opponent finally gives up and checks, you have a hugely profitable shove. The most aggressive opponents may fire three barrels with an extremely polarized range. When they bet the river, they'll have a few very strong hands and a ton of bluffs. Against this unbalanced range, you can make an ever bigger bluff than the standard Mississippi. Call it the "Delta."

In a once-raised pot, you should have room to shove over your opponent's river barrel. Your line will look so strong that some opponents will fold hands as good as sets. That's not the goal, though. The goal is just to knock out all of the bluffs, along with any thin value bets. In a reraised pot with 100-blind stacks, your hyper-aggressive opponent will have a chance to shove his stack in as a bluff, robbing you of your opportunity. So in a 3-bet pot, stacks need to be about 200 blinds deep to try this play.

Use this play with caution! Make sure you have a solid read on your opponent's range and barreling tendencies. When used judiciously, though, the Mississippi Bluff shows just how powerful position is, and how that power grows as stacks get deeper.

If you're still wondering what this play looks like in action, here's an example from a session Dusty played multi-tabling the $5/$10 games online. The opponent in all six of the following hands is the same highly skilled grinder. While his normal game is very aggressive, on this particular day he was betting every street against everyone. While there are many times when it feels like an opponent is betting every street, they're usually only betting most of the time, but this guy was betting every single time. He was playing looser before the flop and never ever checking after the flop. That's not his usual style, which goes to show how important it is to pay attention to how your opponents are currently playing, not just how they usually play.

Upon observing that his opponent was constantly putting in aggressive action, Dusty decided to employ the Mississippi Bluff, a decision he made before the flop. By betting every street, Dusty's opponent was keeping his range wide all the way through his river barrel. The thing is that it's hard to make hands that want to call a river shove so, while his river betting range was enormous, his river calling range was tiny. That means that the Mississippi bluff should work a huge percentage of the time. Given the fact that Dusty and his opponent were playing together at a number of different tables, these hands all occurred within a five-minute time span. That gave Dusty the chance to apply the technique six times in rapid succession without his opponent catching on.

Mississippi Bluff Hand #1

GAME: $5/$10 blinds—6 players
STACKS: $1,200 effective
READS: Villain is under the gun
DUSTY'S HAND: A♦ J♦ on the button
PREFLOP: Villain raises to $30, 2 players fold, Dusty calls, 2 players fold
FLOP: Q♦ Q♣ 8♠ ($75—2 players)
ACTION: Villain bets $65, Dusty calls
TURN: 7♥ ($205—2 players)
ACTION: Villain bets $180, Dusty calls
RIVER: 4♦ ($565—2 players)
ACTION: Villain bets $500, Dusty raises to $925 (all in), Villain turbo-folds

Mississippi Bluff Hand #2

GAME: $5/$10 blinds—6 players
STACKS: $1,000 effective
READS: Villain is the small blind
DUSTY'S HAND: A♦ 7♦ in the big blind
PREFLOP: 4 players fold, Villain raises to $30, Dusty calls
FLOP: 10♦ 8♥ 5♥ ($60—2 players)

ACTION: Villain bets $50, Dusty calls
TURN: 6♣ ($160—2 players)
ACTION: Villain bets $130, Dusty calls
RIVER: Q♥ ($420—2 players)
ACTION: Villain bets $350, Dusty raises to $790 all in, Villain folds

Mississippi Bluff Hand #3

GAME: $5/$10 blinds, 6 players
STACKS: $1,000 effective
READS: Villain is the button
DUSTY'S HAND: A♠ Q♠ in the big blind
PREFLOP: 3 players fold, Villain raises to $30, 1 player folds, Dusty calls
FLOP: K♥ 10♠ 3♦ ($65—2 players)
ACTION: Dusty checks, Villain bets $50, Dusty calls
TURN: 7♥ ($165—2 players)
ACTION: Dusty checks, Villain bets $140, Dusty calls
RIVER: 10♦ ($445—2 players)
ACTION: Dusty checks, Villain bets $360, Dusty raises to 780 (all in), Villain folds

Mississippi Bluff Hand #4

GAME: $5/$10 blinds, 6 players
STACKS: $1,300 effective
READS: Villain is in the cutoff
DUSTY'S HAND: J♥ 10♥ on the button
PREFLOP: 2 players fold, villain raises to $30, Dusty calls, 2 players fold
FLOP: K♣ K♠ 7♦ ($75—2 players)
ACTION: Villain bets $60, Dusty calls
TURN: 8♥ ($205—2 players)
ACTION: Villain bets $175, Dusty calls
RIVER: 5♦ ($555—2 players)
ACTION: Villain bets $480, Dusty raises to $1,035 (all in), Villain folds

Mississippi Bluff Hand #5

GAME: $5/$10 blinds, 6 players

STACKS: $1,200 effective

READS: Villain is in the hijack

DUSTY'S HAND: A♥ J♥ on the button

PREFLOP: 1 player folds, Villain raises to $30, 1 player folds, Dusty calls, 2 players fold

FLOP: Q♥ 10♥ 8♠ ($75—2 players)

ACTION: Villain bets $60, Dusty calls

TURN: 6♣ ($205—2 players)

ACTION: Villain bets $175, Dusty calls

RIVER: 3♦ ($555—2 players)

ACTION: Villain bets $480, Dusty raises to $935, Villain folds

Mississippi Bluff Hand #6

GAME: $5/$10 blinds, 6 players

STACKS: $1,000 effective

READS: Villain is under the gun

DUSTY'S HAND: 6♠ 6♣ in the cutoff

PREFLOP: Villain raises to $30, 1 player folds, Dusty calls, 3 players fold

FLOP: A♦ 9♠ 3♣ ($75—2 players)

ACTION: Villain bets $60, Dusty raises to $180, Villain calls

TURN: 7♥ ($435—2 players)

ACTION: Villain checks, Dusty checks

RIVER: 2♦ ($435—2 players)

ACTION: Villain bets $380, Dusty raises to $790 all in, Villain folds

THE TAKEAWAY

This last hand isn't exactly a Mississippi, but the idea is the same. When Villain calls the flop and almost pots the river, he can only really have air or a set. This is the sort of flop where it can be worthwhile to call a raise out of position as a float (against an aggressive opponent), since they'll give up their bluffs on the turn very often, allowing you to take the pot on the river. That's probably what Dusty's opponent is thinking here, so Dusty checks back and shoves an over the river bluff.

MISCONCEPTION #44
THE MORE YOU BET, THE MORE THEY FOLD

There are situations where betting a large amount will earn more folds than making a small bet. Take the following hand:

GAME: $5/$10 blinds—6 players
READS: BB is straightforward—bets when he has it, checks with whiffs and weak made hands.
STACKS: $1,000 effective
YOUR HAND: You have 8♠7♠ on the button
PREFLOP: 3 players fold, you raise to $30, 1 player folds, BB calls
FLOP: 10♥ 9♥ 3♠ ($65—2 players)
ACTION: BB checks, you bet $45, BB calls
TURN: 2♦ ($155—2 players)
ACTION: BB checks, you bet $130, BB calls
RIVER: 5♥ ($415—2 players)
ACTION: BB checks, you bet $340, BB folds

You've been betting all the way with your straight draw but it's the flush draw that fills in on the river. This opponent is straightforward, so you expect that he would lead into you if he just made a flush. Since all of the straight draws missed, you expect that he may look you up with a hand such as J♣ 10♣ if you make a small bet, but he'll check and fold if you put in a large bet. Given that you expect this guy to virtually always fold to your large river bet, there's no need to worry about saving chips. It doesn't matter how much your bluff costs if it always works and nets you $415. This is a situation where your opponent's calling range is elastic—which hands he calls with depends on how much you bet. Facing a small river bet, he may get curious with one pair, so in this particular instance, a larger bet works better. Don't let him get curious. Make the bet that works.

When you know that your opponent's range is very weak and that he'll almost always fold when you bet, you should bet as much as necessary to take advantage of this very profitable situation. More often, however, your opponent will have a range of hands that he plans to call down with, and a range of hands that he plans to fold. In these situations, you're going to get the same result from a half-pot bet as you would from a three-quarters-pot bet.

Now let's look at another situation. You raise to $30 with **A♠ Q♥** in early position and get called by the small blind. The flop comes **7♦ 5♣ 2♠**. He checks and calls your $50 c-bet. You bet $130 on the **J♥** turn. The river is the **2♦**, a complete blank. It looks like your opponent has a middle pocket pair. You have to decide whether to barrel off or give up. Some opponents will call you down here almost regardless of what you bet. Others will fold unless you make a ridiculously small bet like $80, since their plan was to call two streets and fold to a river bet. That would be a good line for them to take if they don't think you're capable of firing the third shell.

If you decide that this opponent falls into the latter category, don't make a large bet. You don't need to. Betting somewhere between $215 and $260 should get about the same number of folds as betting $360. A bet on the smaller side, like $215, will look like you're trying to entice a calldown without giving a price that's so enticing that you'll actually get it. The range that he calls with just isn't going to change that much based on how much you bet. There are a few hands that will call or check-raise, so don't spend $100 more than you have to.

THE TAKEAWAY

We've gone through this concept four times now, which may seem like overkill. It's not—it's just that important! It comes up on every street. Don't waste money. Don't bet more than you have to.

FOCUS ON THE TOUGH PLAYERS

Have you ever been sitting there, waiting for your opponent to make a reasonable sized bet so you could call, then been taken aback when he makes an obnoxiously large one? Maybe you folded because your pot odds were suddenly terrible. Or maybe you've been sitting on the river, waiting to check and fold, but your opponent makes such a ridiculously small bet that you just have to call because the pot is offering 20 to 1. That's because you're a good player and you understand the fundamental poker concept of pot odds.

Good players usually have a fluid range of hands that they will call a bet with. They are generally willing to call a reasonable sized bet with a reasonable sized range, but when someone makes an unreasonable bet, they need a much stronger hand to call. For instance, betting $400 into a $65 pot will not earn very many calls from a good player. It shows great strength and offers terrible pot odds.

This maxim does not hold true for most fish. Take the following example:

GAME: $5/$10 blinds—5 players
STACKS: $1,000 effective
READS: BB is loose, passive, and stubborn
YOUR HAND: You have 2♣ 2♦ in the hijack
PREFLOP: You raise to $40, 3 players fold, BB calls
FLOP: A♥ A♣ 2♠ ($85—2 players)
ACTION: BB checks, you bet $500

Against a typical player, betting $500 would be a huge risk, since they're likely to fold even some very strong hands such as A-10 and A-J. But this is not a typical player; it's a stubborn player with a wide range. Instead of having a fluid range of hands to call you with, based upon the size of your bet, this player has two types of hands: hands that will call and hands that will fold. Maybe there's a third type of hand that will call a small bet like $50, probably only pocket pairs, but all of those hands have two outs to beat you, and none of them will pay off a turn bet unless they spike a boat and stack you.

You may argue that by making a normal sized flop bet, a normal sized turn bet, and then a big river bet, you can string them along and take the whole stack on the river anyway. Maybe. But even stubborn, showdown bound fish will sometimes wise up when you make that river shove. You're giving them three chances to get away from their hand. With the oversized flop bet, you're giving them one decision point in the hand. You're asking, "Do you want to put all of your chips in with your three aces?" When you ask a fish that question, the answer is invariably yes. If there's any way for them to talk themselves into a call, they're going to call—and the $500 bet was chosen just for that purpose.

What's the first thought you have when someone makes a ridiculous sized bet? "Why did they bet so much?" It's a natural question to ask yourself. By making the bet $500 rather than $900 or $200 or even $510, you've given them an easy answer: "Maybe it's a typo!" Now the fish is thinking, "Yes, it's a typo! I can't fold three aces when this idiot's large bet could have been a typo. He may as well have just dropped $450 in there for me to scoop up. Thank you very much! Oh, you have a full house? Oh well, it could have been a typo anyway."

A lot of good players have highly developed strategies for fending off the attacks of other good players. They have a decent sense of how to play against bad players too. After all, it's easy, right? Yes and no. Sure, it's easy to beat the fish. After all, they're the reason we play. They're not even trying to play well half the time. But here we've got another appearance of lazy edge syndrome. There's a difference between beating the fish, and beating the fish for the maximum—pounding the living daylights out of them! Here's the thing about fish: If you don't catch one yourself, someone else is likely to catch it before you get another chance.

This practice of overbetting is just one example of a way to take maximum advantage of weaker players. It's worth spending some of your thinking time pondering ways to do the same in other situations. Here's another example:

> **GAME:** $5/$10 blinds—5 players
> **STACKS:** $1,000 effective
> **READS:** HJ is loose and bad
> **YOUR HAND:** You have 7♦ 6♦ in the cutoff
> **PREFLOP:** HJ calls, you raise to $50,
> 3 players fold, HJ calls
> **FLOP:** 5♦ 4♥ Q♥ ($115—2 players)
> **ACTION:** HJ checks, you bet $70, HJ calls
> **TURN:** 9♦ ($255—2 players)
> **ACTION:** HJ checks, you bet $150, HJ calls
> **RIVER:** Q♠ ($555—2 players)
> **ACTION:** HJ checks, you bet $60, HJ folds

On the flop, you have an open-ended straight draw and you make a no-brainer continuation bet. You bet again on the turn when you pick up a flush draw. The river is a total blank. Two flush draws and a slew of straight draws all missed. Nothing changed on this card. Your opponent is loose and bad. If he flopped any kind of made hand—probably a pair of queens that just made trips—there's little chance he'll fold to a river bet, almost regardless of the size.

But you have 7-high and there are a large number of missed draws in his range. Sure, you could make a more reasonable looking bet. Maybe $250. But what hands are folding for $250 that won't fold for $60? Those draws are going to check-fold and think nothing of it even if you just sneeze on the pot. Your only goal here is to make the smallest bet possible that your opponent won't just call out of sheer curiosity.

THE TAKEAWAY

Now, a good player might not have that many hands that you beat on this river. He'll check-raise the flop or turn with his draws. But the bad player is perfectly happy to call-call-fold with many of those. Is it a good line? Probably not. But that's what makes him bad. There's nothing more frustrating than checking back with a 7-high busted straight draw and losing to an 8-high busted straight draw. So go ahead and sneeze on the pot. There's no need to bother spitting. Your opponent won't want to catch a cold.

MISCONCEPTION #46

THE GREAT PLAYERS ARE CRAZY

If you watch poker on TV, you've seen some great players make a lot of crazy plays. Maybe it's Tom Dwan calling down with 9-high or Phil Ivey 5-bet bluffing the flop. These are world-class players making insane looking plays based on very specific reads. When these plays work, they look genius. When they don't, they look silly. As sexy as it may seem to make outlandish calldowns, extravagant bluffs, and wicked extortions of value, looking for opportunities for such excess is counterproductive. You don't even need to make plays like that at all.

You don't need to play like your heroes. Tight and solid play will bring home the money.

If you were playing high school basketball, you shouldn't be thinking about being LeBron James. You're probably not

6'8" and if your goal is to make the NBA, you're going to have to conquer your current game before moving up. You would develop your fundamentals, form a sound foundation for your game, and never stop working to improve.

Approach your poker the same way. It's easier to envision yourself playing as well as the best in the world because you can probably slide your chips in the pot just as well as Phil Ivey does it. There are no obvious physical differences that keep you from playing as well as he does. But there is a huge amount of work that has gone into developing every outstanding player's game. There is time spent away from the table, pondering exactly how to combat an opponent's strategy. There are thousands of hours spent at the table, actively practicing the skills honed away from it. Great players are not sitting down, waiting for a lightning bolt of inspiration to strike them. They are reaping the rewards of hours of perspiration.

Hold'em is a simple game to learn and it's easy to fall under the illusion that it's a simple game to master. But it's not tic-tac-toe. No one can give you a cookbook filled with instant recipes for success. We've given you our best advice in this book, but it's up to you to apply it. Learn to make the most of it and never stop working on your game.

A lot of people think they play tight and solid, but still can't beat a $10/$20 game online. It's not for a lack of crazy plays; it's about understanding ranges. Against passive players, this is easy. When they raise, you put them on a strong range and take cover. When they're just calling, you value bet hard and charge them for their fishy ways.

Against aggressive players, hand reading becomes more difficult, but it's still the same game. As you move up in stakes, pay attention to how players' ranges change. In general, high-stakes players will put in aggressive action with wider ranges than lower stakes players.

If a guy 3-bets you at $.25/$.50, maybe you can fold pocket tens. At higher limits, you may want to 4-bet against your opponent's wider range. Some guys may be 4-betting with pocket fours, but you're doing it with tens. You're widening your range as an adjustment, but not going overboard. You may be able to run over most players by 3-betting aggressively at small stakes. At higher stakes, you have to be willing to get it in with some weaker hands, since everyone knows how to play back at you. High-stakes regulars know how to handle an aggressive 3-bettor.

Instead of getting involved in a crazy 3-bet/4-bet/shove war, you can be a conscientious objector. Sidestep the problem. You don't have to fight for every pot. Observe your opponents' ranges, pick your spots, and set yourself up for more profitable opportunities later on in the hand. Many of the chapters in the second half of this section have dealt with sophisticated bluffing lines. These lines can give you a huge edge to replace the smaller edge that you're passing up by avoiding the 3-bet war, but don't go out of your way to find these spots. View your opponent's range objectively and determine which line will yield the highest return.

THE TAKEAWAY

The truth is, the great players don't have to actively look for opportunities to make these crazy plays. They just play their hand against their opponent's range and consider the full spectrum of options. They see more opportunities to make creative plays, but not because they discount the value of making the straightforward ones. They just have a better idea of their opponents' ranges, and how they'll respond to different lines. They're still betting their good hands, folding most of the bad ones, and bluffing at an effective frequency.

MISCONCEPTION #47

A MISTAKE IS A MISTAKE

The above statement is true, at least insofar as "A" is "A" (which it is). However, all mistakes are not created equal. Some mistakes cost a pot, some cost a bet. Some occur occasionally, some recur repeatedly. Mistakes cost more in 2012 cost than they did in 2006. There's a good chance they'll cost even more in 2014.

It used to be common to have multiple bad players at every table, the type of player who would be described as an asset because they're generating income for the other players at the table. These players will often play until they go broke, so if you lose a stack to one of these guys, there's maybe a 20 percent chance that you'll get a good amount of that money back before the end of the session. Some players play so poorly that it's almost like you're lending them money when you lose chips to them because they don't know how to hang onto it.

If you're sitting at a six-handed table with three bad players and two good ones, there's a 60 percent chance that the stack you lose gets "borrowed" by one of the bad players, assuming that you're equally likely to get stacked by a good player as you are by a bad player. This may or may not be entirely true, but the basic point stands nonetheless. Furthermore, they're likely to just pass the money around with their fellow recreational players, keeping it in play and giving you a chance to recoup on your mistake.

On the other hand, if you're at a table with just one bad player (a typical scenario in today's online games), there's only a 20 percent chance that you lose that stack to a bad player. Now it's twice as likely that whatever mistake you make—it doesn't have to cost a whole stack—contributes to the coffers of a winning player. You're not getting that money back. Yeah, they'll make mistakes and you'll make some more, but you're that much less likely to have them return the favor. Good players just don't fork over stacks of chips the way bad players do.

Since mistakes cost more now than they did in past years, it's even more important that you diligently work on your game to maximize your earnings and stay ahead of the competition. You have to grab what's out there right now. This doesn't mean that you should become overly upset every time you make a mistake. To the contrary! If you get so riled up that you can't think straight, that's likely to lead to more and larger mistakes, so stay calm. There's no reason to tolerate the more persistent mistakes, however: Root them out and eliminate them from your game.

The mere fact that you notice mistakes in your own game is a blessing. It presents an opportunity for improvement. You don't need someone yelling at you to change things that you've become aware of yourself. At the same time, when someone is yelling at you about how you're such a donkey for playing a hand a certain way, don't become defensive. While you should never allow the words of others to make you doubt yourself, you should question yourself. "Was this the best way to play the hand? Was my logic sound?" If yes, then great: You've played the hand well. If not, then great: You've found an opportunity for improvement. Don't prohibit your opponents from helping you improve just because they're trying to take your money. And don't let mistakes disrupt the things you do well. Use them to build new strengths.

THE TAKEAWAY

While you're playing, you can't worry about making mistakes. You can only make the best decision you're capable of and move on to the next one. Try using this three-step decision checklist:

3 STEPS TO MAKING GOOD DECISIONS

1. **Observe**

   Put your opponent on a range. What does your opponent's line mean?

2. **Decide**

   Find the best play. What is the best decision you can make against his range, factoring in the strength of your hand and recent history between you and your opponent?

3. **Act**

   Take a deep breath and confidently make the play you have decided on, being willing to accept whatever the outcome may be.

MISCONCEPTION #48
NEVER BACK DOWN

You only make money at poker when you play better than your opponents. Never lose sight of this fact. Every single winning player has something in common. They all play against a field of players inferior to themselves. The single most important decision you can make at a poker table is whether or not to sit in the game. In *Treat Your Poker Like A Business*, Dusty referred to this as choosing a good location for your enterprise. In *Way of the Poker Warrior*, Paul referred to it as picking your battles. It's so important that we're both going to say it again in this book:

Play against players that are weaker than you and take their money!

A swelling collection of poker players, supposed authorities among them, will call you a bum-hunter if you're good at this. Ignore them! Keep finding bad players and keep taking their money. Unless you're playing heads up, playing with bad players doesn't always mean *not* playing with good players. It's fine to have a few good players at the table if there's one soft spot to make up for it. In fact, most online games played at $.50/$1 and higher these days are built around a single bad player.

How do you maximize your winnings at a table with four good players and just one bad one? Try to sit in the seat to the immediate left of the bad player. Having position on anyone will help you take their money—fish are no exception. They'll be entering many pots ahead of you, so you'll have an opportunity to isolate them and take the biggest share of the money they're giving away. That's the most important factor that should keep you at a table. That's what you're looking for—a bad player in the seat to your right.

What's the worst condition that can exist at a table? A tough player on your immediate left. If the tough player is extremely aggressive and goes out of his way to 3-bet your open-raises, this can be the worst seat in the house. It's no fun getting reraised every two minutes, and it's not very profitable either. It's like playing a heads-up match where you're out of position every hand. Phil Ivey says his grandmother could beat him if she always had position, and Phil Galfond doesn't think he could make money in this position either.

Listen to *these* Phils! The simplest solution is unthinkable to those who never like backing down from a fight: Walk away! Don't sit at that table. Unless you're playing in a tournament, there's another more profitable seat somewhere else. Go sit there.

There's another situation where you should not abandon a seat to the right of an aggressive player. If an extremely bad player is sitting to your right, you can put up with an extremely aggressive player to your left. When faced with the best and worst of table conditions, you simply have to weigh the two factors against each other. Is this fish big enough to make it worth dealing with the guy on my left? If so, stay at the table.

But you need a plan for how to deal with the tough player. You have two options: The simplest is to play ridiculously tight when the fish has folded. You still need to get in there and fight for what's yours when the bad player is in the hand. After all, that's why you're still at the table. But when he folds, you should only play hands that you're willing to commit with. Now you're making your commitment decision before the flop. This is a reasonable time to listen to the other Phil and focus on those top ten hands.

Your other option is the polar opposite to option number one. That was the path of least resistance. This is the path of most resistance. Fight fire with fire! You're still going to make a big decision before the flop, but now the decision is to 4-bet every single hand that you opened with. This second option isn't for everyone. It's as drastic as option one, but in the opposite direction. Let's look at an example:

> **GAME:** $5/$10—6 players
> **YOUR HAND:** You have **10♠ 8♠** in the cutoff
> **PREFLOP:** 2 players fold, you raise to $30, BTN raises to $90, 2 players fold, you reraise to $210, BTN calls
> **FLOP:** A♣ 5♦ 5♥ ($435—2 players)
> **ACTION:** You bet $140, BTN folds

You don't have to make your raises or c-bets large. You just have to make them *often*. If you choose this option, don't even think about not 4-betting preflop. You're in full court press, pull-out-all-the-stops overdrive. You're telling your opponent that he's not in control. He's not going to push you around. You have to commit to it, though. You have to play top pair like it's the nuts in these 4-bet pots. Your opponent will be getting it in light and may start shoving back at you. His range is weak, so he'll have to decide between folding a lot or putting tons of money in the pot with some awful holdings. Most semi-rational players will back off. At that point you can resume playing your normal game and eat all the fish you want.

Option two, 4-betting every hand that you open with, is not for everyone! Don't go ballistic if you're not up for dealing with the consequences. It's usually a better idea just to tighten up when the fish has folded. And without the fish at the table, you shouldn't be there either. Again, they may call you a bum-hunter for this. We call it game selection.

Poker is not a contest of egos. It is a contest of intellect.

Rational thought should lead you to the above conclusions. Some players think quitting a bad table is unmanly. Who cares? It's logical. It's profitable! It's the right thing to do. Other players worry that they won't improve if they don't face these tough spots. You're going to face all the tough spots you want just by playing poker and moving up when your skills and bankroll dictate. You don't have to seek them out, they will come to you. It's fine to play at a table with a handful of superstars—just make sure there's enough fish around to feed everyone.

THE TAKEAWAY

You probably don't seek conflict in life: Life *is* conflict. You don't have to make your own. You shouldn't do any differently at the poker table.

MISCONCEPTION #49

WIN RATE IS A CONSTANT

You will see most players who have been playing for a significant amount of time say something like the following: "My win rate is X bb/100." A lot of the time they will have X correctly figured using some hand-history tracking program. They know exactly how many big blinds they've won for every 100 hands they've played. They call that their win rate. What they get wrong is the verb "is."

No one's win rate *is* anything. It *was* X over a given period of hands. Win rate is a historical measure of a player's results. Just like a hedge fund manager can tell you their fund has provided X percent return on investment over the past five years, a poker player can tell you that they have won at X bb/100. But neither can truthfully tell you that's how much they'll grow or win next year.

Win rate can be a useful indicator of future performance, or a reasonable measure of skill over a large number of hands, within the context of certain game conditions. But win rate is not a constant; neither is it an independent variable. It is a function. More specifically, it is the function of six conditions.

WIN RATE IS A FUNCTION OF:

1. Player Skill
2. Opponent Skill
3. The Match Up of Specific Strategies
   Not just the differential between player and opponent skill, but the interaction of their styles.
4. Rake
5. Variance
6. Emotional Control

None of this is to say that win rate is useless. We can use it to calculate various helpful measures. We can use the player's standard deviation along with win rate to calculate how likely it is that this player should expect to run at a certain win rate in the future, given static conditions.

Of course, conditions are dynamic. Some players improve and others don't. The rake may change, and so may legislation. New players will move up to a given level and others may move down. The player whose win rate we're looking at may improve or go on tilt. So we can use win rate as a guideline, but shouldn't take it as an absolute. To complicate matters, we add the element of variance. Again, we can use standard deviation and win rate to calculate how likely it is for a player with a certain win rate to perform at a certain level, given static conditions. Even assuming that conditions don't change, there is no guarantee that a player will get results anywhere near expectation. It's possible to run really, really bad for a really, really long time. Stretches of hands that you wouldn't think possible are, in fact, possible. You can run bad for a million hands. That's a lot of poker. A bad run that long is unlikely and you shouldn't expect to face one—but you should be prepared.

If you plan to play poker for a living, you need to consider the likelihood of running below expectation, and figure out how you're going to deal with it. If your monthly expenses are $2,500, you can't play an amount of poker where your expectation is $2,500. Even if you have savings in the bank, eventually you will run into a stretch worse than you have imagined. Find a way to have an expectation higher than your monthly nut. That way, a few bad months won't put you off track. And if you are lucky enough to run above expectation, you'll have an excellent year-end bonus.

As a prospective pro you should have:

1. **Living expenses saved up.**
   Six to 12 months is a good place to start. Exactly how much you need saved up depends on your living situation. What are the consequences of falling behind in your bills? How hard is it to catch up if you fall behind?

2. **A higher expectation than your monthly nut.**
   Having an expectation of two to three times your expenses will help protect you from bad stretches. It will also give you opportunity to put money in savings or build your bankroll so you can move up in stakes and increase your hourly earnings. If you need $2500 a month to get by, we suggest you play

a number of hands that will allow you to average $5000 to $7500 in profits. It's better to get out in front than it is to fall behind. Don't forget to include rakeback or bonus money in this number, though. That spends just as well as winnings.

3. **A large enough bankroll to withstand the vagaries of variance.**

   The chances of going broke depend on the size of your bankroll, your expected win rate, your standard deviation, and your willingness and ability to move down in stakes should you hit a rough patch. If that sounds like a lot to calculate, we encourage you to follow Dusty's guideline of always maintaining 100 buy-ins for your current limit (assuming you're playing 100-blind games).

Is it possible to succeed without meeting any of the above conditions? Yes. In fact, both authors of this book were lucky enough to survive a complete lack of early planning. But if you plan to have a long poker career, why not give yourself the best chance possible? You'll need to get it together eventually, so why not start off doing things right out of the gate?

THE TAKEAWAY

The fact is that most good players overestimate their ability and their win rate because they ran well when they first started playing. There is a selection bias here. Those who try to play well and get poor results often quit. They won't make it to the long run. The players who start off on the lucky side of variance have a better chance to survive. They eventually see the bad runs of cards themselves, but they've had time to build up the strategic and emotional skills, not to mention the bankroll, necessary to see it through.

Variance can be brutal. Unprepared players quit poker because of it. Be prepared!

MISCONCEPTION #50
POKER IS JUST A GAME

Despite the sheer volume of poker lingo that has seeped into American culture and now throughout the world, many people think poker is nothing more than a game. Yes, poker is *literally* just a game. When things go poorly, it's not a bad idea to remind yourself of that fact. Sure, money is involved, and for some of us poker is our livelihood. But life and death are not at stake, and if we are indeed poker professionals, then we're playing a game for a living. We should feel pretty blessed!

A lot of people also think that poker is a waste of time and contributes nothing to society. Well, fine, it's not some noble endeavor that involves saving lives. Few people are fortunate or brave enough to engage in a living where they do that every day. People do all sorts of things to earn a living, to make money.

Money is power, and having a lot of it gives you the ability to shape the world around you. Sure, some poker players spend their money on frivolous items to give the illusion of a "baller" lifestyle. Others flex their financial muscle in more constructive ways. In fact, the authors of this book have used their poker talents to raise tens of thousands of dollars for various causes. You don't have to take it that far. There's a lot of middle ground. If you're a winning player, poker provides the opportunity for you to make changes in the world, however small. It's up to you what to do with that opportunity.

Poker is also an activity that builds community. A huge number of people across the world enjoy playing poker with their friends and family, or against strangers from all over the globe. Not only is poker a weekly opportunity to connect with your friends, it's also a way to make new ones from all walks of life.

Another concern many have is that poker is a niche skill, and that playing for a living will result in a resume gap that looks bad. Maybe it will look bad on paper, but getting a job is about more than just submitting a resume. People go on job interviews. Instead of having "poker professional" become a black hole on your resume, you can use it as a talking point. The fact is that a lot of people love poker and love talking about poker, especially boss-types. You just need to articulate what broader skills you have developed playing poker.

If you play poker for a living, you should have a thorough understanding of variance, risk management, and equity analysis. These are real skills that apply to a diverse range of fields. In fact, many financial institutions have begun recruiting former poker players for just this reason. Dealing with variance will help you learn to manage anger, frustration, and even overconfidence. Everything in life has variance. There is always an element of chance. Poker shows you this more literally than other activities do. It shoves it in your face. There are factors outside your control. Butterflies are flapping their wings all over the world.

As much as you want to control your opponents' actions, the best you can do is influence them. Acceptance of this fact, combined with an understanding of why people act the way they do, is valuable in all social interactions. The lessons learned from a life in poker can be used to improve both personal and professional relationships. If sportswriters were forced to play poker professionally for a year, their stories would be a lot more objective. When a great player has an off night, it would not be seen as the impending decay of his skills. It would be recognized for what it usually is. Variance.

To use an example from an international sport, look at how writers responded to Roger Federer's losing the 2008

Wimbledon final to Rafael Nadal in perhaps the greatest tennis match ever. They acted like it could be nothing less than the end of his mighty career. They pointed to the fact that it capped a run of three consecutive Grand Slams he hadn't won. The horror! It's true that he lost the match to a younger player who was overtaking his ranking as the number one player in the world. But despite the apparent end of his dominance, he went on to break the all-time Grand Slam record by winning three of the next four. Was there some decline in Federer's level of play? Maybe. Had the distance between him and the next best players contracted? For sure. But the writers always overreact based on a small sample size. Perhaps if they had to deal with the daily variance of poker, they would be better equipped to sift through the transient noise.

THE TAKEAWAY

In order to succeed at poker, you must think logically and objectively. Learning to think more clearly at the table can help you think more clearly in other areas of life. So yeah, poker is a game. A game that teaches lessons. Can't life be viewed the same way?

HAND ANALYSIS

Sit in the game with Dusty as he plays 25 hands of no-limit hold'em in online games with blinds ranging from $3/$6 to $10/$20. You'll see how Dusty puts the principles to work that he and Paul have explained as he tries various maneuvers to outwit his opponents and win the money.

HAND # 1

$3/$6 NO-LIMIT HOLD'EM w/$1.20 ANTE–5 PLAYERS

This hand takes place at a deep-stacked $3/$6 table with antes. Because of the deep stacks and the extra ante money in the pot, the game plays more like a $5/$10 game than a regular $3/$6. The button in this hand is an aggressive and unpredictable player who is capable of making a move at any time.

THE SET-UP

STACKS: Dusty has $1,558; Button has $3,956

READS: Button is erratic and extremely aggressive

PREFLOP ACTION: 2 players fold, Button raises to $18, Small Blind folds, Dusty calls with **A♣ 2♣** in the big blind

DUSTY, BIG BLIND	BUTTON

FLOP ($45)	TURN ($105)	RIVER ($105)

ACTION	ACTION	ACTION
Dusty checks	Dusty checks	Dusty bets $78
Button bets $30	Button checks	Button raises to $156
Dusty calls		Dusty reraises to $668
		Button folds

WHY DUSTY PLAYED IT THIS WAY

Dusty could 3-bet his suited A-2, since it has good equity against the button's range (52.6 percent equity against a 60 percent opening range) and plays well enough postflop. The plan would usually be to *not* go broke with just a single pair of aces, but against this erratic opponent that might be difficult. By just calling instead of 3-betting, Dusty has the opportunity to induce bluffs from his spastic opponent, but still semibluff when he picks up a draw.

The flop is good and gives Dusty about 76 percent equity against the button's opening range. Leading out or check-raising would knock out most of the button's garbage hands that give Dusty such a big edge. This is a better spot to check-call, avoiding building a big pot with a marginal hand. Hopefully, the button will see this as weakness and try to push Dusty off his hand.

Dusty's chances of making a strong hand go out the window when a diamond hits the turn. His **A♣ 2♣** has become a weak bluff catcher; and if the button bets, Dusty has to decide whether to call the turn and river or just give up right away. The button checks back the turn, indicating that he holds a marginal made hand (e.g. a pair of sevens), or that he is surrendering with a hand that missed the board (e.g. Q-10).

When the river card comes down, Dusty doesn't have a firm read on his erratic opponent's range. While he probably has a marginal made hand, he could also hold a weak top pair that hated the turn. Since Dusty plans to call a river bet anyway, he decides to make one of his own. Instead of checking and making a difficult decision, he puts the onus on his opponent to figure out what's going on. When the button raises the minimum, it appears that Dusty is beat. An A-8, A-7 and pocket eights are the button's most likely hands. While it's possible that the button is bluffing, it's unlikely that bluffs make up 19 percent of his range, which is how often he'd have to be bluffing for Dusty to make a profitable call getting 4.35 to 1 odds.

Notably absent from the button's range are flushes. It's almost impossible that he checked back a turned flush; people just don't do that in mid-high-stakes online games. On the other side of the table, Dusty can quite legitimately represent a flush that whiffed on a turn check-raise. Even the top end of the button's apparent range, a set of eights, can't call a reraise when it's so "obvious" that Dusty holds a flush. This guy is erratic, but not terrible. Dusty's bluff should have close to a 100 percent success rate.

THE TAKEAWAY

TWO MAJOR LESSONS TO TAKE AWAY FROM THIS HAND:

1. Beware of making thin value bets and raises when your opponent can represent a much stronger range than you can.

2. Take advantage of situations where the top end of your range crushes your opponent's entire range, particularly when that range consists of thin value bets or raises.

HAND # 2

$3/$6 NO-LIMIT HOLD'EM — 6 PLAYERS

THE SET UP

STACKS: Dusty has $1,041, Hijack has $600, Button has $605

EXTRA BLINDS: Hijack posts $6 live and $3 dead

READS: Hijack is loose and passive; Button is good and extremely aggressive

PREFLOP ACTION: 1 player folds, Hijack checks, Cutoff folds, Button raises to $24, Small Blind folds, Dusty reraises to $72 with K♠ 3♠ in the Big Blind, Hijack folds, Button calls

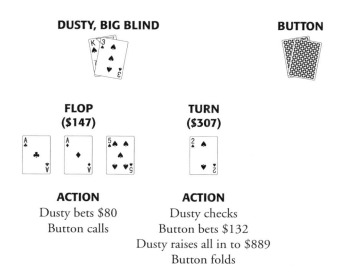

DUSTY, BIG BLIND

BUTTON

FLOP
($147)

TURN
($307)

ACTION
Dusty bets $80
Button calls

ACTION
Dusty checks
Button bets $132
Dusty raises all in to $889
Button folds

WHY DUSTY PLAYED IT THIS WAY

After sitting out a few hands, the hijack has returned to the action by posting a live big blind and a dead small blind. As a result, there is an extra $9 sitting in the middle when the action gets around to the button. His typical open range from this position is about 72 percent. With twice as much money in there to win on a successful steal attempt, it's possible that he's raising even more often, maybe up to 100 percent of his hands.

Knowing that the button has such a wide range, Dusty puts in an aggressive 3-bet. With so much money in there and an opponent with such a weak range, this opportunity is too good to pass up, despite the fact that the button may 4-bet aggressively. In fact, if the button makes a small 4-bet, Dusty may even reraise all in, since he'll be getting good odds against a range with a lot of crap in it. The amount of contentious history between Dusty and the button means they'll be getting all in with unusually wide ranges here.

Once the button just calls Dusty's 3-bet, a lot of hands can be eliminated from his range. He's too good a player to call with a weak offsuit ace, so that's out. With a suited ace or a stronger offsuit ace (think A-K, A-Q, A-J), he would almost always 4-bet with the intention of committing. He would also usually 4-bet shove with all of his pocket pairs. The only hands left in his calling range are suited connectors that he feels are too good to fold, but are in bad shape when all the chips go in.

Given the button's range, the flop is excellent for Dusty. His king is usually good here. More importantly, the button will never have a strong hand. Dusty fires off a continuation bet, planning on firing a second barrel on the turn. He might even shove the turn as a bit of an overbet, mostly to prevent the button from making a play of his own. The button's call does not represent a hand. It simply means that he knows that Dusty will rarely have a hand here himself. There are two aces on board, so it's hard for Dusty to hold one. Aside from pocket pairs, everything else is essentially garbage on this flop.

When the turn gives Dusty a gutshot and a flush draw, he decides to check-raise all in instead of just leading out. If the stacks were shallower, this would be a mistake (unless Dusty had enough equity to call with king high and a ton of outs), since it would give the button a chance to put in the last bet by shoving. With $453 left behind in a $307 pot, there's almost no chance that the button will stick it all in. There's also very little chance that he'll check behind, since we've established that he's calling the flop with the intention of taking the pot away on the turn. From his perspective, he got what he wanted when Dusty checked, and there's no reason for him to risk a large bet when he thinks Dusty has nothing. Actually, he should probably think about jamming just to keep Dusty from playing back at him, as he did in this hand, but it seems that he doesn't expect to face such aggression.

THE TAKEAWAY

On a lot of boards, picking up a huge draw would be an essential factor in making an all-in semibluff. In this hand, however, Dusty could bluff all in with any two cards, since his opponent will almost never have a hand. The added equity does make him more comfortable check-raising the turn instead of betting, just in case the button makes some sort of "Dusty" call with an unlikely pair. This gives him good equity even when he gets called. The check-raise also extracts a turn bet from the button's float, increasing the value of Dusty's bluff.

HAND # 3

$3/$6 NO-LIMIT HOLD'EM— 6 PLAYERS

THE SET-UP

STACKS: Dusty has $780, Cutoff has $609
READS: Cutoff is an extremely erratic but winning regular
PREFLOP ACTION: 2 players fold, Cutoff raises to $15, 2 players fold, Dusty calls in the big blind with A♦ 10♦

DUSTY, BIG BLIND	CUTOFF

FLOP ($33)	TURN ($33)	RIVER ($513)
ACTION	**ACTION**	**ACTION**
Dusty checks	Dusty checks	Dusty checks
Cutoff checks	Cutoff bets $24	Cutoff bets $354 all in
	Dusty raises to $78	Dusty calls, wins pot
	Cutoff reraises to $150	
	Dusty reraises to $240	
	Cutoff calls	

WHY DUSTY PLAYED IT THIS WAY

Ace-10 suited is a strong hand before the flop, but calling allows the cutoff to see the flop with dominated hands like A-9 and J-10, so Dusty just calls. Flopping the nut flush draw with two overcards is always nice. The question is not whether to put money in, but rather how much and in what fashion. Leading out would be fine, but only with the intention of getting the money in if the cutoff raises. Since the cutoff might be willing to get all in with weaker flush draws, it's possible to have about 50 percent equity against the range of hands he'll go all in with.

Checking and calling has its merits as well. It's a deceptive line that may provide more value when an ace or a ten falls. Checking with the intention of raising is fine too. Just like leading out, it's possible to get it in with the best draw often enough to justify shoving over a potential reraise. The advantage the check-raise has over the bet/3-bet is the ability to capture the opponent's continuation bet. Leading out allows him to fold his junk immediately, whereas check-raising will usually get at least $25 from almost his whole range.

After the flop checks through, the turn gives Dusty the nuts. It's okay to lead here and try to get two streets of value, but it's unlikely that the cutoff would fight back and raise. Instead, Dusty check-raises, hoping to represent a naked ace (i.e. just a draw, not a flush). It works well, as the cutoff makes a small reraise. Examined more closely, this guy's turn reraise doesn't make a whole lot of sense. What's he representing? When most players get reraised in this spot, they assume their opponent has a big hand so they try to get the money in immediately, afraid that a bad card will roll off if they just call or make a smaller raise. They shove because they're afraid—but shoving forces the cutoff to have a hand. Otherwise he'll have to fold.

With almost a sure thing to win the pot, this is a time to slow things down and carefully consider the cutoff's range. If he flopped a flush draw, straight, or set, he would have made a continuation bet. This player is erratic, but people just don't check back flops with those hands in mid-stakes games these days. On the off chance that he does hold a hand like that, all the money will go in one way or another. So what does make sense for him to hold? Perhaps a marginal hand that's putting in a small raise as some sort of free showdown play. It's more likely that he has a draw or some other weak hand.

Against an erratic player with a weak hand, what's the best way to extract value on the turn? By feigning weakness yourself. What's the weakest looking play here? Somewhat counter-intuitively, it's a raise!

If Dusty calls in this spot, he has to have a hand. Why else would he call a turn reraise out of position? By making another small raise, Dusty is saying that he either holds the nuts or simply doesn't believe his opponent. It's harder to make the nuts than it is to be skeptical, so the raise looks pretty suspicious. It also gives the cutoff another chance to make a move at the pot. Surprisingly, instead of shoving, the cutoff just calls.

The river doesn't change anything. The cutoff still has nothing. Now Dusty checks to tell the cutoff that he's giving up on his bluff, and his opponent takes the bait. It looks like the cutoff called the turn to get more information on whether or not his bluff would work. This is actually a pretty good play—one that we've recommended earlier in this book. Dusty takes advantage by telling the guy what he wants to hear. The funny thing here is that the cutoff rivers a pair of jacks, a hand with some showdown value. Whatever we may think of his turn reraise, his river bet is awful! There's no reason to turn his pair into a bluff here since Dusty's range is missed draws and the occasional monster.

THE TAKEAWAY

By taking his time and grinding on his opponent's range, Dusty was able to win an entire stack from an opponent who had a very weak hand. He took a line that kept the opponent's weak hands in the pot and eventually got the money from one.

HAND # 4

$10/$20 NO-LIMIT HOLD'EM— 5 PLAYERS

THE SET-UP

STACKS: Dusty has $2,000, Button has $2,000, Cutoff has $2,751, Small Blind has $3,006

READS: Cutoff is very tight preflop, but loose and aggressive postflop

DYNAMIC: Dusty has a tight image and may be viewed as straightforward

PREFLOP ACTION: 1 player folds, Cutoff raises to $60, Button calls, Small Blind calls, Dusty calls with **6♠ 8♠** in the Big Blind

SMALL BLIND	DUSTY, BIG BLIND	CUTOFF	BUTTON

FLOP ($240)	TURN ($840)	RIVER ($840)

ACTION	**ACTION**	**ACTION**
Small Blind checks	Small Blind checks	Dusty bets $785
Dusty checks	Dusty bets $200	Cutoff folds
Cutoff checks	Cutoff calls	Button folds
Button checks	Button calls	Dusty wins pot
	Small Blind folds	

WHY DUSTY PLAYED IT THIS WAY

For whatever reason, Dusty is sitting at a five-handed table with four other world-class players. No one at the table has made less than $1 million dollars playing online poker! That's not the sort of game selection we suggest you sit in, but let's assume that the sixth player who recently left the table was quite bad and justified playing in such a line up. As it is, everyone in the hand can be expected to make rational and high quality decisions.

Despite the high caliber of Dusty's opponents, getting 5 to 1 immediate odds is more than enough to justify playing a good multiway hand like 8-6 suited. When the flop checks around, it's clear that no one has a strong hand. It's possible that someone has A-K or A-J, but that's the top of everyone's collective range. It's also extremely unlikely that anyone holds a flush draw and declined semibluffing at this board. The only player who may have flopped a good hand is the small blind, but he dispels that concern by checking the turn. Since no one has a strong hand and Dusty has a tight image, he decides to represent a failed flop check-raise by making a large bet on the turn. Much to his surprise, he gets two callers.

The cutoff likely holds either A-K or A-J. In fact, it's almost certain. But what could the button have checked through on the flop but decided to call a turn bet with? It's possible that he turned a set of deuces, or perhaps made two pair with A-2. Dusty's plan is to fire any river except an ace, a king, or a jack. The 7♣ is a fantastic card, since it completes his phantom flush draws. Since he's bluffing into two players, each of whom clearly holds something decent but not powerful, he makes a bet close to the size of the pot. Making a smaller bluff here would be a mistake, since it would allow either of his opponents to justify a hero call with a marginal made hand.

THE TAKEAWAY

This is not the time to save a few dollars. It's time to lock up the pot and let the two excellent players make their "good" folds.

HAND # 5

$5/$10 NO-LIMIT HOLD'EM— 6 PLAYERS

THE SET-UP

STACKS: Dusty has $1,030, Button has $1,000, Small Blind has $1,245

READS: Button is absurdly tight, Small Blind is loose and very bad

PREFLOP ACTION: 3 players fold, Button raises to $30, Small Blind calls, Dusty raises to $125 in the big blind with J♦ J♥, Button calls, Small Blind folds

DUSTY, BIG BLIND

BUTTON

FLOP ($280)	TURN ($560)	RIVER ($560)

ACTION	**ACTION**	**ACTION**
Dusty bets $140	Dusty checks	Dusty checks
Button calls	Button checks	Button checks

WHY DUSTY PLAYED IT THIS WAY

Despite the fact that the button is very tight, pocket jacks are doing well against his range. They are also doing fantastic against the small blind's range. Just calling would be an option against the overly tight button, but reraising is mandatory with the small blind in there. He has a wide range and plays terribly postflop, so it's good to get as much of his money in the pot as possible. Dusty makes a considerable reraise, planning to fold to a 4-bet. That's not a good plan against most players: You should usually 3-bet only if you're happy to get all in. But the value in playing a big pot with the small blind outweighs the risk of losing 11.5 blinds without seeing a flop.

The flop is decidedly mediocre. The queen isn't a great card to have sitting out there, but it's not a disaster. Dusty makes a routine half-pot c-bet. The button's preflop calling range is unclear, but the flop calling range could contain numerous floats, along with A-Q, nines, tens, and jacks.

The 4♠ on the turn is a total blank. Betting for value is a consideration, since it's unlikely that the button would slowplay a queen on this draw-heavy board. Most players would raise and get the chips in with top pair here. Overall, the button's range is heavily weighted towards pocket tens and nines. On draw-heavy boards like this one, it's not a bad play to check-raise all in with pocket jacks, especially when the opponent's range is weighted towards nines or tens. You can win an extra bet compared with just betting, and sometimes players will make a hero call, thinking that you could play a draw this way. (Maybe you could.) Dusty decides to go for the turn check-raise, but the turn checks through.

The river ace is an ugly card! Dusty considers turning his jacks into a bluff. The button is unlikely to hold an ace, since he should have bet A-Q on the turn. If Dusty bets the river, he could credibly represent a big ace that 3-bet preflop, make a c-bet on the flop, gave up on the turn, then got there with a free river card. He's still convinced that his opponent holds pocket nines or tens, though, and there's no sense bluffing those. These are exactly the sorts of hands that nitty players hate. They feel like it's too weak to fold preflop, but too scary to 4-bet.

Dusty checks, expecting to win a showdown against nines or tens. Somewhat shockingly, the button turns up with Q-6 suited. His play in this hand is wildly inconsistent. Calling the 3-bet with Q-6 is adventurous, to say the least. His only justification would be that he thinks Dusty's 3-betting range is very wide. That may be unfounded, but fine, it's an angle.

Here's the problem: If the button is calling with a weak hand because Dusty's range is wide, then he has to bet with top pair on the turn! He would have won an entire stack. He wasn't afraid of Dusty's wide range before the flop, but then he was too scared to bet the turn? That doesn't make any sense. It's a clear case of letting emotions overrule logic at the poker table. Flopping top pair is a great result for **Q♥ 6♥** against a wide range. When Dusty checks, it's an easy bet for value: If that hand can't bet the turn for value, it can't call preflop. While he won't always win a stack, there's no way to justify the preflop call without extracting maximum value postflop.

THE TAKEAWAY

If you make a call because you think your opponent's range is wide, then you have to commit with hands that are strong against wide ranges.

Top pair/no kicker is weak compared to the strong ranges this player is used to playing with, but it's strong against the range he has to put Dusty on to justify the preflop call.

HAND # 6

$3/$6 NO-LIMIT HOLD'EM—
8 PLAYERS

THE SET-UP

STACKS: Dusty has $651, Cutoff has $624

READS: Cutoff is an unknown player

PREFLOP ACTION: 4 players fold, Cutoff raises to $18, 2 players fold, Dusty calls with **10♦ 9♦** in the big blind

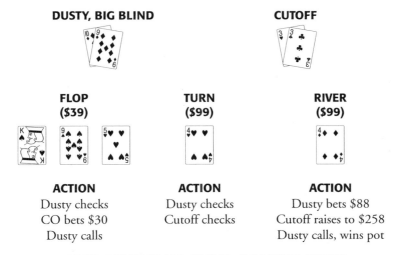

DUSTY, BIG BLIND		CUTOFF

FLOP ($39)	TURN ($99)	RIVER ($99)

ACTION	ACTION	ACTION
Dusty checks	Dusty checks	Dusty bets $88
CO bets $30	Cutoff checks	Cutoff raises to $258
Dusty calls		Dusty calls, wins pot

WHY DUSTY PLAYED IT THIS WAY

Against a cutoff raise, 10-9 suited is a borderline call in the big blind. Playing against an unknown opponent can make it more difficult to play the hand accurately, but with the number of hands Dusty plays, most unknowns are going to be part-time players at best. In other words, there's a reasonable chance that the cutoff is a weaker player.

On this draw-heavy board, Dusty takes a passive line to get to showdown. The plan is to check-call the turn and check-call most river cards, though **Q♠, J♠, Q♥,** or **J♥** would be likely exceptions. Calling the turn with the intention of folding every draw-completing river would be an awful plan. With two flush draws and a bevy of straight draws available, only cards that pair the board will not complete draws. Even a third of those will fill in one flush draw or the other. When you check-call a turn like this, you may want to fold certain rivers. Stick to the river cards that complete multiple draws, particularly the most likely ones for your opponent to hold.

As it turns out, the cutoff checks through and the river is one of those innocuous board-pairing cards. That's the good news. The bad news is that Dusty has no idea where he is in the hand. That's one of the tradeoffs for playing a hand passively. The cutoff could have a moderately strong hand that was afraid of getting check-raised on the turn—K-Q, K-J, and K-10 fill the bill. Pocket pairs such as queens, jacks, tens, eights, sevens and sixes also make sense.

What should you do when you're out of position on the river and you don't have a firm idea of your opponent's range or plan? In this case, Dusty decides to make a nearly pot-sized bet. It's an unorthodox play, but there are a lot of good things that can happen. The cutoff may interpret Dusty's weird line as a missed draw, and make some loose calls. Even a hand such as A-Q beats the missed draws, and pocket pairs have to feel pretty good. It may be interpreted as a nuts or a bluff bet. In other words, Dusty's range looks polarized. If the cutoff thinks Dusty has the nuts more than twice as often as he's bluffing, he can fold hands as strong as top pair. Hands like A-9 and pocket tens through queens will certainly hit the muck. If the cutoff interprets the river bet as the nuts or a bluff, he may raise with his own missed draw (such as 8♣ 7♣ or 7♦ 6♦), hoping to push Dusty off of a larger draw. Since there are so few legitimate hands that the cutoff can hold, Dusty can snap call the river with little to fear.

It may seem illogical to argue that better hands will fold and weaker hands will call. The point is that Dusty's bet looks like either he beats everything or nothing. Therefore, top pair and ace-high are roughly the same from the cutoff's perspective: They're bluff catchers. If Dusty had checked, his opponent would have bet and put Dusty in a tough spot.

THE TAKEAWAY

By betting here, Dusty goes from thinking, "I have no idea what's going on," to making his opponent think, "I have no idea what's going on." He flips the situation on its head and makes his opponent make the tough decision.

When the cutoff raises the river, there are not many strong hands that he can hold—**A♠ 4♠** and **A♣ 4♣** are just about the only ones. Getting 2.6 to 1, Dusty doesn't need the cutoff to be bluffing very often to justify a call. It's strange that the cutoff chose to turn his bluff catcher into a bluff against a range that should usually be comprised of bluffs and monsters. He clearly didn't buy Dusty's story about having a polarized range. But Dusty didn't buy the cutoff's story either and as a result, he took down a huge pot with a small hand.

HAND # 7

$5/$10 NO-LIMIT HOLD'EM— 9 PLAYERS

THE SET UP

STACKS: Dusty has $1,005, Early Position Player has $1,062, Cutoff has $1,407

READS: Early Player is a relative unknown who plays decently; Cutoff is tight and tricky

PREFLOP ACTION: 2 players fold, Early Player raises to $20, 2 players fold, Cutoff calls, Button folds, Dusty calls in the small blind with **A♣ J♣**, Big Blind folds

DUSTY, SMALL BLIND	EARLY PLAYER	CUTOFF

FLOP ($70)	TURN ($130)	RIVER ($310)

ACTION	ACTION	ACTION
Dusty checks	Dusty checks	Dusty bets $255
Early Player bets $30	Early Player bets $90	Early Player folds
Cutoff folds	Dusty calls	Dusty wins pot
Dusty calls		

WHY DUSTY PLAYED IT THIS WAY

Even though A-J suited is a quality hand, reraising against an early position raise in a full ring game would be foolhardy. The draw-heavy flop gives Dusty a double gutshot. It's hard to say what the early position player's small flop bet means, so raising is a viable option. Against this unknown, however, Dusty decides to just check and call. The plan is to either improve to the best hand or hit something to bluff at (like a flush-completing heart). Dusty can also bluff the river if his opponent checks the turn.

The 6♠ on the turn presents a second flush draw, which gives Dusty more fake outs to bluff at on the river. In addition to the heart and spade bluffing outs, an A, K, or 9 would also give him a strong hand. Early Player's three-quarters-pot bet on the turn is somewhat odd after his preflop min-raise and small flop bet. If he has a big hand, then Dusty may be able to win the guy's whole stack if a king comes on the river. Instead, the jack gives Dusty second pair, which is all but useless. It does complete some straight draws and the backdoor flush, however, so Dusty decides to make a substantial bluff. His opponent may fold a hand as strong as three queens on this awful river.

Earlier we dispelled the myth that you never act out of turn, but most of those examples were where you should donk bet for value. As this hand illustrates, it's also a good line to use as a bluff. The board has become so ugly that you can't rely on your opponent to bet for you anymore.

THE TAKEAWAY

Whenever you can lead out for value, you can represent the same hand with a bluff.

HAND # 8

$5/$10 NO-LIMIT HOLD'EM— 5 PLAYERS

THE SET-UP

STACKS: Button and Dusty each have $1,000

READS: Button is a tricky, tight regular who has a penchant for making moves against Dusty; Big Blind is a weak player

PREFLOP ACTION: 2 players fold, Button raises to $30, Dusty calls with Q♥ 10♥ in the small blind, Big Blind folds.

DUSTY, SMALL BLIND   **BUTTON**

FLOP **($70)**	**TURN** **($370)**

ACTION	**ACTION**
Dusty checks	Dusty bets $65
Button bets $50	Button raises to $140
Dusty raises to $150	Dusty reraises to $820 all in
Button calls	Button folds

WHY DUSTY PLAYED IT THIS WAY

With a stronger player in the big blind, Dusty would usually prefer to 3-bet preflop and avoid getting squeezed. In this hand, however, the big blind is a weak player, so Dusty cold calls, inviting him to join the pot. Unfortunately, the big blind folds and the flop comes out heads up.

Despite the fact that Dusty just called before the flop, there is no reason to let the button win the majority of pots. The plan is to check-raise any flop that Dusty catches a piece of (a gutshot, a backdoor flush draw, etc.) The flop is reasonably good, as it provides some obvious draws that Dusty can represent (clubs and straight draws) and some less obvious ones that he actually holds (backdoor hearts, overcards, running straight draw). The plan after check-raising the flop is to follow through when he picks up a draw (heart, jack, 9, or 7); bluff if an ace or a king comes out; and value bet a queen or a 10. A 3, 4, or 5 will also hit some of the straight draws, so those aren't bad bluffing cards either.

The turn gives Dusty a double gutshot—any jack or 7 completes the straight. It's hard to put the button on a range at this point, but there's a reasonable chance that he's waiting until the turn to raise with a big overpair. The question now becomes how to get some fold equity against the button's range. Making a standard sized bet will allow the button to shove over the top with all of his good hands. If Dusty had made a bet like $320, he would be getting 3 to 1 on a turn call against a shove. That would be just about the right price to call with eight to fourteen outs, but the money wouldn't be going in very good at all. Instead, Dusty makes a tiny bet, effectively reducing the stack sizes. Now when the button raises, there's room to make a convincing shove and put the onus on the button to have a hand. If the button just calls the tiny turn bet, Dusty can shove the river, comfortably knowing that the button should never have a strong hand.

As the hand plays out, the button makes a weird little raise of his own. This looks like a free showdown play—a small raise intended to freeze Dusty from putting in any more action. It's supposed to be a cheap way to get to showdown, but its transparency causes it to backfire.

THE TAKEAWAY

Since Dusty feels that his opponent isn't capable of making a big hero call with a hand like A-8 or 10-9, he goes ahead with his plan, jams the money in on the turn, and takes down the pot with his semibluff.

HAND #9

$3/$6 NO-LIMIT HOLD'EM–
6 PLAYERS

THE SET-UP

STACKS: Dusty has $1,563, Button has $1,091,
Big Blind has $541

READS: Button is an aggressive regular, Big
Blind is a fish

PREFLOP ACTION: 3 players fold, Button raises to $18, Dusty calls
with **6♠ 6♥** in the small blind, Big Blind folds

DUSTY, SMALL BLIND

BUTTON

FLOP ($42)	TURN ($42)	RIVER ($772)
ACTION	**ACTION**	**ACTION**
Dusty checks	Dusty checks	Dusty checks
Button checks	Button bets $30	Button bets $708 all in
	Dusty raises to $120	Dusty folds
	Button raises to $210	Button wins the pot
	Dusty raises to $365	
	Button calls	

WHY DUSTY PLAYED IT THIS WAY

While the button is a solid player, the big blind is not. Pocket sixes would usually be a 3-bet from the small blind, but with deep stacks of almost 200 blinds, they play well for a call. The weak player in the big blind is not a squeezer, so all signs point toward his having a wide cold-calling range.

The flop is a disaster and Dusty checks, planning to give up, but the button also checks, giving a free look at the turn **6♣**, which gives Dusty the relative nuts. No one ever checks back sets these days, so there's simply no way that he's beat. Hoping to represent a total air bluff, Dusty goes for a big check-raise, four times the size of the button's delayed c-bet. The button takes the bait and makes a min-reraise. There's almost no real hand he can represent. The only reasonable hand he can claim to have is three sixes, but of course that would be impossible unless someone slipped an extra one into the deck.

The button's tiny reraise is sized to prevent Dusty from jamming it in with a draw, since there's so much money left behind. Since the button can never hold a real hand here, Dusty makes a smallish 4-bet, planning to check-call the inevitable river shove. Betting any river in Dusty's position would be awful because his opponent can never have a hand good enough to call. The button is calling the turn either because he has a draw or because he wants to bluff the river if Dusty gives up. The only way he can bluff is if Dusty checks, so betting would be a mistake on his part. Unfortunately, the river is the absolute joker! Every turned draw (8-7 and clubs) that the button could have been semibluffing with just came in. While the plan was to call a river shove, the second worst card in the deck (the **9♣** is marginally worse) commands a retreat.

THE TAKEAWAY

The button made an interesting play here on the turn, calling Dusty's $155 reraise in an attempt to take the pot away on the river. He applied the concept of waiting to bluff until more information is presented. Had the river not been a disaster, Dusty would have presented the information he was looking for, although it would have been false.

HAND #10

$5/$10 NO-LIMIT HOLD'EM— 6 PLAYERS

THE SET-UP

STACKS: Dusty has $2,157, Small Blind has $1,005, Big Blind has $267

READS: Small Blind is a weak regular, Big Blind is a fish

PREFLOP ACTION: 3 players fold to Dusty on the button, Dusty raises to $30 with **J♥ 10♥**, Small Blind calls, Big Blind calls

SMALL BLIND	BIG BLIND	DUSTY, BUTTON

FLOP ($90)	TURN ($190)

ACTION	ACTION
Small Blind bets $50	Small Blind bets $110
Big Blind folds	Dusty raises to $285
Dusty calls	Small Blind folds

WHY DUSTY PLAYED IT THIS WAY

There's not much to say about raising preflop with J-10 suited, particularly from the button, but there's plenty to say about the small blind's flop donk. To begin with, it doesn't make much sense. Let's look at his range: The only strong hands he can represent are A-Q, A-3, and pocket threes. It's possible that he cold called with pocket aces or queens, hoping that the short stack in the big blind would squeeze. Even then, why would he lead out with a flopped set, particularly aces that have the deck crushed? No, it's unlikely that he holds one of the few strong hands possible.

It's much more likely that he holds something marginal such as A-J or A-10, or something weaker like a gutshot draw with K-J, K-10, or J-10. Against this weak range, Dusty plans to make a move with his gutshot. He could raise the flop, but raising the turn is better. Here's why: Waiting captures a second (and larger) bet from the small blind on the turn. Raising the turn represents a stronger range—the line looks stronger than a mere flop raise. By just calling the flop, Dusty can represent a queen if a second one hits the turn, whereas his opponent can never really hold one—people rarely donk the flop with second pair when an ace is on board. He would need to have flopped at least two pair for the queen to be a good card for him.

It's harder for the small blind to re-bluff against a turn raise than against a flop raise because it requires committing almost an entire stack and usually works less often. All in all, the small blind will be bluffing (or bet-folding a marginal hand) on the turn so often that raising the turn should be hugely profitable. It's true that Dusty is also representing a narrow range, but his line looks more credible than the small blind's. The sliver of equity provided by the gutshot subsidizes the bluff, meaning it doesn't have to work as often as it would with a total air ball.

"But wait!" you may ask, "If waiting for the turn is so much better than raising the flop, then why not wait for the river?"

THE TAKEAWAY

There are spots where waiting for the river will capture a third (and even bigger) bet, as demonstrated by the Mississippi bluff. Unfortunately, those situations are rare. In this particular hand, the small blind's range is split between top pair and air. By raising the turn, there's a good chance Dusty can get all of those hands to fold—everything except an unlikely monster like A-Q or pocket threes. But waiting for the river would allow the small blind to check and call with his top-pair hands. Passing up the opportunity to bluff those out of the pot would be a huge mistake.

HAND #11

$3/$6 NO-LIMIT HOLD'EM— 4 PLAYERS

THE SET-UP

STACKS: Dusty has $600, Big Blind has $619

READS: Big Blind is active and bluff happy

PREFLOP ACTION: 1 player folds, Dusty has **Q♦ Q♥** on the button and raises to $18, Small Blind folds, Big Blind raises to $57, Dusty calls

DUSTY, BUTTON	BIG BLIND

FLOP ($117)	TURN ($237)	RIVER ($483)
ACTION	**ACTION**	**ACTION**
BB bets $60 Dusty calls	Big Blind bets $123 Dusty calls	Big Blind checks Dusty bets $360 all in Big Blind calls, wins pot

WHY DUSTY PLAYED IT THIS WAY

The big blind's range is so wide when he 3-bets that Dusty decides to just call before the flop and let him barrel off with all of his garbage hands. Putting in a 4-bet would allow him to get off cheap with those hands. The flop is good for Dusty's hand. While overcards are never something to rejoice over, the presence of a second king on board makes it 33 percent less likely for the big blind to hold one. It also eliminates the opportunity for him to make two pair with a hand like 8-7 or 9-8.

Just like the preflop decision, there is no reason to force the big blind to fold his garbage. There's nothing to get value from and not much to protect against. The only bad card in the deck is an ace. By calling, Dusty represents a range of jacks, tens, nines, and various pairs of eights. He could also have some random hands calling as a float. Nothing changes on the turn. The reasons for calling are the same as they were before and on the flop.

When the big blind checks the river, Dusty will almost always have the best hand. The big blind is either giving up with a bluff, or checking a marginal pair. In fact, discarding the irrelevant garbage from the big blind's range (irrelevant because it will check-fold), Dusty and the big blind should have very similar ranges at this point in the hand. Since pocket queens are the absolute top of that range, it's an easy value bet.

The big blind calls the river and turns over **A♣ A♦**, raking in the pot. While he wins the pot and the rest of Dusty's stack, he made a clear error. Unless he thinks (which he shouldn't) that Dusty is pulling the Mississippi bluff all over town, there are no bluffs in Dusty's range that the big blind can induce a bet from. Dusty's hand should look like a middle pair, which is much more likely to call a bet than it is to make one. The big blind has a clear value bet on the river, since he's ahead often enough to see the showdown and because the money will go in better when he puts it in himself.

THE TAKEAWAY

The moral of the story is: Don't check and call the river when the money goes in better if you bet it.

HAND #12

$5/$10 NO-LIMIT HOLD'EM— 6 PLAYERS

THE SET-UP

STACKS: Dusty has $1,061, Small Blind has $1,411

READS: Small Blind is solid, aggressive, and capable of making moves

PREFLOP ACTION: 3 players fold, Dusty raises to $30 with **10♠ 4♠** on the button, Small Blind calls, Big Blind folds

DUSTY, BUTTON	SMALL BLIND

FLOP ($70)	TURN ($160)	RIVER ($160)

ACTION	ACTION	ACTION
Small Blind checks	Small Blind checks	Small Blind bets $120
Dusty bets $45	Dusty checks	Dusty raises to $290
Small Blind calls		Small Blind folds

WHY DUSTY PLAYED IT THIS WAY

Opening with 10-4 suited on the button is standard, as is making a two-thirds pot sized continuation bet on this board, which is unlikely to have hit the small blind's range. The 2♣ is the ultimate brick on the turn. This opponent is extremely unlikely to check-call the flop and then check-fold this particular turn card, so Dusty checks back.

When the small blind bets the river, it would be the easiest thing in the world to simply give up. After all, Dusty has no hand. He's checked the turn, pretty much announcing that he has no hand. But let's take a closer look at each player's range. To begin with, it's very difficult for the small blind to have a hand that he's excited about. He could possibly have called the flop with pocket twos, but a pair that weak will usually fold. He could also have check-called with a hand like Q-J. Given the preflop cold call, this would probably have to be Q-J suited, which is only three combos. Combined with pocket twos, that's only six remotely possible combinations of hands that are happy to get chips in the pot. It seems extremely unlikely that this player slowplayed a hand as strong as a seven or a full house.

Let's look at the rest of his range. He could have a small pocket pair that is making an ill advised and overly thin value bet. He could also have a hand like A-J, K-J, or J-10 making a similar value bet. Missed gutshots like 9-8 and 10-9 are also possible. There is some chance for the small blind to hold a hand like A-Q or K-Q that floated out of position, but these usually would have 3-bet preflop. Taken as a whole, the small blind's range is very weak and can rarely stand a raise. Looking at Dusty's range, there are few very strong hands possible, but there are many possible queen hands he could hold: A-Q, K-Q, Q-10, or any suited queen. When he raises, it's very easy for his opponent to give him credit for this and fold a smaller pair.

A common mistake that mediocre players make is to check out of a hand early. You can see it in their mannerisms in live games. They'll twirl their finger to the dealer like, "Come on, let's see another card. Let's get this over with." Their more observant opponents will notice their attitude and take advantage. Would you rather be the player who gives up every time you don't have something, or the one who takes advantage of the guy who does? The idea is not to blindly raise at every turn (or river), but rather to always keep your eyes open.

THE TAKEAWAY

Never stop thinking about your opponent's range and how he'll play it. When an opponent can never be strong, it's usually a good time to take a stab at a lonely pot.

HAND #13

$3/$6 NO-LIMIT HOLD'EM— 9 PLAYERS

THE SET-UP

STACKS: Dusty has $1,221, Cutoff has $713
READS: Cutoff is a regular who is on tilt
DYNAMIC: Dusty has been 3-betting a lot, Cutoff has check-raised several flops in a row
PREFLOP ACTION: 5 players fold, Cutoff raises to $18, Dusty reraises to $54 on the button with **A♥ A♣**, both blinds fold, Cutoff calls

DUSTY, BIG BLIND

CUTOFF

**FLOP
($117)**

ACTION

Cutoff checks
Dusty bets $65
Cutoff raises to $138
Dusty reraises to $211
Cutoff reraises to $284
Dusty reraises to $1,167 all in.
Cutoff folds

WHY DUSTY PLAYED IT THIS WAY

This hand illustrates how reads can have a huge effect on which line you should take. Dusty had 3-bet the cutoff in five consecutive orbits. After check-folding the first couple of flops, the cutoff check-raised the next two. It seemed that he was taking the reraises personally and had decided to fight back. What better time to pick up aces?

After getting check-raised on three consecutive flops, a player in Dusty's shoes will often get fed up and do something stupid in return. So after this guy's tiny flop raise, Dusty makes a tiny reraise of his own, feigning irritation. This gives the cutoff another chance to try to run Dusty over. He takes the bait and puts in another min-raise.

After putting in the 4-bet, it's unlikely that the cutoff has much of anything. People rarely play monsters this way, and any moderately strong hand would be better off letting Dusty keep the lead. It's worth considering putting in another min-raise, but Dusty decides it's highly unlikely that this guy will 6-bet with air, so he jams in the rest of the chips. There's no sense in letting him draw for free, since it seems he's unlikely to bluff at the pot again.

THE TAKEAWAY

While making a min-reraise often looks like a stupid play, sometimes it's those stupid-looking plays that can push your opponents over the edge. When you see someone tilting and spewing off chips, don't let him off the hook too easily. It would be easy to jam over this guy's flop check-raise, but it's worth it to give him one more chance to do something stupid. The antagonistic and weird-looking line probably earned Dusty an extra $146 on this hand alone, and quite possibly set the guy off for further losses.

HAND #14

$3/$6 NO-LIMIT HOLD'EM— 4 PLAYERS

THE SET UP

STACKS: Dusty has $633, Small Blind has $601

READS: Small Blind is a very solid regular who is currently tilting

DYNAMIC: Small Blind has been playing extra aggressively

PREFLOP ACTION: 1 player fold, Dusty raises to $18 with K♠ 3♠ on the button, Small Blind calls, and the Big Blind folds

HAND ANALYSIS

SMALL BLIND

DUSTY, BUTTON

FLOP ($42)

TURN ($186)

RIVER ($450)

ACTION
Small Blind checks
Dusty bets $24
Small Blind raises to $72
Dusty calls

ACTION
Small Blind bets $132
Dusty calls

ACTION
Small Blind checks
Dusty bets $411 all in
Small Blind folds

WHY DUSTY PLAYED IT THIS WAY

Dusty's preflop raise on the button is standard. The small blind is an aggressive 3-bettor, but only reraises with very strong hands, small suited connectors, and junky middling cards. His cold-calling range is mostly pocket pairs and suited Broadway hands such as A-Q, A-J, K-Q and K-J. The small blind will almost never hit this type of flop, so Dusty throws out a standard continuation bet. When the small blind check-raises, the only value hand in his range is pocket fives; however, there should be plenty of overcards in his range. Dusty clearly has no hand, but since the small blind has so many bluffs in his range, he decides to call the flop and make a small turn raise. Despite the fact that the small blind is tilting, it's unlikely that he would be willing to shove against a turn min-raise. It simply represents too much strength.

When the turn pairs Dusty's bottom card, it's time to change the plan. A pair of threes is enough to call down against this tilting opponent. There's no longer any reason to bluff. It's more profitable to allow the opponent to continue bluffing. When the river queen comes out, the small blind checks after a long pause. There's a good chance that he would fire the river if he still had air, but there's also virtually zero chance that he intends to call a bet.

If he spiked a queen and was willing to call a large bet, it would make more sense for him to put the chips in himself instead of trying to induce a bluff. After all, what can he induce a bluff from? A double float? Most players calling the flop raise would have put their bluff in on the turn. Calling the turn would allow the small blind to bluff all in on the river, thus stealing the button's opportunity. No, the only reasonable hand that could bluff the river is exactly what Dusty is holding. It's so unlikely that the small blind has this type of hand that it's not worth giving too much thought to. So what happens on the river? Dusty turns his turned pair into a bluff. The small pair may be good as often as 80 percent of the time, but bluffing is like a freeroll here. He'll almost never get called.

This hand is an example of a situation where you can come up with a plan on the flop, but modify that plan as the board and your opponent provide you with new information. Dusty called the flop planning to bluff the turn, then called the turn trying to catch a bluff, then turned his hand back into a bluff on the river.

THE TAKEAWAY

It is important to have a plan early in the hand, but it's just as important to keep your eyes peeled for unexpected developments.

The irony here is that the small blind may have backed into a hand with showdown value, and as a result didn't get to show down. If the queen gave him a pair, then he may have checked, hoping to show down for free, and gotten bluffed by a hand that would have called a shove! This means that he lost a 75-blind pot instead of winning an entire stack.

HAND #15

$3/$6 NO-LIMIT HOLD'EM— 8 PLAYERS

THE SET UP

STACKS: Dusty has $780, Early Position Player has $645

READS: Early Player is very tight

PREFLOP ACTION: 1 player folds, Early Player raises to $18, 3 players fold, Dusty calls with **K♠ J♠** on the button, both blinds fold

EARLY PLAYER

DUSTY, BUTTON

FLOP ($45)	TURN ($105)	RIVER ($453)
ACTION	**ACTION**	**ACTION**
Early Player bets $30 Dusty calls	Early Player bets $72 Dusty raises to $174 Early Player calls	Early Player checks Dusty bets $558 all in Early Player folds

WHY DUSTY PLAYED IT THIS WAY

The early position raiser has a tight range of approximately 7 percent of all hands (6-6+, A-K, A-Q, A-Js, K-Qs). Reraising with K-J suited would be terrible against this range, since Early Position will almost always either 4-bet or fold. It would be just as good to 3-bet with 3-2 here. Given the fact that the early position player folds too much after the flop, folding K-J suited would also be a mistake, so Dusty calls.

The flop is excellent, giving Dusty a spade draw and providing little help to his opponent's range. In fact, it's possible that he would fold everything except a set of eights if he were raised. He might decide to commit with his big pairs, though, since there are so many draws on board. Raising with Dusty's hand would be profitable here, but waiting for the turn is more profitable.

There are a number of reasons why waiting to raise on the turn would be more profitable in this situation: First of all, waiting for the turn allows the early position player to put another bet in the pot, providing more reward for the risk. Secondly, Dusty's opponent is likely to make a better flop decision than turn decision. Most players use a statistic in their HUD to display how often their opponents raise the flop, but rarely use a statistic to display how often they raise the turn. The sample size on the latter stat would be smaller anyway, rendering it less useful. Any time you can take a tool away from your opponent, it's worth considering. Finally, Dusty can represent more strong hands with a turn raise than with a flop raise. Flopped sets could be played either way, but there are more sets available on the turn (because there is another card out there to hit). If a 6 or a 7 falls, Dusty can represent a straight. When the 3 comes out, Dusty can represent A-2 suited.

If his opponent had checked the turn, Dusty would have bet and won the pot immediately almost every time. But the guy bets! Dusty follows through with his plan to raise and Early Position calls. If this particular player had shoved over the turn raise, Dusty would have had to fold: His opponent's shoving range would be too strong and the pot odds too small. Against an aggressive player, however, Dusty would call the turn shove, knowing that his K-J would be live some of the time. And occasionally he would actually get the chips in with the best draw (i.e. king-high would be in the lead). He also wouldn't want to let an aggressive player run him off of strong draws in too many big pots.

Dusty's turn raise is on the small side to leave room for a pot-sized river bluff. (Note that the bet is a little less than a pot-sized bet, since the effective stacks were only $645 before the flop.) Having a credible river bet is important. The smaller turn raise also puts Dusty's opponent in a worse situation. He's calling, hoping that Dusty gives up—but the smaller the turn raise, the less he wins when Dusty does give up. Actually, the risk is the same if he calls down, but the reward is less when there is no river bet. There is a counter argument to the small turn raise: If Dusty knows that his opponent will often call the turn but fold the river, he'd like to get as much money in as possible on the turn before taking the pot away on the river.

THE TAKEAWAY

Arguments often pull in multiple directions. The job of a good player is to decide which factors weigh the heaviest.

The queen is a bad river card, since pocket queens comprise a fair portion of the early position player's range at this point. Still, there are more than enough combinations of pocket aces, kings, and jacks to justify firing the last missile on the river. Calling the turn and waiting to raise the river would be a mistake in this hand, since so many moderately strong hands can bet the flop, bet the turn, then shut down and check-call the river. If his opponent had bet the river, there wouldn't be enough chips left for Dusty to make a threatening raise. This would result in not enough folds and too many frustrated calls. Giving his opponent that happy surprise win at showdown would be a mistake!

HAND #16

$5/$10 NO-LIMIT HOLD'EM— 6 PLAYERS

THE SET UP

STACKS: Dusty has $1,100, Cutoff has $1,207

READS: Cutoff is a high-stakes regular who is playing below his usual limits. He's tight preflop and good postflop.

PREFLOP ACTION: 2 players fold, Cutoff raises to $30, Dusty reraises to $90 with **3♠ 2♠** on the button, both blinds fold, Cutoff calls

CUTOFF	DUSTY, BUTTON

FLOP ($195)	TURN ($615)	RIVER ($615)
ACTION	**ACTION**	**ACTION**
Cutoff bets $70	Cutoff checks	Cutoff checks
Dusty raises to $210	Dusty checks	Dusty bets $300
Cutoff calls		Cutoff folds

WHY DUSTY PLAYED IT THIS WAY

Deuce-trey suited is not exactly a powerhouse hand before the flop, and flopping bottom pair is not an excellent result. Nonetheless, Dusty decides to take a couple of shots at his tight opponent with it. The plan is not just to get immediate folds on the flop and preflop streets (though that would be nice), but also to take the pot away with big bets on the right turn and river cards.

Before the flop, the cutoff is opening a modest range, but he's also folding a large portion of that range to a 3-bet. When he calls, his range is approximately pocket nines through queens, A-Q and A-J suited. The cutoff makes a weird donk bet on this super dry board that has no draws and only one high card. Dusty continues his charade with a raise and the cutoff calls. This small donk-and-call line is so weird that it's hard to put him on a range. It's possible that he's taking a bizarre line with three jacks in an attempt to get the money in. He's twice as likely to hold pocket tens, however (due to card removal from the jack on board), or pocket nines for that matter.

The ace on the turn is not hugely threatening, since it only improves A-J, which was unlikely to go anywhere anyway. Still, it's a bad spot to get trapped, and the cutoff may be thinking that if he induced a bluff raise from Dusty on the flop, he can induce another bluff on the turn. Another problem with making a decent sized bet on the turn is that it would make the remaining stacks too small to make a threatening river bet.

Since betting the river should earn as many folds as betting the turn, Dusty checks it back. The advantage to bluffing the river instead of the turn is having more information. At this point in the hand, the cutoff either has a huge hand or a very marginal one. There's little risk that he'll turn his marginal hand into a bluff on the river, and the risk of seeing him making a hero call is just as small—if this guy has a flaw, it's that he doesn't like to take risks.

A turn bet would work as a bluff just as often against a marginal hand as a river bet would, but it would be a donation against the monsters in the cutoff's range. By checking back, Dusty waits for his opponent to tell him whether or not his bluff will work. In this case, the cutoff admits to his marginal hand by checking, and Dusty takes the pot away with a mid-sized bet. There's no reason to make a large bluff on the river flush card, since Dusty would probably try to sell his hand if he actually had the A-K or A-Q that he's representing. Against observant opponents, it's a good idea to keep your bluffs in line with what they expect to see from your real hands.

It is worth noting that the half-pot bet only has to work about 33 percent of the time to be profitable. Compare this to a full pot bet, which needs to succeed 50 percent of the time, or a shove, which needs to succeed about 57 percent of the time. Also heed this:

THE TAKEAWAY

If an opponent folds the same percentage of his hands against each bet size, the smaller bet will always be more profitable. Lower risk, same reward!

HAND #17

NO-LIMIT HOLD'EM $1.20 ANTE— 4 PLAYERS

THE SET UP

STACKS: Dusty has $2,030, SB has $1,500

READS: Small Blind is an aggressive 3-bettor

PREFLOP ACTION: Dusty has **Q♠ 10♠** in the cutoff and raises to $18, Button folds, Small Blind raises to $60, Big Blind folds, Dusty calls

DUSTY, BIG BLIND

CUTOFF

FLOP ($130.80)	TURN ($298.80)	RIVER ($934.80)
ACTION	**ACTION**	**ACTION**
Small Blind bets $84 Dusty calls	Small Blind bets $132 Dusty raises to $318 Small Blind calls	Small Blind checks Dusty bets $1,567 all in Small Blind folds

WHY DUSTY PLAYED IT THIS WAY

Playing with 250-blind stacks, Dusty has a lot of options for making the 3-bettor's life difficult. With such deep stacks, he could 4-bet often and still not give the Small Blind good odds to shove over the top. With position, he can call, raise a lot of flops, float others, and exert a lot of pressure on his opponent. Everything but the nuts tends to shrink up when you're playing big pots deep-stacked and out of position, particularly against good, aggressive players.

With hands like A-5 offsuit, Dusty would be inclined to 4-bet before the flop. Holding an ace makes his opponent half as likely to hold pocket aces and 25 percent less likely to hold A-K or A-Q, meaning that Dusty is that much more likely to win immediately. It also plays terribly for a call, so it's in raise-or-fold territory. On the other hand, **Q♠ 10♠** is a good hand to see a flop in position. Dusty calls.

After flopping a flush draw, raising is an option. The drawback is that hands like pocket aces through queens can happily commit on this flop since there are so many flush and straight draws that they can get it in against. Big overpairs only lose to sets, and sets are hard to flop. Calling the flop and raising the turn will often look stronger than raising right away, so that's what Dusty does.

The turn **K♣** is a mixed bag. It hits the small blind's range, especially A-K, which may or may not fold to pressure with these deep stacks. On the other hand, it's such a good bluffing card that the small blind will likely bet all of his weak hands. Dusty's flop call looks a lot like a medium pair, so the small blind will bet his strong hands as well. Overall, raising this turn will show a huge profit, since all of the bluffs and many of the weaker value hands will fold. The draw in spades subsidizes the bluff, meaning that it doesn't even have to work that often. Dusty is not thrilled that the small blind calls the turn, but there's another chance to bluff on the river.

Let's look at the small blind's turn call. If he held a very strong hand, it's likely that he would have just reraised all in on the turn. When he calls, it is much more likely that he has a hand such as tens through queens or A-K. He's probably thinking, "What the hell is this stupid little raise? Folding A-K here is too weak. Hopefully, he'll give up on the river." What the small blind is *not* thinking here is, "I hope he bets the river. I can't wait to snap off a bluff!"

It doesn't appear that the small blind's plan is to call down. It doesn't seem likely that he wants Dusty to bet. This brings up an important point:

THE TAKEAWAY

When your opponent doesn't want you to do something, it's usually a good idea to go ahead and do it.

Think about what you'd hate to see if you were in your opponent's shoes, then show it to him. Odds are you're going to have them clicking the time bank. Sometimes they'll call and sometimes they'll fold. But once they click the time bank, you've done your job. Most of your bluffs only have to work somewhere between 33 percent and 50 percent of the time. From experience, we've seen that people fold more often than not once they really start to think about things. Hero calls happen, but they're called "hero" calls for a reason. How many people try to be a hero in real life? It's not much more common at the poker table.

HAND #18

$5/$10 NO-LIMIT HOLD'EM— 6 PLAYERS

THE SET UP

STACKS: Dusty has $1,400, Hijack has $1,286

READS: Hijack is an aggressive and excellent player

PREFLOP ACTION: 1 player folds, Hijack raises to $30, Dusty calls in the Cutoff with **A♠ Q♥**, Button and both blinds fold.

HIJACK

DUSTY, CUTOFF

FLOP ($75)

TURN ($175)

ACTION

Hijack bets $50
Dusty calls

ACTION

Hijack checks
Dusty bets $135
Hijack raises to $400
Dusty raises to $665
Hijack folds

WHY DUSTY PLAYED IT THIS WAY

With deeper than usual stacks, Dusty calls preflop with A-Q to keep dominated hands in the hijack's range. The flop is excellent, as Dusty only trails flopped sets and A-K here. With an ace in hand, that's only 15 possible combinations. Despite the strength of his hand, Dusty is unlikely to get much action from worse hands by raising. An A-J or A-10 may call, and there's a chance that flush draws will play back. If Dusty were to raise and get reraised, it would be impossible to tell whether his opponent was playing a set aggressively, bluffing, or semibluffing. The pot would get big in a hurry, and stacks are too deep to commit with A-Q on this flop.

The only real argument for raising is so that Dusty can represent a flush draw himself, hoping to get the chips in. Considering the range of hands the hijack is likely to commit with, that's not such an exciting proposition. It's better to call in this spot, as Dusty does, trying to get three streets of value. If a diamond comes off, it would be possible to get away from the hand if the hijack bombs on both the turn and river.

The turn check from the hijack is disappointing, since it's so likely that he's giving up. Still, it's important to put in a value bet here in case he's planning to check-call with A-10 or A-J. Dusty puts in the bet—and surprisingly, the hijack raises. There are even fewer hands that beat Dusty now (only 10 combinations), and they're unlikely to be played this way. It's also hard for the hijack to have a weak ace, since he wouldn't expect to get paid off by anything weaker. His range consists of some semibluffs, a few pure bluffs, and the rare monster.

Calling with the intention of calling a river bet would be a reasonable option, but Dusty doesn't want to miss getting value against an A-J when a red card comes on the river to complete a flush draw. He also doesn't want to give combo draws such as 5♦ 4♦ or 5♥ 4♥ a free shot to take his stack.

THE TAKEAWAY

Since a shove will really only get called by better hands (and maybe A-J), Dusty makes a funny looking min-raise, literally clicking it back to his opponent. This may allow some draws to shove, perceiving the illusion of fold equity. It also has a high "bastard" factor, which has the potential to incite irrational behavior from even solid players.

HAND #19

$3/$6 NO-LIMIT HOLD'EM
$1.20 ANTE—9 PLAYERS

THE SET-UP

STACKS: Dusty has $2,153, Hijack has $2,317, Big Blind has $601

READS: Hijack is a solid regular, Big Blind is weak

PREFLOP ACTION: 4 players fold, Hijack raises to $18, Dusty calls with **9♥ 8♥** in the Cutoff, Button folds, Small Blind calls, Big Blind calls

SMALL BLIND	BIG BLIND	HIJACK	DUSTY, CUTOFF

FLOP ($82)	TURN ($232)	RIVER ($232)

ACTION	ACTION	ACTION
Small Blind checks	Big Blind checks	Big Blind checks
Big Blind checks	Hijack checks	Hijack checks
Hijack checks	Dusty checks	Dusty bets $54
Dusty bets $50		Big Blind folds
Small Blind folds		Hijack folds
Big Blind calls		
Hijack calls		

WHY DUSTY PLAYED IT THIS WAY

With stacks of 350 blinds, 9-8 suited becomes a must-play hand against the hijack's open. Reraising would ordinarily be fine, but with a weak player in the big blind, calling has more value. When three players check to Dusty, he makes a modest bet. This is the type of board that most folks will either raise or fold. In other words, they'll either be very happy with their hand, or looking forward to getting dealt a new one.

Since the pot is already large on the flop, it won't be a stretch for Dusty to get the money in when he makes his hand. By making a smaller bet, he also gives himself an easy call to hit his draw with nice implied odds. People are more likely to call these small bets and then give up when they don't improve, so Dusty plans on firing most turn cards. It is surprising to see the hijack check and call this board, but perhaps he holds a hand like A-K or A-Q.

The board-pairing **10♦** is one of the few cards that cause Dusty to check back. While his opponents are unlikely to have flopped anything to be proud of, a pair of tens fits that bill and will have just made trips. When the **10♠** comes on the river and again everyone checks to Dusty, his opponents can hold two types of hands:

1. They can have a decent made hand like A-6, pocket sevens through nines, or possibly a jack; or
2. It's more likely that they have some sort of busted straight draw.

Since the pairs will always call a bet and the straight draws will always fold, it doesn't matter how much Dusty bets. That is to say, it doesn't matter in terms of how many folds he'll get. And if the size of his bet makes no difference in how often his opponents will fold, then it makes sense to bet as little as possible—so the size *does* matter in terms of how profitable the bluff is. Now, betting something ridiculous like $6 might incite a curiosity call from queen-high, or even prompt one of his opponents to re-bluff, so he bets the smallest amount he can get away with. This illustrates an important principle:

THE TAKEAWAY

When your opponent's range is entirely polarized and his calling range is "inelastic"— that is, your bet size will not affect which hands he chooses to call with—make the smallest bet you can get away with.

Note that Dusty can quite credibly represent a jack on the river. His line tells a story: Value bet the flop, get afraid of a 10 on the turn, value bet the full house on the river. It would make sense for him to make his value bet small here, since his opponents can never really have a hand.

HAND #20

$5/$10 NO-LIMIT HOLD'EM— 4 PLAYERS

THE SET-UP

STACKS: Dusty has $1,622, Small Blind has $2,676
READS: Small blind is an excellent player
DYNAMIC: Small blind has been hyperaggressive recently
PREFLOP ACTION: Dusty raises to $30 with A♠ Q♥ in the cutoff, Button folds, Small Blind raises to $110, Big Blind folds, Dusty calls

SMALL BLIND	DUSTY, CUTOFF

FLOP ($230)	TURN ($760)	RIVER ($1,490)
ACTION	**ACTION**	**ACTION**
Small Blind bets $110	Small Blind checks	Small Blind checks
Dusty raises to $265	Dusty bets $365	Dusty bets $882 all in
Small Blind calls	Small Blind calls	Small Blind folds

WHY DUSTY PLAYED IT THIS WAY

With the small blind reraising so aggressively, A-Q has good equity. Four-betting would likely be an immediately profitable play since Small Blind will fold a large portion of his range. With position and effective stacks of 162 blinds, however, calling gives Dusty a chance to outplay his opponent postflop and make a larger profit with the hand. If Dusty flops a strong hand, there's a good chance he can let his opponent fire off three barrels. Inducing bluffs like that can have huge value with big stacks in a reraised pot.

As it turns out, the flop is of no help. That's the bad news. The good news is that it doesn't hit the small blind's range very hard either. With stacks this deep, there is room to make a small flop raise, a moderate turn bet, and still fire a significant river shell. This is a line that few players take as a bluff, so it looks very credible, despite the fact that it represents a fairly narrow range—basically, just sets (10-10, 6-6, 5-5), straights (8-7s), and big pairs (A-A, K-K).

The critical aspect of this hand is bet sizing. Let's imagine for a moment what would happen if Dusty raised the flop to

$330. Assuming the small blind called, the pot would be $890 heading to the turn with stacks of only $1,182. That leaves just a little more than a pot-sized bet on the turn. Even by betting only half the pot on the turn ($445), the river would feature a pot of $1,780 with stacks of only $737. That leaves less than a half-pot bet on the river, which would offer the small blind better odds and command less fold equity. By making a larger flop raise, Dusty would be giving his opponent only two chances to fold instead of three. By betting less on the flop and turn, he leaves room to make a significant enough river bet to earn a fold from everything except a set or an extremely curious opponent.

One related point is that calling a raise to $265 instead of $330 on the flop, or $365 instead of $445 on the turn, should be even less attractive to the small blind. It's true that his immediate pot odds will be better. That would help if he were on a draw or if he expected Dusty to give up on his bluff with a high frequency. But if he expects Dusty to follow through often enough to justify a calldown, he still needs to put in the whole enchilada—so the price is the same when Dusty commits to shoving the whole stack in. But what about the times Dusty gives up? Now the small blind wins less. So, he wins or loses the same amount when all the money goes in, but wins less when the turn or river checks through. By betting less, Dusty is presenting the small blind with the same risk but less reward.

Despite the fact that Dusty is representing a narrow range, the only hands the small blind is likely to call the river with are pocket jacks, J-10 suited, and maybe 10-9 suited. That's a small portion of his range. There are tons of hands he could fold on the flop (all of his air and small pairs), fewer hands he is likely to fold on the turn, and hands such as pocket aces, kings, and queens, along with A-10, K-10, and Q-10, which will all fold the river the vast majority of the time.

Aside from bet sizing, the other key to this hand is this: Few players have the heart to bomb off almost two buy-ins on a cold bluff! Doing so indiscriminately would be a huge leak. But if you can find specific situations where your opponent will have a hell of a time calling you down, you can turn a hell of a profit. The only way to take advantage of those situations is this:

THE TAKEAWAY

Give yourself permission to make a mistake from time to time!

You will run into sets here and there, but if you avoid making these moves on draw-heavy boards, you'll get a lot of folds too.

HAND #21
$2/$4 NO-LIMIT HOLD'EM— 6 PLAYERS

THE SET-UP

STACKS: Dusty has $428, Button has $400
READS: Button is a solid and aggressive mid-stakes winner
DYNAMIC: Button has been playing back at Dusty a lot
PREFLOP ACTION: 2 players fold, Dusty raises to $10 in the Cutoff with K♥ Q♦, Button calls, both blinds fold

DUSTY, CUTOFF

BUTTON

FLOP ($26)	TURN ($54)	RIVER ($254)
ACTION	**ACTION**	**ACTION**
Dusty bets $14	Dusty bets $36	Dusty checks
Button calls	Button raises to $100	Button bets $172
	Dusty calls	Dusty calls, wins pot

WHY DUSTY PLAYED IT THIS WAY

Dusty makes a standard preflop open and gets cold called by the contentious player on the button. The flop is extremely good against the button's calling range. Top pair with a queen kicker is basically the third nuts here since the button can have pocket threes and fours, but almost never aces, A-K, or two pair. Dusty bets for value and gets called.

The turn looks like an ugly card, but there are not too many aces in the button's flop-calling range. A bet will usually go in better if Dusty puts it in himself than if he checks and calls. Another consideration is that checking this turn with hands as strong as flopped top pair would result in a bluff-heavy range. While balance is not always the primary concern, it is an important consideration against regular opponents, particularly observant ones. When the button raises the turn, it's unlikely that he has just hit the ace unless he has specifically A-3 or A-4 suited. Even with a hand as strong as A-Q, he can't get paid that often. He's more likely to call with an ace, since Dusty is very likely to put a bet in on the river either as a bluff or a thin value bet. This leaves only pocket threes and fours in the button's value range, and even those should wait to raise the river since most players will bet/fold the turn with a single ace. Even against A-K, waiting until the river is fine, since all the money will go in regardless of the turn action.

All told, the button's turn raise doesn't make much sense. It looks like a float more than anything, perhaps a turned draw like 7♠ 6♠ or 6♠ 5♠. Dusty calls, planning to call a non-spade river. Against a more conservative opponent, the turn would have been an easy fold. But this hand was being played against an aggressive player who had been even more active than usual.

THE TAKEAWAY

It can be hard to deal with players putting a lot of pressure on you, but you can't let them get away with representing narrow ranges all the time or they'll run you over. It doesn't pay to be roadkill.

The only hands that the button can value bet here are Q-J (which floated and semibluffed the turn), or a small set (which slowplayed the flop). That's 18 combinations of hands: Q-J is 12; 3-3 is 3; and 4-4 is another 3. It's just as likely that the button is bluffing with Q-10 or J-10. That's 21 combinations of hands: Q-10 is 9, and J-10 is 12. There are also five combinations of suited connectors that picked up spade draws on the turn but missed the river. Getting better than 2 to 1 makes this an easy call for Dusty.

HAND #22
$5/$10 NO-LIMIT HOLD'EM— 9 PLAYERS

THE SET-UP

STACKS: Dusty has $1,125, Under the Gun has $1,000

READS: Under the Gun is a very tight full-ring player. He value bets until he's told his hand is no good and will only put the money in when he has a very big hand.

HAND ANALYSIS

PREFLOP ACTION: Under the Gun raises to $30, Early Position Player calls, 3 players fold, Dusty calls in the Cutoff with **Q♠ J♠**, Button folds, Small Blind calls, Big Blind folds

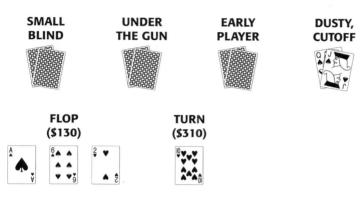

SMALL BLIND	UNDER THE GUN	EARLY PLAYER	DUSTY, CUTOFF

FLOP ($130)	TURN ($310)

ACTION	ACTION
Small Blind checks	Under the Gun bets $240
Under the Gun	Dusty raises to
bets $90	$1,050 all in
Early Player folds	Under the Gun folds
Dusty calls	
Small Blind folds	

WHY DUSTY PLAYED IT THIS WAY

The preflop call with two big suited cards is standard. **Q♠ J♠** plays very well in position in a multiway pot. With four players in for a raise, the pot is already getting large when the flop comes out. Dusty picks up the second-nut flush draw and calls with the intention of raising the turn unless the board pairs. Against certain players, it wouldn't be horrible to raise to something like $260 with the plan of getting all the chips in the center. Some players will shove with smaller flush draws, giving Q-J the chance to actually be the best hand.

The trouble here is that Under the Gun is likely to have a hand such as A-K or A-Q and go all in on the flop. His large flop bet looks like he has something strong but vulnerable, and he's afraid of getting drawn out on. Under the Gun is also unlikely to have any flush draws in his range except perhaps **K♠ 10♠**, which would be a nightmare. With nothing more than a flush draw, it's hard for Dusty to get the chips in with good equity on this flop. On the turn, however, it's easy to represent a hand like A-10. If the turn were a 3, 4, or 5, Dusty could represent an unlikely wheel. Even without a great turn card (the 10 is nice since it adds a gutshot to Dusty's draw), it would be okay to jam the flush draw here since this is an opponent who sees monsters under the bed. By calling the flop and raising the turn, Dusty has allowed him to put in a big turn bet before showing him the monsters he's so afraid of. It doesn't matter whether or not they're really there.

The key to this play is that it is consistent with how a flopped monster like a set could be played. In fact, it's so in line with what the opponent expects to see that he actually types a message in the chat box: "Unbelievable! Nice A-10. You donks always get there with your weaker aces." He just *knew* Dusty had turned two pair because that's what *always* happens to him! That's what he thinks, anyway.

Not only can the turn raise generate more fold equity by essentially risking the same amount of money as the flop raise (since the plan would be to call a shove), it also earns more money the times when it works.

THE TAKEAWAY

Against aggressive opponents, it's a good idea to let them put that extra turn bet in before you convince them that they're beaten.

That's why it's a reasonable way to play a set (although against this opponent it might be better to raise the river), and that's why it works with a draw.

HAND #23

$3/$6 NO-LIMIT HOLD'EM— 6 PLAYERS

THE SET-UP

STACKS: Dusty has $1,711, Button has $600

PREFLOP ACTION: 1 player folds, Dusty raises to $18 with **A♦ J♠** in the Hijack, Cutoff folds, Button calls, both blinds fold

DUSTY, HIJACK

BUTTON

FLOP ($45)

TURN ($105)

ACTION

Dusty bets $30
Button calls

ACTION

Dusty bets $70
Button raises to $188
Dusty raises to $1,663 all in
Button folds

WHY DUSTY PLAYED IT THIS WAY

From the hijack, A-J is a standard open. The button's cold-calling range is roughly pocket twos through jacks, A-Q, suited Broadway hands, and some suited connectors. Out of position against a good player on this moderately coordinated board, giving up would be a reasonable option. The button's entire range consists of pairs and overcards, often with a straight draw to boot. What's worse, a good player will often float with any two cards, knowing that there are many troublesome turn cards for the out-of-position bettor. If the turn comes 5, 6, 7, 10, J, or Q, there will be a possible straight for the button to represent, along with feasible two-pair holdings as well.

Despite those considerations, Dusty decides to fire out a continuation bet, planning to fire three barrels a fair amount of the time. Several of the scare cards will improve Dusty's hand: A 7, 10, or Q will give him a straight draw, while a J or an A will give him a good top pair. Since the effective stacks are not that deep, hands like J-9 and J-8 are unlikely to be in the button's range. He would likely only play those weaker suited hands with the better implied odds that deeper stacks would provide. That means that hitting a jack would give Dusty a strong hand that beats all of the button's likely holdings except for Q-10. If the board comes out with a couple of blanks, firing off three shells will get the button to fold a large percentage of his range.

The **A♠** on the turn is obviously a good card as it gives Dusty top pair. Checking and calling would be a reasonable option, hoping to induce bluffs from all of the air hands that floated the flop. It may be the best play in a vacuum—but poker is not played in a vacuum and check-calling the turn presents some problems to an overall strategy. Namely, this is a great card to fire a second barrel on. If Dusty wants the right to bluff this card with all of the hands that miss here, he should also be betting when he hits the card, so that's what he does.

THE TAKEAWAY: 1

If you want to bluff when you don't have it, you should usually value bet when you do. This is particularly true in common situations like turning an ace and firing a second barrel.

Another benefit to betting the turn is inducing a bluff raise. Hands like **7♠ 6♠** and **J♠ 10♠** may raise the turn, since there are not many hands the button expects Dusty to jam with in this situation. He'll expect Dusty to call here a lot and often fold the river. The button's turn raising range has very few value hands: A-9 and A-8 suited, along with some unlikely to be-slowplayed sets. He could also be raising any two cards as a bluff, as this is a prime bluff card. Dusty hates jamming the turn if only better hands will call, but this guy is pretty well priced in with combo draws. It's also hard to tell which river cards are scary, so it will be difficult to play the river accurately.

THE TAKEAWAY: 2

When you think you're doing well against your opponent's range but can't come up with a good plan for the river, it's good to just jam the money in.

If something like the **Q♠** comes on the river, folding would be quite reasonable, but there are enough bluffs left in the button's range that it would still be rather distasteful. Dusty avoids making a questionable fold on the river by jamming the turn. In years past, he would have been more inclined to play it safe and check-call or bet/fold. But thinking through and understanding people's ranges lets him make a confident turn shove.

HAND #24

$5/$10 NO-LIMIT HOLD'EM— 8 PLAYERS

THE SET-UP

STACKS: Dusty has $3,184, Early Position Player has $2,136, Under the Gun has $1,273, Cutoff has $456, Button has $1,000, Small Blind has $1,826, Big Blind has $1,623

READS: Early Player is tight and conservative, Under the Gun is extremely tight

PREFLOP ACTION: Under the Gun raises to $40, Early Player calls, 1 player folds, Dusty calls in the Hijack with **A♠ K♣**, Cutoff calls, Button calls, Small Blind calls, Big Blind calls. With Dusty in the Hijack, we go to the flop seven-handed!

FLOP ($280)	TURN ($610)	RIVER ($1,510)
ACTION	**ACTION**	**ACTION**
Small Blind checks	Early Player checks	Early Player bets
Big Blind checks	Dusty bets $450	$1,000
Under the Gun checks	Early Player calls	Dusty folds
Early Player checks		
Dusty bets $165		
5 Players fold		
Early Player calls		

WHY DUSTY PLAYED IT THIS WAY

Against an extremely tight opener and a tight cold caller, 3-betting A♠ K♣ would be a mistake. Even against only one player with a very tight range, A-K is an underdog. Adding the second player with a tight range makes matters worse. It's now likely that one player has a pair and the other has another A-K, killing outs and cutting down on implied odds. A-K is easily strong enough to cold call, which is what Dusty does, allowing him to play a well-disguised hand in position. Somewhat surprisingly, four more players call behind him and they all take a flop seven ways.

As a result of all the callers, there are already 28 blinds in the pot when the flop comes down. It's unlikely that either Under the Gun or Early Player would check a set with so much money in the pot and draws on board. It's also very difficult for them to hold pocket aces or kings with two of each card accounted for; there is only one combination of each. The only way Dusty's top two pair is no good here is if someone called behind him with pocket twos.

All of this is to say that Dusty is not considering whether to make a value bet, but rather how to size it. If he makes a very large bet, flush draws may just fold outright since there won't be room for them to make a big enough raise to generate fold equity. Instead, Dusty makes a bet slightly larger than half the pot. The idea is to bait someone into thinking they have fold equity. Everyone folds around to the original cold caller, who calls again.

The 4♣ on the turn is an excellent card for a number of reasons. First, it's almost impossible that Dusty's opponent will have drawn out on him. Tight players don't cold call with 5-3, and pocket fours would surely have folded the flop, so Dusty's A♠ K♣ is still the relative nuts. When the early position player check-calls Dusty's three-quarters-pot bet, it seems likely that she has a hand such as A-Q. On a blank river, Dusty can comfortably place a pot-sized bet to get the rest of the money in. But the river is not a blank. The 8♦ prompts some hesitation and a large bet from Dusty's opponent.

Given what he knows about his opponent, Dusty knows almost exactly which two cards she holds. Back when everyone played tight, it was possible to put players on very narrow ranges. In fact, there were a number of times when you could put a player on his exact two cards.

THE TAKEAWAY

When a tight player cold calls from early position against an even tighter under-the-gun player, he will have a very narrow range.

Big pocket pairs, A-K, and A-Q suited will surely call. Smaller pocket pairs, A-Q offsuit, and other suited Broadway cards may also call. Once she checks and calls the flop, her range can be narrowed down to flush draws with top pair and A-Q almost exclusively. It is very likely that she would bet the flop with any naked flush draws, since it's hard for anyone to flop a very strong hand on this board. With top pair to go with her flush draw, her check-call line makes more sense since she has strong showdown value. There is no need to semibluff.

So why is she leading the river now? Almost certainly because she holds exactly **A♦ Q♦**. She leads out to prevent Dusty from checking back with a strong hand that's afraid of the flush. It's also possible but less likely that she would play **A♦ J♦** or **A♦ 10♦** this way. There's almost no chance that this conservative player would be turning A-Q without a flush into a bluff on the river. Some players might, but that's not a play likely to be in her arsenal. No, she almost definitely holds the nuts.

HAND #25

$5/$10 NO-LIMIT HOLD'EM— 6 PLAYERS

THE SET-UP

STACKS: Dusty has $2,121, Cutoff has $1,289, Button has $1,787

READS: Button is very loose, aggressive, and bad; CO is a good regular

PREFLOP ACTION: Dusty raises with **8♠ 8♦** in the Lojack, Hijack folds, Cutoff calls, Button calls, the blinds fold

DUSTY, LOJACK	CUTOFF	BUTTON

FLOP ($105)	TURN ($245)	RIVER ($585)

ACTION	ACTION	ACTION
Dusty bets $70	Dusty bets $170	Dusty checks
Cutoff calls	Cutoff calls	Cutoff bets $270
Button folds		Dusty calls, wins pot

WHY DUSTY PLAYED IT THIS WAY

Playing with somewhat deep stacks, Dusty opens under the gun and gets called by two opponents. Despite having an overpair, this is the sort of flop that Dusty will sometimes check and fold against wildly aggressive and tough opposition, since it's so hard to get to showdown while getting the money in good. The button, however, is capable of paying off with some weak hands, so Dusty value bets. The fact that the flop is rainbow also helps, since fewer gross cards will show up on the turn.

While the K♠ on the turn is not fantastic looking, it doesn't particularly hit anything the cutoff should be holding, so Dusty sticks in another bet. It's possible that the cutoff slowplayed a set, particularly with the fishy player in the hand behind him, but he'll probably let Dusty know by raising here, so there will be no further losses. The cutoff could also hold a hand like pocket sixes or fours, giving him a pair and a gutshot, or 7-6, which does the same. He could also have a stronger hand like nines through jacks or A-7. Dusty's bet can get value from some of these hands, particularly the pairs with a draw, and occasionally folds from pocket nines or tens (though not that often). When the cutoff calls the turn, it is clear that he has a small to medium pair.

THE TAKEAWAY

Dusty's turn bet is also motivated by a particular river dynamic that it sets up. When the river pairs the board and Dusty checks, which hands is the cutoff likely to bet with? Not any of the ones that beat Dusty. Pocket nines through jacks will be delighted to take a showdown here, hoping they're good, but fearing a weak king. Weaker hands like pocket sixes and fours may get turned into a bluff, and missed draws like 9-8 and 8-6 will almost surely bet.

This is a somewhat strange situation in which, by betting the turn and checking the river, Dusty often gets two bets in against the hands he beats, and only one bet in against the hands that beat him. A lot of times, the situation will be the opposite: Betting twice will get the money in against a weaker range. It pays well to learn the difference.

SECTION 3

STUDY

1. **Which street(s) of poker should you focus on the most to improve your game?**
   A. Preflop
   B. Flop
   C. All postflop streets
   D. Turn

2. **Warren Buffet felt that it was best to be an:**
   A. Innovator
   B. Imitator
   C. Idiot
   D. What does Warren Buffett know anyway?

3. **In poker, the profit comes from:**
   A. 3-betting your opponents liberally
   B. Getting to showdown cheaply
   C. Betting the flop
   D. Making a better decision than your opponent would have made

4. **Mastering preflop play will instantly make you a winning poker player:**
   TRUE
   FALSE

5. **If you are under the gun in a 9-handed game, you should play the following hands:**
   A. 9-8s
   B. 4-4
   C. K-Qo
   D. 6-6
   E. None of the above

6. **You are on the button in a 6-handed game with a 100 big blind stack and hold 7-4s. You should:**
   A. Fold
   B. Raise
   C. Limp
   D. Shove all in

7. **If you are in the Lojack in a 9-handed game, you should play the following hands:**
   A. K-Jo
   B. 4-4
   C. J-10s
   D. A-10s
   E. None of the above
   F. A, C and D only

8. **If the button is abnormally tight and you are in the cutoff position, you should:**
   A. Open up your starting hand requirements as if you are on the button.
   B. Play fewer hands than you normally would.
   C. Leave the table.
   D. Limp in preflop more frequently.

9. **A huge fish in the big blind. You are in the lojack. You should:**
   A. Tighten up preflop.
   B. Leave the table.
   C. Open raise with the same hands you would normally play from the cutoff in our starting hand chart.
   D. Open raise the same starting hands you normally would from the lojack in our starting-hand chart.

10. **Every decision you make at the poker table should be based on:**
    A. How big the fish is at your table
    B. A math-based approach
    C. What you think will win the most money
    D. I'm sorry, sir, we don't sell cranes.

11. **Which statement is true:**
    A. Playing loose makes you a great player.
    B. Great players often play loose because they are great.

12. **Which statement is true:**
    A. The smaller your stack the looser you should play.
    B. The larger your stack the looser you should play.

13. **Ignoring bonus money, who makes more money per hour?**
    A. An online player who plays a 30 VPIP, wins 14 cents a hand playing 400 hands an hour
    B. An online player who plays a 20 VPIP and wins 8 cents a hand playing 1,200 hands an hour
    C. An online player who tries to play loose like Tom Dwan

14. **All other things being equal, who makes more money playing poker?**
    A. A player who diligently studies the game, focuses on advice from other proven winners, and consistently tries to play his best each and every session
    B. A player who just purchased the Phil Hellmuth DVD set and is all set to go to his local casino and play the top 10 hands
    C. A player who is trying to play loose like Tom Dwan
    D. A player who tries out the latest tip given out by whoever won the latest WPT event

15. **Assuming you want to play your hand, you should always raise:**
    A. The same amount no matter what the situation
    B. Less than your default raise size when there are short-stacked players in the blinds
    C. More than your default raise size when there are players who limp in ahead of you
    D. Then, on second thought, fold if Phil Hellmuth is at the table. You can't beat an Eagle!
    E. Both B and C
    F. None of the above

16. **If you are considering whether to raise a limper, a good rule of thumb is to:**
    A. Raise any two cards
    B. Raise only the top 10 hands
    C. Raise your standard opening range, depending on what position you are in
    D. Loosen up your starting hand requirements by one position
    E. None of the above

17. **Good reasons for raising limpers include:**
    A. You might win the pot when the limper folds.
    B. If your opponent calls, you can often win the pot with a c-bet on the flop.
    C. You can bloat the pot for the times when you do indeed have a strong hand.
    D. You can put the limper on tilt and induce large mistakes from him when done repeatedly.
    E. All of the above

18. **If someone folds to a 3-bet 69 percent of the time, you should:**
    A. Be more inclined to 3-bet this person instead of folding or calling.
    B. Always 3-bet these opponents when they open raise.
    C. Disregard this statistic and play your game.
    D. None of the above
    E. All of the above

19. **Which statement is true?**
    A. You should design your game so that you fold less than 67 percent of the time to a 3-bet. Failure to do so would be a leak in your game.
    B. If you find an immediately profitable opportunity to win the pot preflop, you should always take it.
    C. If someone folds to a 3-bet 72 percent of the time according to your HUD, they will always fold 72 percent of the time regardless of how often you 3-bet them. They will not adjust.
    D. You should make the play that you believe will make you the most money based on the information you have gathered about your opponent(s).

20. **If the tight and aggressive hijack raises, everyone else folds, and you hold A-Qo on the button, you should:**
    A. Fold because your hand is not ahead of their range.
    B. Call because you have position and want to play pots postflop against a range you dominate.
    C. 3-bet because you are ahead of their range and are likely to get enough folds to make your 3-bet immediately profitable.
    D. 3-bet because the more you 3-bet, the tougher an opponent you are.

21. **If a very loose fish raises from the cutoff and you hold A-Js on the button, you should:**
    A. Call because you don't want to lose your customer.
    B. Fold because the fish plays crazy and you are never going to be able to put him on a hand.
    C. 3-bet because the loose fish is likely to call your 3-bet with hands you dominate, giving you an opportunity to play a big pot in position against a bad player.
    D. Fold because A-Js is not among the top 10 hands.

22. **Which statement is true:**
    A. You should defend your blinds liberally. Don't let people take your blinds without a fight.
    B. The money in the blinds belongs to the pot, not you.
    C. If someone continues to raise your blinds, you should shove all in to send them a message.
    D. Doyle Brunson famously said, "The key to no-limit Texas hold'em is to fiercely defend your blinds."

23. **You are in the small blind with K-K. The button open raises first in, as he does 74 percent of the time. The big blind is the most aggressive player preflop that you play against. What should you do and why?**

   A. Call because the button is very unlikely to have a hand that will give you action if you 3-bet him and the big blind will often make a squeeze play when he sees a raise and a call in front of him.

   B. Fold because—I'm sorry, I can't even come up with anything clever here. The answer is not B.

   C. 3-bet because you want to 3-bet a wide range of hands against a loose button opener. If you always trap your big hands and 3-bet your marginal ones, your opponent will likely figure this out and exploit you.

   D. None of the above

   E. Mix it up between A and C

24. **You are in the small blind and the button open raises the pot. You should almost always 3-bet which of the following hands:**

   A. A-Qo

   B. K-Qo

   C. A-Js

   D. K-Js

   E. All of the above

25. **You have 7-6s on the button. The tight aggressive cutoff raises and the big blind is a fish. Stack sizes are 100 BB effective. You should:**

   A. Fold because suited connectors are not profitable hands under any circumstances in a 100 BB structure.

B. Call because, while suited connectors aren't typically great hands in a 100 BB structure, having position and possibly a fish in the pot makes calling a profitable option.

C. 3-bet because you want to always put pressure on your opponents to have a hand.

D. Call because "they can never put you on a hand that way."

26. **You have 7-6s on the button. The tight aggressive cutoff raises and both of the blinds are very tough and very aggressive players who are known to frequently utilize the squeeze play. Stack sizes are 100 BB effective. You should:**

A. Fold because you stacks are only 100 BB, there are no fish left in the hand, your hand is behind the cutoff's range, and you are not assured to see the flop because of the aggressive blinds.

B. Call because suited connectors are great hands that your opponent can't put you on.

C. 3-bet occasionally because it is a good way to mix up your play and avoid becoming too predictable.

D. Usually A and sometimes C

E. None of the above

27. **You are in the big blind with A-4o. The button open raises to 3 blinds as he has historically done 77 percent of the time. The very aggressive small blind 3-bets 14 percent and 3-bets the button to 11 big blinds. Stacks are 100 BB effective. You should:**

A. Fold, your hand is too weak to withstand a raise and a 3-bet preflop.

B. Call because you have a pretty good hand against these aggressive opponents.

C. 4-bet and call an all-in reraise.

D. 4-bet to 25 big blinds with the intent to fold to an all in reraise. 4-betting here will induce enough folds to be a profitable option and you have an ace, which reduces their chances of having a big hand.

28. **The cutoff open raises to 3 big blinds. The tight aggressive button calls. You have 7-4s in the big blind. The cutoff folds 84 percent of the time to a 3-bet squeeze play. Stacks are 100 BB effective. You should:**

A. Attempt a squeeze play by raising to 12 big blinds.

B. Attempt a squeeze play by raising to 19 big blinds.

C. Fold

D. Call

29. **You are in the small blind with K-Qo. The button open raises to 2 blinds. You decide to 3-bet the tight aggressive button. Stacks are 100 BB effective. What should your 3-bet raise size be?**

A. 11 blinds

B. 7 or 8 blinds

C. All in

D. 3 blinds

30. **You are on the button with A-Ko. A tight aggressive player open raises to 3 blinds from the cutoff. You decide to 3-bet your opponent. Stacks are 100 BB effective. What should your 3-bet raise size be?**
    A. 9 blinds
    B. 13 blinds
    C. 6 blinds
    D. All in

31. **When you are about to enter the pot with whatever holding you have, the best approach is to:**
    A. Enter the pot and take a wait-and-see attitude.
    B. Develop a default plan for the entire hand with the intent of deviating if information is presented to you that is powerful enough to alter your decision.
    C. Enter the pot and begin looking into your opponent's soul.
    D. Enter the pot and check-raise your opponent on the flop no matter what cards come.

32. **You should do most of your preparation for difficult situations:**
    A. Away from the table so that when the hand arises, you already have a solid sense of what you intend to do
    B. While playing as many tables as possible
    C. During the play of your hand
    D. Never. The great ones feel out the situation and make the best decisions on the fly.

33. **The first thing you should ask yourself every time you see a flop is whether or not you are willing to get your chips in. You should actively look to get all in with which of the following types of hands:**
    A. Strong hands that will be ahead of your opponent's all-in range
    B. Anytime you have top pair
    C. With all your bluffs
    D. Strong draws with excellent equity
    E. Draws that can be the best hand now
    F. Answers A, D and E

34. **A vital consideration in deciding whether to commit to your hand is:**
    A. Stack size and its relation to the pot
    B. How much you are winning at the table
    C. How many tables you are playing
    D. Whether or not you're feeling lucky

35. **When deciding whether to make a continuation bet, the first thing to consider is:**
    A. How hard the board hits your opponent's range
    B. The strength of your hand
    C. Your opponent's propensity to try to play you off of your hand
    D. All of the above

36. **When you raise preflop, get a caller, and the flop is terrible for your hand, you should consider:**
    A. Giving up on a continuation bet and likely surrender the pot
    B. A compromise of making a smaller than usual continuation bet
    C. A balance between A and B

D. You should always make a continuation bet regardless of the situation

37. **When trying to figure out which hand your opponent has to determine the best course of action, you should:**
    A. Put him on a specific hand and stick with your read.
    B. Read your opponent's soul like Phil Hellmuth does.
    C. Assign your opponent a range of hands based on all the information you've obtained about your opponent.
    D. Pick one or two hands you think he has and base your strategy around those one or two hands.

38. **When you flop a marginal made hand out of position in a raised pot, you should:**
    A. Lead out and find out where you stand.
    B. Determine the best course of action against the range of hands your opponent can have.
    C. Check and fold if your opponent bets.
    D. Check and call to keep your opponent honest.

39. **You open-raise with 3-3 in the small blind to 3 times the big blind. The big blind 3-bets you to 9 times the big blind. Stacks are 100 BB and your opponent is a solid regular at your limits. You should most often:**
    A. Fold
    B. Call
    C. 4-bet your opponent to 22 blinds and fold to an all-in reraise.
    D. Call and be willing to call down for your stack if no cards above a 10 come on the board.

40. **When you have a hand that is almost always best and are considering how much to value bet, you should:**
   A. Always bet the size of the pot.
   B. Bet two-thirds the pot as that is the best way to keep your bets a consistent size.
   C. Treat your poker like a retail store. Choose the bet size that is the highest amount you think your opponent will pay off, while considering potential inflection points.
   D. Bet about half the pot to make sure you get called.
   E. Both A and C

41. **You become involved in a 3-bet pot against competent opposition and you have the initiative in the pot. You decide that betting the flop is the best option. Stacks are 100 BB. Your bet size should almost always be:**
   A. About the size of the pot
   B. About one-half to one-third the pot size
   C. Determined only after attempting to look into your opponent's soul
   D. Three quarters the size of the pot

42. **By making relatively large bets on the flop in a 3-bet pot, you are effectively reducing your skill advantage on future streets:**
   TRUE
   FALSE

43. **You become involved in a pot against a highly aggressive opponent. You decide to bluff your opponent on the turn because you feel he is unlikely to have a big hand. With the pot at $400, your opponent bets $280. Your bluff raise size should be approximately:**
   A. $560
   B. $695

C. $880
D. $1,225

44. **You raise first in on the button to 3 blinds. Stacks are 100 BB. A tight aggressive player in the big blind calls your raise. He checks and calls a two-thirds-pot bet from you on the flop. Your opponent checks the turn. You consider betting, but are contemplating the possibility that your opponent may check-raise you. Against most opponents a check-raise on the turn is:**
   A. Common. Expect to get check-raised here a high percentage of the time.
   B. Uncommon. Most opponents check-raise the turn infrequently and this should not play a major role in your decision to bet the turn.

45. **You have won 2 BB/100 over the last 100,000 hands you have played at your limit. For the next 100,000 hands you play, you should expect to:**
   A. Win 2 BB/100. 100,000 hands is a huge and reliable sample size that should accurately predict how well you will do in the future.
   B. Win 4 BB/100. 100,000 hands is a lot of poker and there is no reason you shouldn't win more after gaining so much experience.
   C. Not be able to reliably give an answer. All you can control is how hard you work at your poker game, how well you control your emotions, and how well you are able to manage your bankroll.
   D. Win "one meeeelion" dollars.

46. With stacks of 100 BB, which flop should you be more inclined to bet with the intention of betting the turn and river as a bluff, assuming your opponent never raises you and the turn and river cards don't improve your opponent's likely holdings?
   A. 9♦ 5♥ 2♠
   B. A♥ 7♦ 2♠
   C. K♣ 9♦ 3♠
   D. 7♥ 8♥ 9♥
   E. Both B and C

47. You come across some new ways to bluff your opponents and are curious if they will work. You decide that you don't want to risk a lot of money to test out these bluffs. A good option for you is to:
   A. Try them anyway. After all, it's only money.
   B. Drop down in limits and test them out so it will be less costly in the event you decide that the new plays you learned are not ones you want to add to your arsenal.
   C. Test them out in the World Series of Poker. If they work there, they will work anywhere.
   D. When these situations arise, bet or raise only when you actually have a strong hand. If your opponents rarely call your value bets or raises in these spots, then you know you found a good bluffing opportunity.
   E. Both B and D
   F. Both A and C

48. When faced with a situation where you are out of position with a weak made hand on a draw-heavy board, and you are unsure if your opponent has a weak made hand or a draw, betting the minimum can be a good way to:
    A. Freeze up the bottom end of your opponent's value betting range, which is more likely to simply call your minimum bet.
    B. Induce bluff raises from busted draws.
    C. Both A and B
    D. None of the above

49. Which step does not belong in a 3-step decision checklist that you should use before every important decision at the tables:
    A. Act: Take a deep breath and confidently make the play you have decided on, with a willingness to accept whatever the outcome may be
    B. Observe: Put your opponent on a range. What does your opponent's line mean?
    C. Decide: Find the best play. What is the best decision you can make against his range, factoring in the strength of your hand and recent history between you and your opponent?
    D. Tilt: If you get the money in good and your opponent draws out on you, berate your opponent in the chat box or in person at a live poker table.

50. **The best way(s) to approach a mistake you are making in your game is to:**
    A. Realize that you have spotted a great opportunity for yourself to improve your game.
    B. Become depressed and realize that if you keep making mistakes, you will never beat Phil Hellmuth.
    C. Get angry and let the steam out.
    D. Do some work away from the tables to figure out how you might be able to prevent making the same mistake in the future.
    E. Both A and D
    F. None of the above

51. **When considering whether or not to semibluff all in with a flopped draw, you should weigh the following factors:**
    A. Whether or not your opponent is a Super Nova Elite
    B. How often you think your opponent will fold
    C. What your equity is when he calls
    D. The size of your bankroll
    E. All of the above
    F. Both B and C

52. **With 100-blind stacks in a $5/$10 game, you raise to $30 with A♦ 8♦ on the button. The very aggressive big blind calls. The flop comes J♦ 10♦ 3♥. Your opponent checks and you bet $45 into a $65 pot and get raised to $140. You should almost always:**
    A. Call and hope to make your hand on the turn.
    B. Raise to approximately $350 with the intention of calling your opponent's shove. Your aggressive opponent can have a lot of worse draws he will commit with and you will never get outplayed on later streets by a worse draw if you end up all in on the flop.

C. Raise and fold to a shove. If your opponent shoves all in on a board like this, he will almost always have a set or two pair at the worst.

D. Fold. Your opponent's raise indicates a lot of strength and you only have ace-high.

53. **A tight-aggressive opponent raises first in from the button to 3 blinds, the small blind folds and you call from the big blind with 10♥ 9♥. The flop come Q♦ 9♣ 5♥. Stacks are 100 BB. You should usually:**

A. Check the flop and call if your opponent bets.

B. Lead out for 4 blinds and find out where you stand.

C. Check and fold if your opponent bets.

D. Check and min-raise your opponent because you always want to be applying pressure to your opponent at every opportunity.

54. **Playing your opponent off of his hand is not a macho thing. It is a math problem:**
TRUE
FALSE

55. **You have A♦ J♠ in the cutoff and raise first in to 3 blinds. The tight aggressive button, who isn't known to run a ton of bluffs, calls. The blinds fold. The flop comes A♥ 7♦ 2 ♠. You bet 5 blinds and your opponent raises you to 13 blinds. Stacks are 100 BB. With no draws present on the board, your best option is to:**

A. Call now and re-evaluate the turn.

B. Raise to 30 blinds and call a shove.

C. Raise to 30 blinds and fold to a shove.

D. Fold. While your opponent can be bluffing some of the time, on this dry board you have very little equity when he is value raising.

56. A tight-aggressive opponent who is well capable of
4-betting preflop as a bluff, open raises to 3 blinds on
the button. You have two black jacks in the big blind.
Your plan for the hand should usually be to:
   A. 3-bet to 11 blinds and if your opponent 4-bets you,
      shove all in.
   B. 3-bet to 9 blinds and if your opponent 4 -bets you, fold.
   C. Call
   D. Fold preflop

57. You raise first in on the button with 8♥ 7♥ to 3 blinds.
The small blind folds and the solid regular in the big
blind calls. Stacks are 100 BB. The flop comes J♦ 6♣
K♥. Your opponent checks and you decide to check.
The turn is the 2♠ and your opponent again checks.
You should almost always:
   A. Bet 4 or 5 blinds in an attempt to pick up the pot
      with your bluff. Once your opponent checks twice,
      there is a good chance he has a weak hand.
   B. Check again and give up on trying to win this pot.
   C. Check the turn and bluff raise the river if your
      opponent bets.
   D. None of the above

58. You open raise first in from the cut off to 3 blinds with
A♦ 3♦. Everyone folds except the tricky big blind.
Stacks are 100 BB. Assuming the big blind checks the
flop, which board(s) should you almost always make a
continuation bet on?
   A. A♥ 9♠ 5♦
   B. 8♥ 7♥ 6♥
   C. Q♣ 10♣ 9♠
   D. K♣ 8♦ 4♥
   E. A and C
   F. A and D

59. **A tight aggressive opponent raises to 3 blinds before the flop from the cutoff. You have A♦ 10♦ on the button and choose to call. The blinds fold and the pot is heads up. Stacks are 100 BB. The flop comes 10♥ 6♠ 3♦. You should usually do what and why?**
    A. Fold the flop because you feel that if your opponent raised before the flop and bet the flop, he is too likely to hold an over pair to your tens.
    B. Call because, while you decide you are ahead of your opponent's range, by raising you will typically only get raised back by your opponent when you are behind. Calling keeps the pot size small and can induce bluffs or value bets on later streets from worse hands.
    C. Call because, while you are afraid of overpairs, you can't bring yourself to fold top pair.
    D. Raise because you have top pair/top kicker. If you aren't happy to raise this flop, what kind of flop were you hoping for?
    E. Raise and if you get reraised, you can safely fold. You raised to find out where you stood.

60. **As a prospective professional poker player you should have which of the following:**
    A. At least 6 to 12 months living expenses saved up.
    B. A willingness to play 2 to 3 times the amount of poker you typically need to play to cover your monthly nut.
    C. At least 100 buy-ins for your limit in your poker bankroll so that you can withstand the vagaries of variance.
    D. All of the above
    E. None of the above. I don't need to have any of those—I can read souls, baby!

ANSWERS

1. C	21. C	41. B
2. C	22. B	42. True
3. D	23. E	43. B
4. False	24. E	44. B
5. E	25. B	45. C
6. B	26. D	46. A
7. F	27. D	47. E
8. A	28. A	48. C
9. C	29. B	49. D
10. C	30. A	50. E
11. B	31. F	51. F
12. B	32. A	52. B
13. B	33. F	53. B
14. A	34. A	54. True
15. E	35. D	55. D
16. D	36. C	56. A
17. E	37. C	57. A
18. A	38. B	58. F
19. D	39. A	59. B
20. B	40. C	60. D

GRADING

58–60 = High Stakes Regular

54–57 = Mid Stakes Regular

48–53 = Low Stakes Regular

42–47 = A pro career may still be in the cards for you, but you'd better work hard for it

36–41 = We strongly recommend reading this book a few more times

35–0 = Poker does not come naturally to you. Please reread the book a few more times and take this test again. If your score doesn't improve dramatically, you may want to reconsider a poker career.

 # GLOSSARY

3-bet

The second raise on a round of betting. "When someone is making big raises with a wide range of hands before the flop, you can often steal a lot of money by **3-betting** aggressively."

3-bet light

Reraise with a less than premium hand. "Once everyone realized that everyone else was opening with a wide range of starting hands, **3-betting light** came into vogue."

4-bet

The third raise on a round of betting. "There's so much 3-betting going on that people have started to **4-bet** cold with air."

Air

A hand with no intrinsic value.

Balance (your range)

Adjust the range of hands you play in certain situations. "This is a spot where you absolutely need to **balance** your range. If you want to raise flush draws and straight draws on this flop, you have to be raising strong hands like your sets."

BB

See Big Blind.

Barrel

Bet, raise or reraise. "Most players don't **barrel** the turn often enough."

Bet for value

A bet made to increase the size of the pot (rather than to get your opponents to fold) when you have either the best cards, the best draw, or cards that may not the best but still have a good chance of winning. "Whenever you can lead out **for value**, you can represent the same hand with a bluff."

Big Blind (BB)

The second position to the left of the button and the last to act to before the flop.

Bluff catcher

A hand that can only beat a bluff. "If he has a properly balanced barreling strategy, it will be very difficult for you to find a profitable way to show down your **bluff catcher**."

Bomb

Make a huge bet. "This guy's rarely going to have better than one pair, so I'm going to **bomb** all three streets and get him to fold."

Button (BTN)

The last player to act on every round of postflop betting.

BTN

See Button.

C-bet

Short for continuation bet, in which you continue with a bet on the flop after raising preflop. "You don't have to make your raises or **c-bets** large. You just have to make them often."

Call down

To call a bet or a raise (verb); calldown (noun). "If he expects Dusty to follow through often enough to justify a **calldown**, he still needs to put in the whole enchilada."

CO

See cutoff.

Cutoff (CO)

One seat to the immediate right of the button, or the player who is seated there.

Donk

(a) Lead out with a bet into a previous round aggressor when you're out of position. "In this case, you should **donk**. Just lead right out into the preflop raiser/flop bettor." (b) An abbreviation of "donkey," meaning an inexperienced or poor poker player. "**Donk** is short for donkey, a not so affectionate term for a bad player."

Dry board

A board that has no apparent draws and no pairs; for example, 10-6-2 in three suits. "You can also check-raise weaker draws like overcards with backdoor flush draws on **dry** boards."

Early Position (EP)

Approximately the first third of players to act in a nine- or 10-handed game or the first or second to act in a six- or seven-handed game. Often simply referred to as "early," as in "an early player."

Effective (stack size)

The size of the smallest stack that is active in the hand. "The next time you see a player cold call with 5-3s, take a look at his **effective** stack size in relation to the blinds."

Equity

The amount of money in the pot multiplied by the perceived or actual chances of winning it. "Players see a chance to end the hand early by getting it in with decent **equity** and jump all over it. They're trying to avoid tough postflop decisions."

EV

Expected value; the long-term outcome of a play.

Float

Call a bet or raise with weak cards, with the intent of bluffing later in the hand. "When your opponent c-bets the flop but frequently gives up on the turn, it's a good time to **float**. You call the flop with the plan of betting the turn when your opponent checks."

Hijack (HJ)

2 seats off the button

HJ

See Hijack

HUD

A computer program that analyzes an opponent's play in real time. "Most players use a statistic in their **HUD** to display how often their opponents raise the flop."

Lazy-edge syndrome

Mindlessly 3-betting hands that play better if you call.

Line

An approach or plan for playing a hand. "Your **line** needs to represent something in order to maintain credibility."

Lojack

3 seats off the button, or under the gun in a six-handed game

LJ

See Lojack

Min-bet

The minimum bet allowable in the game. "It's hard to know what a **min-bet** means since it occurs so infrequently."

Min-raise

Raise the minimum. "There are players who **min-raise** with any two cards preflop, then massively overbet every flop."

Monotone

A flop in which all the cards are the same suit.

Nit

A very tight player. "A standard sized bet will avoid giving information to the observant player and avoid pushing the **nit** out of the pot."

Open-raise

Always entering the pot with a raise. "In today's games with 100 big-blind starting stacks, loose and aggressive **open-raising,** where players always enter the pot with a raise, is the norm."

Polarized (range)

A range that consists primarily of very weak or very strong hands with few medium-strength hands in it. "It may be interpreted as a nuts or a bluff bet. In other words, Dusty's range looks **polarized**."

Pot control line

An approach to playing that allows you to control the size of the pot. "When your hand is too weak to commit your stack, you should often take **pot control** lines."

Range

(a) The group of hands you normally play in each type of situation; (b) All the likely hands an opponent can have based on his actions and his usual style of play. "Some players may naturally be better at playing a wide **range** than others, while some may be better served by hunkering down and playing a more disciplined and conservative style."

Read

Your evaluation of another player's actions or holding. "My **read** on the cutoff is that he's a decent regular who usually plays the standard starting hands."

Small Blind (SB)

The first position to the left of the button, sandwiched between the button and the big blind, and the first to act after the flop if still in the hand.

SB

See Small Blind.

Shove

Go all-in. "Maybe you've been playing loose all day and a super tight and oblivious player **shoves** over your 3-bet."

Stack off

Put all your chips in the pot and go broke as the result. "The small blind **stacked off** against the button and got broke to the hand."

Thin (bet)

A bet with a marginal hand. "Your alternative to giving up is to judiciously fire continuation bets, second barrel bluffs, and **thin** value bets."

Thin (drawing)

Drawing to a hand that has very few outs or chances of winning in a showdown. "The cutoff was drawing **thin** with his pocket deuces."

Turbo fold

To fold a hand without hesitation.

VPIP

Voluntairly Put In Pot. VPIP is the percentage of hands where a player puts money in the pot on purpose. "An online player who plays a 20 **VPIP** and wins 8 cents a hand playing 1,200 hands an hour wins more money per hour."

POWERFUL WINNING POKER SIMULATIONS
A MUST FOR SERIOUS PLAYERS WITH A COMPUTER!
IBM compatible CD ROM Win 95, 98, 2000, NT, ME, XP

These incredible full color poker simulations are the best method to improve your game. Computer opponents play like real players. All games let you set the limits and rake and have fully programmable players, plus stat tracking, and Hand Analyzer for starting hands. Mike Caro, the world's foremost poker theoretician says, "Amazing... a steal for under $500... get it, it's great." Includes free phone support. "Smart Advisor" gives expert advice for every play!

NEW! Windows Versions More Features!

1. TURBO TEXAS HOLD'EM FOR WINDOWS - $59.95. Choose which players, and how many (2-10) you want to play, create loose/tight games, and control check-raising, bluffing, position, sensitivity to pot odds, and more! Also, instant replay, pop-up odds, Professional Advisor keeps track of play statistics. Free bonus: Hold'em Hand Analyzer analyzes all 169 pocket hands in detail and their win rates under any conditions you set. Caro says this "hold'em software is the most powerful ever created." Great product!

2. TURBO SEVEN-CARD STUD FOR WINDOWS - $59.95. Create any conditions of play; choose number of players (2-8), bet amounts, fixed or spread limit, bring-in method, tight/loose conditions, position, reaction to board, number of dead cards, and stack deck to create special conditions. Features instant replay. Terrific stat reporting includes analysis of starting cards, 3-D bar charts, and graphs. Play interactively and run high speed simulation to test strategies. Hand Analyzer analyzes starting hands in detail. Wow!

3. TURBO OMAHA HIGH-LOW SPLIT FOR WINDOWS - $59.95. Specify any playing conditions; betting limits, number of raises, blind structures, button position, aggressiveness/ passiveness of opponents, number of players (2-10), types of hands dealt, blinds, position, board reaction, and specify flop, turn, and river cards! Choose opponents and use provided point count or create your own. Statistical reporting, instant replay, pop-up odds high speed simulation to test strategies, amazing Hand Analyzer, and much more!

4. TURBO OMAHA HIGH FOR WINDOWS - $59.95. Same features as above, but tailored for Omaha High only. Caro says program is "an electrifying research tool...it can clearly be worth thousands of dollars to any serious player. A must for Omaha High players.

5. TURBO 7 STUD 8 OR BETTER - $59.95. Brand new with all the features you expect from the Wilson Turbo products: the latest artificial intelligence, instant advice and exact odds, play versus 2-7 opponents, enhanced data charts that can be exported or printed, the ability to fold out of turn and immediately go to the next hand, ability to peek at opponents hand, optional warning mode that warns you if a play disagrees with the advisor, and automatic mode that runs up to 50 tests unattended. Tough computer players vary their styles for a great game.

6. TOURNAMENT TEXAS HOLD'EM - $39.95

Set-up for tournament practice and play, this realistic simulation pits you against celebrity look-alikes. Tons of options let you control tournament size with 10 to 300 entrants, select limits, ante, rake, blind structures, freezeouts, number of rebuys and competition level of opponents. Pop-up status report shows how you're doing vs. the competition. Save tournaments in progress to play again later. Additional feature allows quick folds on finished hands.